CHINA
and the
CROSS

By the same author

THE SHEEPFOLD AND THE SHEPHERD

CHINA AND THE CROSS

A Survey of
Missionary History

BY

COLUMBA
CARY-ELWES
O.S.B.

P. J. KENEDY & SONS

NEW YORK

NIHIL OBSTAT: JOANNES M.T. BARTON, S.T.D.,L.S.S.
CENSOR DEPUTATUS
IMPRIMATUR: T. MORRAGH BERNARD
VIC. GEN.
WESTMONASTERII, DIE 142 APRILIS, 1956

Library of Congress Catalog Card No.: 57–5760
© Copyright 1957 by P.J. Kenedy & Sons, New York
PRINTED IN THE UNITED STATES OF AMERICA

CONTENTS

LIST OF ILLUSTRATIONS

PUBLISHER'S NOTE

We are indebted to the following for permission to quote copyright material:

The editor's representatives for extracts from *Contemporaries of Marco Polo* edited by Manuel Komroff; Messrs. George Allen & Unwin Ltd. for *The Two Red Towers*, by Po Chü-i from *170 Chinese Poems* by Arthur Waley; and The Council of The Hakluyt Society for extracts from *Cathay and the Way Thither* by Sir Henry Yule.

THANKS AND ACKNOWLEDGEMENTS

As I cast my mind back over the quarter of a century during which, off and on, I have been working at this book, the names of a group of friends present themselves; those who helped me, those who reassured me, those who encouraged me to complete the task. The first name is that of Fr. Stephen Marwood who, when asked what he thought of the idea, said, 'start'. So I did. Then comes that of Fr. Abbot, who let me go here and there in search of material. I remember too Mrs. Raymond Asquith, who set me on my course by presenting me with a copy of Sir Henry Yule's *Cathay and the Way Thither*. Arnold Toynbee never despaired of my completing the course, though I almost did. On several occasions he looked through parts of the manuscript and gave useful advice. Then there come to mind the names of Père Combaluzier and Père Monjean, archivists and librarians of the Maisons Mères of the Lazarists and the Missions Étrangères respectively, who gave me of their time and plied me with books and archives. In Paris, too, the Jesuits of Rue Monsieur loaned me manuscripts and made me free of their library. Then I remember Br. Henry Wansbrough, who went through the manuscript in detail, and also Mr. Otto B. van der Sprenkel of the School of Oriental and African Studies, London University, whose minute care over the typescript has been of immense assistance to me. I thank them all and many others too numerous to name. The faults in it are mine and many a precision and a grace will be theirs.

Mrs. Gatling I wish to thank for her labours in typing this MS., and Miss Barbara Chrisler and Mrs. Margaret Trouncer whose help was invaluable, the editor for two extracts from *The Times*, and finally my publishers for the care they have taken.

Let me not to the marriage of true minds
Admit impediments. Love is not love
Which alters when it alteration finds,
Or bends with the remover to remove:
O, no! it is an ever-fixed mark,
That looks on tempests, and is never shaken;
It is the star to every wandering bark
Whose worth's unknown, although his height be taken.
Love's not time's fool, though rosy lips and cheeks
Within his bended sickle's compass come;
Love alters not with his brief hours and weeks,
But bears it out even to the edge of doom.
    If this be error, and upon me proved,
    I never writ, nor no man ever loved.

WILLIAM SHAKESPEARE

CHINA
and the
CROSS

INTRODUCTION

WHEN I was working at the head House of the Missions Étrangères in Paris at the rue du Bac, one of the most important centres of information for the Chinese mission, Père Monjean, the friendly and helpful *archiviste*, expressed surprise that I should be writing a history of the Church in China. I was hard put to it to explain my reasons in a phrase. The same thought will have occurred to the reader. The answer simply is that the story is both immensely important and outstandingly interesting. It remains to be seen whether either of these elements emerges from the reading of the pages which follow.

As soon as one really appreciates the fact that a quarter of the world is Chinese, it becomes evident that taking Christ to the Chinese is one of the most important, if not the most important, task for the Church in the missionary field. Not only is China vast in extent, it is also a land of profound tradition, one of the ancient centres of civilization. It is one of the half-dozen cultural units on the earth. Thus the significance of this story is incontestable.

There is something mysterious and heroic about the missionary endeavours to the Chinese. The story goes back to the very distant past; the circumstances,. though known to historians, are not known to the cultured reader, certainly not to the general public. To study these happenings is to resurrect for oneself great periods of history of the Middle and Far East which are generally ignored by Westerners: the eastern thrust of the Moslems, the rise of the Mongols, the Portuguese conquests in eastern waters, the travellers of every century across the tracks of Asia or over the eastern seas. The tenacity of the missionaries, their skill, their endurance, all these things have drawn me for twenty years to study the Chinese mission.

A complete and definitive history of the Church in China is not as yet possible. The Archives of the Roman Congregations, those of the Jesuit Order in many countries, the Archives of the Franciscans, of the Dominicans, to mention but a few, would all have to be ransacked. The writer would have to know the languages of most European countries and the Chinese writing. And, now that North America has come into the picture, since last century, the scholar would also have to travel widely there in search of facts.

It was evident to me from the start that this history I was engaged on could not be of that calibre; and yet there is enough information scattered here and there to give a true picture of the tremendous enterprise, courage and endurance of those who entered upon that great labour: the winning of the Chinese to Christ. This book then has been written to put together these bits and pieces into a coherent whole. The last Catholic author to attempt the task was the Abbé Huc,[1] of happy memory, at the beginning of the nineteenth century.

Twenty-five years ago Professor Latourette in his *History of Christian Missions in China* gave a masterly and most scholarly account of the whole matter. He is uniformly most fair to Catholic missionaries, though, quite naturally, his chief emphasis is upon the Protestant activities of the last hundred years. One salutes him as a master. In so vast a field there is room for two labourers.

A little, very little, must be said in preface upon the spelling of proper names. Every country in Europe has its own version of Chinese names, and some at various times have adopted different methods. Take for example the name of the province Szechwan; it becomes in French Sseu-Tch'ouan. There is a further difficulty that cities in China, rather like streets in France, change their names with the change of the political complexion of the rulers. The major cities through the course of their history have often had at least three names. I have shamelessly used a name which is known to the general reader. In this whole matter I am

[1] cf. bibliography, p. 302.

restored to a sense of humour by re-reading the correspondence
between Lawrence of Arabia and his publishers over the spelling
of names in his book *The Seven Pillars of Wisdom*.

★   ★   ★

It is sometimes asserted that the religion of Christ is for the
West only. The East, so the argument runs, has its own Ways
of the Spirit. The argument is based either on the historical fact
that this in the event has proved to be the case, or on a precon-
ceived notion that Christianity of its nature does not suit the
Eastern mind. Or to put the point the other way round: the
Eastern mind does not suit Christianity. A study therefore of one
portion of the story, that of Christianity in China, should help
to create a truer perspective. Not only has the religion of Jesus
Christ spread east, but it has proved itself as suitable to the souls
of the Chinese as it has to those of the English, American, Irish,
French or German. The reasons why 'the marriage of true minds'
has not yet been consummated must be sought elsewhere, in
political impediments, wars, difficult communications, in misunderstandings, persecutions and the like.

The missionary effort in China, which stretches back in time
certainly to the seventh century, is only part of an immense
eastward expansion of the Church. Church history books for
Western readers naturally enough stress the progress of the Church
within the confines of the Roman or Byzantine Empires; but
that is only half the story, even if the more important half. The
News of Christ spread as rapidly in the early Church eastwards
as it did westward.

A Christian Church existed in Mesopotamia long before
Eusebius, the historian and Constantine's contemporary, wrote
of it. From such Centres as Nisibis and Edessa in Syria and
Ctesiphon in Mesopotamia Christian missionaries had pressed on
eastwards into Central Asia. Before the break between East and
West, episcopal sees had been established at Samarkand, Kashgar,
Balkh and other cities on the great Asian highways. India

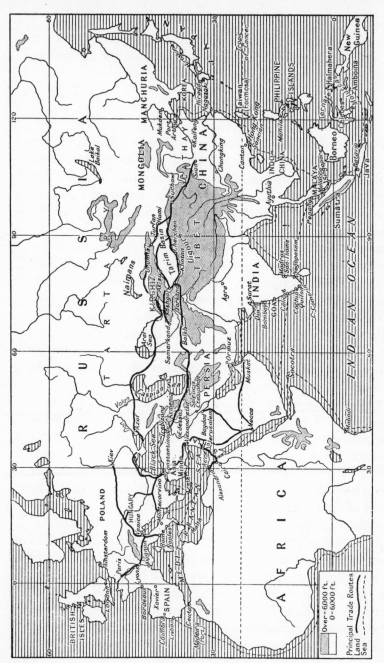

Land and Sea Routes to China in the Middle Ages

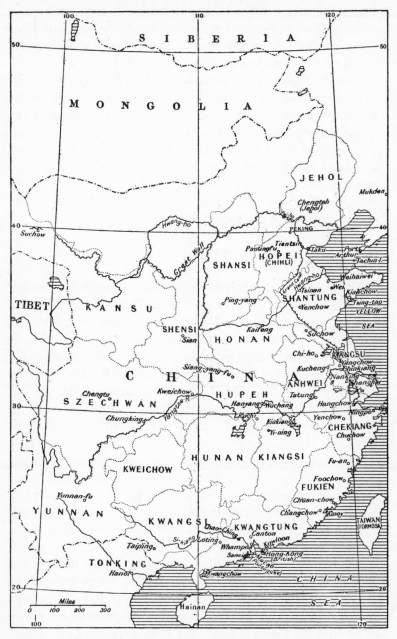

China, showing principal Missionary Stations

certainly had Christian communities in the second and third
centuries. St. Thomas the Apostle himself is said to have penetrated even into its deep south.

Thus the Chinese story, described in the following pages, is no
isolated excursion from the Mediterranean basin, a freak of
history, something unique in the annals of the Church: far from
it; it is merely a fragment of an even greater story: the eastward
expansion of the Church. The followers of Christ have encountered many a Diocletian in those parts but never a Constantine. Yet the truths of the Christian revelation have certainly
been, throughout the long story of the apostolate in the East, as
acclimatized and acceptable, as they are in the West.

★   ★   ★

The story in outline is this: a legend has it that St. Thomas the
Apostle landed on the coast of China. This we shall show has
little or no foundation. We may safely assert that the first
Christian missionaries to reach Cathay—the old name for North
China—were the *Nestorians* in the seventh century, going overland. After a period of success, their Church fell on evil days, its
members were persecuted and only a remnant survived in Central
Asia. Into China itself the Nestorians were reintroduced probably
in the wake of the Mongol invaders of the twelfth and thirteenth
centuries.

The second main contact between Christ and China, the second
act of the drama, occurred when from the Far West came
Franciscans, travelling the land and sea routes to the court of
Kublai Khan in the thirteenth century. In its turn this missionary
Church was swallowed up a hundred years later with the collapse
of the Mongol Empire.

When the third great effort was made, in the time of the
Renaissance, the sixteenth century, very few traces remained to
tell of the previous heroic endeavours. This third act, perhaps
the most brilliant of them all, is rightly associated in the minds
of all with the *Society of Jesus*. But there were other groups and

Orders at work at the same time, as we shall see. The missionary advance of this period came to an end with the Rites controversy which reached its peak at the beginning of the eighteenth century. This was followed by a hundred years of intermittent persecution.

The fourth act of the drama began with the breaking down of the wall of isolation that the Chinese had maintained as best they could for centuries. The first breach was the Opium War the Chinese lost against the British in 1842. This period is one when not only almost all the Orders of the Catholic Church but also all the Protestant bodies gained a foothold on Chinese soil; it was *Everyman's Century* in China.

The last act is upon us, and it would appear to have a tragic end: the triumph of Communism. But love is stronger than death, and no Christian play is ever a tragedy, because the Cross is always, though upon a higher plane, a triumph.

Chapter One

THE LEGEND OF SAINT THOMAS, THE APOSTLE

Bird's-eye View

The scanty evidence. In the sixteenth and seventeenth centuries the Augustinian, Dominican and Jesuit missionaries remark upon the legend. The medieval Franciscans seem to be ignorant of the tradition. Other medieval documents do mention it. The earliest documentary evidence comes from two liturgical sources not later than the eighth century. The very early Church is silent on the matter. But Arnobius of the third century has a famous veiled reference. The conclusion is that there is little or no ground for supposing that St. Thomas went to China.

It would have been a pleasure to begin the ecclesiastical history of China with the arrival on its shores of one of the twelve Apostles of Christ. St. Thomas has been cast for the role, and certain sects in the East are still convinced that it is true. But modern scholars, after examining the evidence or the lack thereof are now convinced that the story is wholly without foundation. The problem is not a little tedious and it would not offend the present writer if the less unhurried readers omitted this portion of the book.[1]

According to the legend St. Thomas reached China via India, converted some Chinese and then returned to Meliapur, on the south-east coast of India, where he died. We have the story in this precise form only from a sixteenth-century source, from no less a personage than St. Francis Xavier, who, as is well known,

[1] All the relevant data has been collected by A. C. Moule in that princely work of scholarship: *Christians in China before the Year 1550*, S.P.C.K., London, 1930.

made a pilgrimage to Meliapur and the tomb of the Apostle before setting off farther east. He relates the legend, but does not give it his blessing. 'Many people say that Saint Thomas the Apostle went to China, that he made many Christians. . . .'[1]

A Dominican contemporary of St. Francis, one Gaspar da Cruz, whose exploits are almost as remarkable as St. Francis' and who landed in China in 1556, wrote: 'The Armenians have it in their true and authentic writings that before the Apostle suffered martyrdom in Meliapur he went to China to preach the Gospel, and, after being there some days and seeing that he could not bear fruit among them, he returned to Meliapur, leaving in China three or four disciples whom he had made there.'[2] That is a typical statement of the story.

There is nothing inherently impossible in the idea that St. Thomas did go to China. St. Paul travelled over a great deal of the Roman Empire on the same errand. Asia Minor, Greece, Spain and Rome were among his stopping places. When we hear that it is a generally accepted proposition, today, that most probably St. Thomas travelled through Asia to India, that his tomb is at Meliapur in South India, it would appear not completely unlikely that he even went farther, arriving, as one legend has it, in a Chinese junk off the coast of China, the Middle Kingdom. But possibilities do not make history. There is no nearly contemporary evidence. The origin of the legend can be traced up to a point, and no farther.

From the Middle Ages we have only one important reference to the legend, and one surprising silence. Indeed the strangest part of the whole story of this legend is that the medieval Franciscans, who passed through India on their way to Cathay or China in the thirteenth century, make no mention of St. Thomas going to China at all, in spite of the fact that they visited his tomb at Meliapur. Bl. John of Montecorvino, the future

---

[1] Moule, *op. cit.*, p. 12.

[2] *op. cit.*, p. 13. For the full text of Gaspar da Cruz's *Tratado* cf. Boxer (ed.), *South China in the XVI century*, Hakluyt Society, 2nd series, Vol. cvi, London, 1953, pp. 44–239. The passage quoted above, p. 213.

Archbishop of Peking in that century, spent thirteen months in Meliapur on his way out, yet never once does he mention the story. In fact he goes out of his way to say that no apostle or disciple of one had reached those regions.

On the other hand a contemporary of these great medieval Franciscan travellers and missionaries, one Abd-Ishu, a Nestorian in Mesopotamia, and scribe to Mark, Nestorian Patriarch to those parts in the thirteenth century, makes the following statement:

'The laying on of hands from the Apostles was received by India and the regions belonging to it and round about it even to the ultimate sea, from Thomas who was ruler and bishop in the Church which he built there and served.'

This passage, which in itself would carry no weight, is nevertheless itself, according to Professor Burkitt, a quotation from a work of the fourth century, and so at a bound carries the tradition back nearly a thousand years. But note that China is not expressly mentioned, although it may perhaps be inferred from the phrase 'even to the ultimate sea'.[1]

On the other hand a more judicious but equally obscure writer, a Syriac Nestorian chronicler of the same century, a certain Ebedjesus, stated that there was a metropolitan see in China in the eighth century. The origins of the see he puts back to the fifth century. But he admits that he is doubtful of this. All we do know is that in the seventh century the Nestorians were the first Christians to reach China.

There are, however, two liturgical sources which take the legend behind the Middle Ages, and at least as far back as the eighth century, possibly much earlier. One comes from South India in the old Malabar rite, the other from a Syriac Breviary, unconnected with South India. A certain early Jesuit missionary, John Maria Camponi, discovered that in the ancient Malabar liturgy on the feast of St. Thomas the Apostle in the lessons of the

[1] cf. Moule, op. cit., p. 18.

second nocturn of Matins the following statement is to be found:

The error of idolatry was banished from India by St. Thomas. The Chinese and Ethiopians were converted to the truth by St. Thomas. From St. Thomas they received the sacrament of Baptism and became children of adoption. Through St. Thomas they believed in and professed the Father, Son, and Holy Spirit. Through St. Thomas they preserved the faith in one God which they received from him. Through St. Thomas the splendour of a life-giving faith flourished through all India. Through St. Thomas the Kingdom of Heaven took wings and sped its flight to the Chinese.

One of the antiphons reads: 'The people of India, of China, of Persia and others on the islands, together with those of Syria, Armenia, Greece and Roumania, venerate thy Holy Name, in memory of St. Thomas.'[1] We may add that the Metropolitan of the pre-Jesuit Malabar Christians styled himself Metropolitan of India and China.

An identical passage was found by Professor Burkitt[2] in another Syriac Breviary, whose provenance was not South India but Syria. Though these two areas are thousands of miles apart, Malabar was dependent on the East Syrian Church, so the evidence points to the source of this story being not South India but Mesopotamia or Syria. Professor Burkitt would date his source as not later than the eighth century and possibly earlier. It is relevant to remark that the work of the expedition, which set out for China overland from that area one hundred years before, had begun to flourish, and by the eighth century the Christians in China were fairly numerous. Were these lessons only the imaginative effusions of a contemporary monk? It is possible.

When we have mentioned this liturgical evidence of uncertain date have we said all? The documents of the early Church in the first two centuries say nothing of St. Thomas's movements. The argument from silence is very strong to prove that St. Thomas

[1] The above references to the Breviary of the Malabar Christians is from *The China that Was* by Nicholas Trigault, S.J. Transl. by L. J. Gallagher, S.J., pp. 188–9. Milwaukee, 1942.

[2] *Breviarium Chaldaicum*, ed. P. Bedjam, 3 vols. Paris, 1886, 1887, Vol. III, p. 476, quoted by Moule, *op. cit.*, p. 11, and notes.

never set foot in China. For example the *Acts of St. Thomas* make no mention of that kingdom. A certain Christian writer, Philip, who came in the second century from the Syrian Edessa, an important episcopal centre of the Syriac Church, describes the morals of the Chinese, but does not take occasion to mention their evangelization by the apostle, from which we conclude he knew nothing of his ever having gone there. Nor does he mention that there were Christians among them, though he points out how the Parthians, men of Kashan, had turned to Christ.[1]

The first mention in Christian literature of the Chinese having embraced Christianity comes from a very tedious apologist, Arnobius, who lived towards the end of the third century and wrote a long-winded book entitled *Disputes against the Gentiles*. In the eighth book, second chapter, he recounts the triumphs of the Church and gives there a list of countries which had been at least partly won . . . 'for the evangelizing of India must be counted, and for the purposes of reckoning we must include the work done among the Seres (Chinese), the Persians and Medes, in Arabia and Egypt, in Asia . . .' and so on interminably.[2] That is hardly a precise mention. The Chinese on their side, who were most careful to record the arrival of Buddhist monks from over the mountains, say nothing whatsoever about the arrival of a Christian Apostle.

We conclude therefore that, unless further evidence is produced, the legend of St. Thomas going to China is non proven, and the honour of being the first missionary to China belongs to Alopen, the seventh-century missionary from Syria. That story must now be told.

---

[1] cf. Moule, *op. cit.*, p. 23.

[2] Arnobii, *Disputationum Adversus Gentes*, Libri octo, ii, 448, Max. Biblioth. Patrum 1677. cf. Moule, *op. cit.*, p. 23.

Chapter Two

THE NESTORIANS

Bird's-eye View

Those who relish the discovery of ancient and distant things will find a dish to their taste here; those who find such tales too remote and unfriendly will find this of little interest. But no account of China and the Cross is complete without a retelling of the story of the Nestorians in China and of China's first Christian missionary, Alopen.

This chapter will therefore be divided into five main and unequal sections. The first will deal with the discovery of the Nestorian Tablet, the chief source of our knowledge of this most remote and distant Christian missionary effort. Then comes some account of events: the political background in 635, the facts in so far as they can be pieced together. This will be followed by the story of the suppression of the Nestorian Church in the ninth century. The way that the Christian message is presented on the Tablet is so unusual that this section concludes with some account of the Technique of Adam, the writer of the Tablet, for that is of interest to us even today. Lastly there comes the second wave of Nestorians and the aftermath. This includes the curious case of the Chinese Christian wine merchant, descendant of the maker of sherbet to Genghis Khan.

i. The Rediscovery

HAD a European traveller, wandering through the streets of Hsianfu—the ancient capital of China—at the beginning of the seventeenth century asked any native whether the Christian religion had ever been preached there, he would have gazed at the traveller with amused amazement, and answered, of course not. But in fact he would have been wrong. One thousand years before, missionaries had entered by the western gates of Hsianfu and had been received with pomp and ceremony by the great

Emperor of the day. All that story was lost and buried. The evidence still lay under the earth not far away, written in that most beautiful calligraphy of the ninth century, upon a stele or stone monument. Its discovery was not far off. It is reasonable then, when dealing with the Nestorian chapter of the Christian infiltration into China, to begin with the unearthing of that tablet, in the year of Our Lord 1625.

The Fathers of the Society of Jesus who reached China in 1583 and first settled in Peking in 1601 were deeply conscious of the fact that the Chinese venerated anything, particularly ideas, only if they could be proved to be of great antiquity and indigenous to their country. It was galling therefore to these missionaries not to be able to point out to their neophytes or sympathetic listeners some ancient Christian monument, some church or statue, book or monastery, which in ages past had been Christian, and so prove that Confucianism and Buddhism and Taoism were not the only three 'Laws' or 'Ways' which had, one might say, a pedigree. In these matters the Chinese were snobs, and with a form of snobbery which had some justification: a way of life which had stood the test of time was one worth careful examination; Christianity seemed not only foreign but new-fangled.

Moreover when the Fathers had passed through India, they had been shown an ancient Breviary in which St. Thomas had been called the Apostle, not only of that country but also of China. While that scrap of evidence has not stood the test of historical scrutiny, it left them with the conviction that there must long ago have been Christians in the Middle Kingdom. Father Ricci, the founder of the Peking mission, had besides gleaned some trifling evidence: an ancient sacring bell with Christian writing upon it in Greek characters.[1] As will appear in the sequel, he

---

[1] It is also a strange fact that at this time no mention is made of the Franciscan medieval mission to China, nor of their records. They too seem to have been submerged and forgotten until rediscovered by Wadding, the great Irish Franciscan scholar, who published his *Annales Ordinis Minorum* in eight vast tomes between the years 1625 and 1654, beginning the very year that news of the yet earlier missionary effort was discovered; they were, however, too late for Ricci, who died in 1610, to benefit by their information.

also heard of, though he never saw, the descendants of an earlier missionary effort, Christians only in name, families who still made the sign of the Cross but knew not why. Daily these Jesuit missionaries hoped to find some record of an early Christian Church, some enclave of Christians, which would prove the ancient lineage, as it were, of their religion.

And so the hunt went on until one day in 1625 news reached the mission house in Peking of a great find. The story is best told in the words of the first historian of the Church in China, Fr. Bartoli, a contemporary of the events he here records, whose account, according to Fr. Havret—a considerable authority on the subject—is the most authentic and reliable.[1] Fr. Bartoli provides us with the date of the discovery, much disputed among scholars:[2]

A treasure of precious documents, buried for God knows how many years, so many indeed that they were not only lost, but were already completely forgotten, has fortunately been discovered in 1625. Published in China, it has since been communicated to the whole Christian world in the East, in Europe and in the New World, as a thing of public interest for the whole Church. . . . We must now tell in some detail, where, when, how and by whom it was discovered.

Among all the fifteen provinces of China, that of Shensi is held in particular veneration as the mother province, where in very distant times, the first fathers and founders of the Chinese nation lived, and whence their descendants, as they multiplied, spread over the other fourteen provinces. . . .

[1] It is here translated from the French version found in Yule, after being diligently compared with the original Italian (and with a previous translation made from the Italian) whose Baroque style with its endless parentheses and flourishes scarcely admits of translation; Fr. Bartoli knew some of those intimately connected with the find, e.g. Fr. Semedo, who first translated the inscription. cf. Appendix I, pp. 285 ff. The text of the account is to be found in Daniello Bartoli, Dell' Istoria della Compagnia di Gesù, La Cina, Terza parte, dell' Asia, Florence, 1832, Bk. IV, pp. 793–5.

[2] The two chief sources for this section are the texts and commentaries of Fr. Havret and Professor Saeki on the Nestorian Tablet. Henri Havret, La stèle chrétienne de Si-ngan-fou (Variétés sinologiques, Nos. 7, 12 and 20—Parts I, II and III—Shanghai, 1895, 1897, 1902). Saeki, P. Y., The Nestorian Monument in China. London, 1916.

Now the Fathers were on the point of evangelizing that province of Shensi and its majestic capital Hsianfu when, some months before their arrival there (and not several years before their arrival in China, as has been written, which would be an error of at least forty-five years), whilst excavations were going on in making foundations for some building or other near Chouchih, a town of secondary importance, about thirty miles east of the capital, the workmen came across the remains of a building, and whilst clearing this away they found a great slab of marble which was taken out and carefully cleaned. It was then noticed that it was all covered with characters, some Chinese, the others of a strange shape, belonging to a language which no one understood, but the former carved with rare perfection.

In a country such as China this discovery was sure to create a sensation, for nowhere had men such veneration for antiquity as in China, and this monument so evidently aroused not only the curiosity but also the veneration of the people of the locality, that it soon became the object of pious rites and of endless speculation. How old was it? What was the language used? What was the subject?

Bartoli goes on:

The Governor, after having adored this marble slab, which was very venerable on account of its age, being nearly 850 years old (as it indubitably appears from the period at which the kings mentioned in it had lived), and containing in his native language mysteries which he little understood, while he understood nothing of the foreign language, gave orders for it to be transported into a Taoist temple, one mile from Hsianfu, near Chouchih, where he was governor, to be raised up on a pedestal under a fine campanile supported by four pillars, and to one side another marble slab bearing on it in carved characters the history of the discovery of that ancient monument. All Hsianfu went to see it, and the most learned vied with each other in trying to decipher the meaning of the inscription. This presented the greatest difficulty partly because the style was very elevated and partly because of the figurative language in which the mysteries of our faith, which had not yet been published abroad in that part, were expressed.

The whole discovery might have remained a mystery but for the fact that two of Ricci's most distinguished neophytes became involved. The story is again told by Bartoli. The names of these two famous converts were Dr. Leo and Dr. Paul, Chinese *literati* of considerable eminence.

No one could be found to appreciate the significance of the find, except a scholar of second degree or chü-jên. This person had been in close contact with Ricci at Peking nearly eighteen years before. What he had heard him say about the Christian Law now came back to his memory, and finding it again in what he read upon the stone, he became convinced that this was the matter with which it was concerned. He took a rubbing of the inscription in white on a black background, as the Chinese method is, and sent it by express [post] to his old friend Doctor Leo at Hangchow, whom he knew quite well was a Christian.

Such are the facts, so far as I can gather them from an account made by Dr. Leo himself, who came with great pleasure to notify the fact to the Fathers. This same Dr. Leo, and after him Dr. Paul, had the inscription printed in smaller characters, with the addition of explanations and the necessary comments; they distributed these throughout the empire.

Dr. Leo himself describes how he first came to hear of the discovery:

I was living in retirement in the country near Ling-Chu [wrote Dr. Leo Li at the beginning of his Appendix], when my friend Chang Kang-yu of Shensi had the kindness to send me a copy of the Tablet of the T'ang, saying to me: 'it has recently been discovered at Chang-nyan[1] while men were digging the earth. It has as its title: "Praise of the monument recalling the propagation in the middle kingdom of the Illustrious Religion."' We had not heard speak of that religion before. Could it be the holy religion that Ricci had come to preach from the farthest West?

[1] Chang-nyan—this has caused some confusion as previously we have seen Chouchih is mentioned as the place of the discovery. But Chang-nyan can be understood to mean a neighbourhood which included part of Chouchih. cf. Saeki, *op. cit.*, p. 18.

ii. The Facts Discovered

When deciphered, the information regarding this early Christian church proved more detailed than the wildest hopes of the missionaries had led them to expect. We shall begin by giving the facts in outline, and then we shall reprint as an appendix the old translation given by Fr. Semedo in his *History of China* translated in 1655 into English, the quaint seventeenth-century English which gives something of the flavour of the ancient Chinese. The reader will find this translation given in full in Appendix I, pp. 285-90.

But first it might be as well to describe the monument itself. Its height is just over 9 feet, it is about 3½ feet across and not quite 1 foot thick. The material is black oolitic limestone. The carving on the top is of Buddhist origin, used by the Nestorians for their own purposes. It shows two monsters holding a pearl. The pearl, according to Professor Saeki, is the pearl of great price of the Gospels.[1]

Just above the large letter-inscription at the top is a carved figure of a cross, somewhat like those found in South India on the tomb of St. Thomas at Meliapur. The cross surmounts a lotus and a cloud. The former is the Buddhist emblem, the latter a Taoist symbol and one used also by Mohammedans.

This document starts with a heading, then comes a statement of the Christian doctrine in Chinese dress, followed by an account of the Apostolic Age, then is given the story of the arrival in China of the first missionary, Alopen. This is followed by an account of the fortunes of the Church there up to the erection of the stone (A.D. 781). Finally comes the eulogy, a recapitulation of the history, this time in verse. The Chinese section concludes with a statement of who set up the stone and when. At this point some Syriac remarks are interjected. The sides are covered with names in Syriac and Chinese; they are those of the clergy of the time.

The facts as recorded in Chinese style on the monument may

[1] *ibid.*, pp. 12-13.

be summarized as follows: in the year 635 Alopen, coming over-land from the West from a country named Tachin, arrived in the capital of China. The Emperor of the time, T'ai Tsung, paid him great honour, sending one of his chief ministers to receive him.

Alopen was brought to the palace and there, at this fabulously remote place, the Christian books were translated. The Emperor, after an examination of them, promulgated a decree in 638 com-manding a church and a monastery to be built in the capital, and, more important, he gave Alopen and his followers the right to propagate their faith. Thus the beginning of the mission was all favourable; but during the two centuries of its existence it had periods of persecution alternating with peace; in 845 the Christian monasteries, together with the Buddhist and Taoist, were suppressed.

In the Syriac section of the inscription the name is given of the Patriarch of Seleucia-Ctesiphon in Mesopotamia, who was con-temporary with the setting up of the monument. Thus proof is provided that in the eighth century at least the Chinese Christian Church was Nestorian, for this Patriarch is known from other sources to have been head of the Nestorian Church.

What was the political background when Alopen set out across Asia?

The text of the inscription does not suggest that Alopen's arrival in Hsianfu was connected with the Mohammedan con-quests, but the dates if compared are so remarkably close as to make some connection not impossible. Thus, the year that Alopen reached Hsianfu is given on the stone as A.D. 635. Now Mohammed died in 632, and the close proximity of these dates cannot be mere coincidence. Indeed some account of the Moham-medan explosion from the desert into the 'sown' must be given in order that we may catch the spirit of that tumultuous period. It will be found that Alopen came precisely from that region which felt the first impact of that terrifying attack, the Syriac world, which was the first to be overrun by the soldiers of the Prophet. Further, the fate of the Nestorian Church was later to be closely linked with the fortunes of this rival religion. So sudden was the blow, so completely were the Christians taken by surprise, that by the year A.D. 634 the Byzantine Syriac provinces already lay completely at the mercy of Islam.

On Mohammed's death, his followers wasted no time in propagating his teaching. The following year they took the road of conquest, which was to lead them almost to the ends of the earth. Two armies set forth northwards from Arabia, the one attacking Mesopotamia from the south, the other Palestine. Both were successful. The Mohammedans were thus established at the cross-roads of three continents, Asia, Africa and Europe. Operations in all three directions proceeded apace. They went west along the Africa coast towards Spain and France, north towards Byzantium and east to attack and subjugate Persia and beyond.

Persia was in decay, and, when roused by the news of the Arab inroads, was ruled, or misruled, by a beardless boy of fifteen supported by a general, Rustam. In the circumstances no help could come to Mesopotamia from Persia; Ctesiphon was sacked in 637 after the Persian forces had been crushingly defeated at Kadisiya. Yezdegerd III, the youthful King of Persia, sent an embassy to China in 638 asking for help. He also sent his treasure, including 7000 vases of gold. In the end (642) the whole of Persia was overrun.

Tibet, on the southern flank of the highway across Asia, was at this time turbulent and warlike. Much to the relief of China, the Tibetan monarch, with the help of two Buddhist wives, one from Nepal and the other a daughter of the Chinese Emperor, T'ai Tsung, reverted to peace, in which condition Tibet remains to this date.

So much for conditions along the route. What of the situation within China itself? The scene was one of barbaric splendour. Alopen appeared at one of the supreme moments of Chinese history. T'ai Tsung had just come to the throne over the dead bodies of his elder and younger brothers, whom he killed (622) because they had conspired to murder him when they had first persuaded his father to abdicate. He was, nevertheless, from a political point of view, one of the greatest rulers China had ever had. His first act was to save the capital from an insurrection, his second was to found a mighty library of 200,000 books. And he is said to have swept 3000 women out of the imperial palace.

The major preoccupation of his reign was the turbulent condition of the Turkish hordes on his far western frontier. An ambassador had arrived in 627 from Samarkand, a State ruled by descendants of a Chinese princess married to a Turkish khan. The ties between China and this distant outpost became closer with the years and guaranteed the route which Alopen, the missionary bishop, was to take in 635. For that route was the chief highway to China: Samarkand, Kashgar, Cherchen, through the Tarim Basin and so to Hsianfu.[1] It began, in the west, at 'the golden gates of Samarkand' and ended, in the distant east, at the western gate of the capital of the Celestial Kingdom, the great city of Hsianfu. Along this route all trade went, especially the bales of silk, the secrets of which were so closely guarded by the Chinese. Along this route too, behind the mighty massif of the Tibetan mountains and the Himalayan ranges, moved the armies of the great Emperor and his ambassadors; there travelled too the representatives of all his subject principalities in Central Asia; along this famous road travelled Alopen.

It becomes clear why the potentates of the Farthest East should take so favourably to the adepts of this alien religion, treat them so courteously, seem even to encourage them. The answer undoubtedly is partly to be discovered in the dangerous international situation in Central Asia, where China was now staking a claim, and partly in the upset of the balance of power between the empire of Islam and China. The prize was the trading area of Bactria and beyond, the old silk route over the roof of the world.[2] The people who lived in those parts were, not a few of them, Christian. The Chinese Emperor, perhaps at his wits' end to know how to deal with the new and ominous situation in the

[1] It is now proved that a northern route over the steppe and north or south of the Gobi desert was also used.

[2] See Sir Aurel Stein, On Ancient Central-Asian Tracks, London, 1933.

interior, heard of the arrival of an embassy from the Far West; it was a golden opportunity both to make friends with the Children of Light and to serve one's own ends too. The situation was complicated by the question of many languages, the difficulty of controlling mercenaries, Uighurs and the like, whose dialects were often unknown to the Chinese generals. These missionaries would be, and were, of inestimable use in acting at least as interpreters in the long-drawn-out campaigns against the power of the Prophet.

The Christian religion had spread to such rich cities as Balkh, the capital of Bactria, certainly by 635, for in Balkh there was already a metropolitan see. It was from such points as these that the zealous missionaries converted their nomad overlords, the Turkish tribes. These tribes and these cities, according to Professor A. J. Toynbee,[1] had the makings of a Far Eastern Christian civilization, had it not been for the rising tide of Islam which overcame them. The cities were rich in trade, entrepôts between the West and the Far East, once again prosperous under the T'ang dynasty.

Thus it was that T'ai Tsung and his successor saw, in the bolstering up of the Christian principalities, a bulwark against the common enemy from Arabia.

Where precisely did Alopen come from? Where was his home? The inscription reads 'there was a man of high virtue by name Alopen, who came from Tachin'.[2] The same thing is stated in the Chinese imperial decree of 638 recently discovered. Tachin is probably Syria.

Whether Alopen was Catholic, Nestorian or Jacobite, the church he had founded in China was Nestorian by the time the stone was erected, for we find, as already said, the name of the Nestorian Patriarch of Seleucia-Ctesiphon as being its spiritual superior in 781.

The life of the Nestorian Church in China was not entirely without reverses. These swings of the pendulum are faithfully recorded on the Nestorian Tablet. Thus in 638 the Emperor

[1] *A Study of History*, Vol. II, Oxford, 1934, pp. 375-7.
[2] Other spellings: Ta-ch'in, or, Ta Tsin.

T'ai Tsung issued his edict. It is laudatory but cautious. We must remember that he favoured the Buddhists as much as, if not more than, the Christians. That edict, given below, contemporary with the Nestorian mission, proved to the scholarly world that the insinuations of fraud made against the Jesuits by Voltaire and others were entirely unfounded.

Monastery of Tachin. In Chên-kuan, the 12th year (A.D. 639 *corrige* 638) in the 7th month, the following imperial edict was promulgated. 'Religion has not yet an invariable name: Saints are not of constant form: They establish doctrines in accordance with the countries and mysteriously save living beings. The monk A-lo-pen from Po-sze[1] has come from afar with the Scriptures and the doctrines; we find this religion excellent and separate from the world, and acknowledge that it is quickening for mankind and indispensable. It succours living beings, is beneficial to the human race and [therefore] is worthy of being spread all over the Celestial Empire. We decree a monastery to be built by the appropriate Board in the quarter of Yi-ning, and twenty-one priests to be appointed there.'[2]

The Emperor knew how to be non-committal. He also knew how to be helpful. The Christian religion was State-supported as a result of the above decree.

The reign of the next Emperor was one of prosperity for the Christian mission. Kao Tsung (650–83) the son of T'ai Tsung, continued the policy of his father, extending the influence of the Christians by setting up monasteries in every prefecture of the ten provinces of his dominion. But it would be an error to suppose that this Emperor was exclusively favouring the 'Luminous religion'. In the Chinese annals he emerges as perhaps the most fervent Taoist Emperor the Chinese had ever had. In any case he seems to have been a slave to his passion for a certain concubine

[1] The name for Persia. One would expect Tachin. But Alopen would certainly pass through Persia on his way from Tachin to China.

[2] This is a translation made by the Archimandrite Palladius, the discoverer of the Decree of A.D. 638, mentioned and quoted in the Nestorian Tablet, found by him in the forty-ninth chapter of the T'ang-Hui-yao in the imperial library. Quoted here from Havret, *op. cit.*, part II, p. 255.

who ultimately made history as the Empress Wu. It was through her animosity, we learn from the inscription, that the Christians in China had a serious set-back. Some years before his death (683), Kao Tsung was already a nonentity in the government of the country and the infamous Wu already completely dominated him. A short account of her activities will give some idea of the difficulties the Christians in the Far East experienced at this time.

Wu had been a concubine of Kao Tsung's father, but upon the latter's death had been put, doubtless to her chagrin, into a Buddhist nunnery. However, Kao Tsung, having conceived a passion for her from afar, on becoming Emperor, found her, took her from the nunnery, and all this with the co-operation of his wife, the Empress. Wu, as soon as she felt her power over the Emperor was absolute, seized the imprudent Empress, cut off her hands and feet, put her in a vat of wine and finally cut off her head. This was only the first of her recorded crimes. It seemed only necessary to be heir to the throne in order to be assassinated by this bloodthirsty woman. For years she terrorized the court, first her unhappy lover, the Emperor, then her son, a mere puppet. Not until her death in 705 did hope for the Christians return.

The inscription picks out two years of her reign—without mentioning her—as particularly evil times, 698-9. It was in the latter year that she threw off any pretence there might have been that she was merely Regent, and proclaimed herself Empress and foundress of the new Chou dynasty. As recorded above, Wu had spent some of her youth as an inmate of a Buddhist nunnery. She now attempted what is so often done by tyrants—she attempted to set up a State religion, in this instance Buddhism, to which end she established monasteries throughout the Empire and richly endowed them. This surely must have been a reward for their supporting her party. And here then is the background to the sentence in the inscription: 'During the period Shêng-li (698-9) the Buddhists, taking advantage of these circumstances, exercised a great influence and raised their voices (against the Luminous Religion) in the Eastern Chou.' (Saeki's translation.)

In A.D. 705 death took the once beautiful and now cruel Wu; her son, whom she had deposed, reigned in her stead until he was assassinated in 710. During the short reign of his successor it was the turn of the Taoists to deride the religion of Christ. As the inscription put it: 'Some inferior scholars (i.e. Taoists) ridiculed and derided it.' This was in the year 712. But that same year proved to be also the year of delivery for the persecuted Christians, since it was then that the Emperor Hsüan-Tsung succeeded to the throne (712–55). The position was immediately eased. The inscription puts it delicately thus: 'The consecrated rafters, which had been temporarily bent, were once more straightened.'[1]

This was the advent of one of the longest and the most glorious reigns in the whole long history of China. Only the K'ang-Hsi Emperor of the Manchu dynasty may be compared to Hsüan Tsung. This period coincided with an intense literary and artistic renaissance, significant of internal peace; yet externally it coincided with one of the greatest struggles for power on the grand scale in the history of the world: Islam was challenging Chinese hegemony in Central Asia. The Chinese marshalled the warlike tribes of those areas to support them in the struggle. In the end the war went against Hsüan Tsung, but not without a protracted resistance. He therefore needed all the help he could get. Here was the opportunity for the Nestorian Church to exert its greatest influence in China, and the political background explains some of its power, linked as it was with the Nestorian churches in Central Asia, battling against the Mohammedan intruders.

The inscription faithfully reflects this politico-religious activity. Two incidents of this century stand out. In 732 a Persian embassy arrived at the Western capital, and accompanying it was a priest named Chi-li. Twelve years later went another, Chi-ho.

'In the third year of the same period (A.D. 744) there was a priest named Chi-ho in the kingdom of Tachin. Observing the stars, he decided to engage in the work of Conversion . . . and looking towards the east he came to pay court to the most

[1] Saeki, op. cit., p. 168.

honourable emperor.' The inscription goes on to explain how he was ordered to perform the Christian ceremonies in the Hsing-ching Palace. This is extremely significant as it was this very palace which the Emperor had built for the royal princes. It adds weight to the hypothesis that the Emperor and his family might even have become Christian. Hsüan-Tsung also gave the Nestorian monasteries special names, a sign in those days of imperial protection. From this we can be certain that there were the closest relations between him and the Nestorian missionaries.

From other sources we know that after the deposition of Hsüan Tsung China entered a period approaching chaos and that this lasted for several hundreds of years with occasional spells of comparative peace. The inscription says little about the next two emperors and then arrives at the one contemporary with the setting up of the Tablet in A.D. 781, the Emperor Teh Tsung. The usual laudatory things are said and then the Tablet mentions one I-ssŭ who apparently came from Balkh. His significance is that he was not only pious, but martial, somewhat like the medieval fighting bishops. On the one hand he was noted for his liberality to the poor and on the other for his military efficiency. He was made 'Lieutenant Governor-General of the Northern Region, Assistant Overseer of the Examination Hall'. The Tablet also mentions that he was ordered by the Emperor to accompany a certain Duke Kuo Tzŭ-i on his expedition to the Northern Region. This would be in A.D. 750 and this Duke is a well-known figure in those troubled times, as he twice saved China, once from a rebellious general who captured the capital, and now from the Uighurs, a nomadic tribe who had created a vast but fluid empire north of China proper. These Uighurs now become important in Chinese history for several hundreds of years. The Duke made an alliance with them against the Tibetans, but for some time it was really the Uighurs who ruled. Now these Uighurs were either Manichean or Nestorian, perhaps Manichean at this time and a little later Nestorian. It is certain that in the thirteenth century many of them were Christian. But the situation is still so obscure that all one can say is that Iss-ŭ may have been sent with the Duke because the Uighurs had already become Christian, and also because the Chinese armies included Uighur mercenaries.

For many years the only evidence of the Nestorian entry into China and the flourishing Church there was the Nestorian Monument. But gradually more facts have come to light, scattered, obscure and incomplete, but nevertheless of great interest.

Adam, the author of the Monument, is mentioned later; but far more important was the discovery by local pagan priests in the nineteenth century of the hoard of documents in the cave temple near Tun-huang. Sir Aurel Stein and Professor Pelliot both visited the place in 1908, and took some precious MSS. away with them. Pelliot found among his treasure-trove what is now called the Tun-huang *Gloria in excelsis Deo*. It contains, however, not only the Syriac version of the *Gloria* turned into Chinese verse of lines of seven syllables but also a list of books used by the Christian community of China in the T'ang period including perhaps the Psalms, under the title 'The David, Sage King, Book'. There is a Breviary, 'The Heavenly Treasure Store', but strangely enough a Manichean book too, 'The Book of the Three Moments'. Is this yet another example of the eclecticism of these early Nestorians, or was it a present from Adam, that enterprising translator of all and sundry? The roll says that altogether they had three hundred and fifty works, all in the Sanskrit (perhaps Syriac?) tongue. It then recounts the arrival of Alopen in the Middle Kingdom, thus confirming the Monument. It also makes reference to the industry of Adam and says he was ordered to translate thirty rolls and more by imperial command.

iii. *The Suppression of the Nestorian Church*

The end of this Nestorian Chinese Christianity came in A.D. 845. In that year, the Emperor of the time (Wu Tsung), was particularly under the influence of the native Taoist bonzes or monks; he was losing wars on the Western frontiers, and these bonzes persuaded him to persecute all foreign religions, Buddhist, Manichean, and Christian alike.

As the Nestorians were, if we may go by their names upon the Tablet, mostly of foreign extraction, especially their leaders, the chance of survival was remote. They were foreigners, they were cut off from their base in Mesopotamia by war between the Chinese and their levies on the one hand and the Moslems on the other, whilst the region we may call Transoxania, formerly Bactria, was overrun by the Arabs. Thus the first twilight of the Christian religion in China was a false dawn; it flushed dimly for a space in the Far East, only to darken again and to remain for centuries obscured by the heavy clouds of paganism.

The decree dissolving all foreign monasteries in A.D. 845 is still extant, as is a contemporary poem which gives some idea of the feeling against foreigners at that time.

The Two Red Towers, written in 820 by the great poet Po Chü-i (A.D. 772–846), is a fine piece of pamphleteering. He is incensed by the power of the monks, not only Buddhist—of whom there were thousands—but all monks, and nuns too. All elegant pleasures have been abandoned or suppressed. He longs for music and the ballet. Mr. Arthur Waley calls it 'a satire against Clericalism'.

At this period the foreign religions, Buddhism and Christianity, had become very popular, and the instinctive reaction of the traditionalists was bound to express itself violently. Po Chü-i wrote as follows:

The Two Red Towers

North and south rise facing each other.
I beg to ask, to whom do they belong?
To the two Princes of the period Cheng Yuan[1]
The two Princes blew on their flutes and drew down fairies from the
sky,
Who carried them off through the Five Clouds, soaring away to
Heaven.
Their halls and houses, that they could not take with them,
Were turned into Temples planted in the Dust of the World.

[1] A.D. 785–805.

In the tiring-rooms and dancers' towers all is silent and still;
Only the willows like dancers' arms, and the pond like a mirror.
When the flowers are falling at yellow twilight, when things are
   sad and hushed,
One does not hear songs and flutes, but only chimes and bells.
The Imperial Patent on the Temple doors is written in letters of gold;
For nuns' quarters and monks' cells ample space is allowed.
For green moss and bright moonlight—plenty of room provided;
In a hovel opposite is a sick man who has hardly room to lie down.
I remember once when at P'ing-yang they were building a great
   man's house
How it swallowed up the housing space of thousands of ordinary
   men.
The Immortals are leaving us, two by two, and their houses are
   turned into Temples;
I begin to fear that the world will become a vast convent.[1]

The legal suppression of the monasteries was not long delayed.
It was issued by Wu Tsung in A.D. 845. It is a typical appeal to
nationalism, and also an attack by the active on the monastic
ideal of the contemplative. 'Why don't these people do something useful?' is the cry.

Under our three famous dynasties, never did anyone hear of Foe.[2]
It is since the Dynasties of Han and Wei that the sect, which has
introduced the statues, began to spread through China. Since that
time those foreign customs have established themselves without our
people being sufficiently on their guard. Every day they gain more
ground. Unfortunately the people is imbued with them, and the
State suffers in consequence. At the two courts, in all the cities, in
the mountains there are nothing but religious of both sexes. The
number and magnificence of the monasteries grow daily. Any
number of workmen are occupied in making their statues in all
manner of materials. A great deal of gold is used up in embellishing
them.[3] A number of persons forget their Prince and their relations

---

[1] Arthur Waley, *170 Chinese Poems*, London, 1939, pp. 135–6.
[2] 'Foe', from Chinese 'fo', the common expression for Buddha and
Buddhism.
[3] The opposition to the making of these things was mainly economic.

in order to put themselves under a Master Bonze. There are even some wretches who abandon wife and children and go and find among the Bonzes a sanctuary against the laws. Could anything more pernicious be found? Our forefathers had a maxim that if there were a man who did not work or a woman who did not busy herself in the silk-making, someone in the State felt the effect and suffered hunger or cold. What then is the state of affairs today, when an infinite number of bonzes, men and women, live upon and dress by means of the sweat of others and take up the time of an infinite number of workmen for building on all sides, and for furnishing at great expense magnificent edifices? Need we seek any other cause for the exhaustion of the Empire under the four dynasties, Chin, Liu Sung, Ch'i, Liang (265-556) and for the wickedness that reigned in those days?

As for our Dynasty of T'ang, the Princes who were its founders, after having used with success force of arms, in order to give back to the State its ancient tranquillity, concerned themselves with ruling it by wise laws; and in order to achieve this, far from borrowing anything from this vile foreign sect, from the very first of the years called chên-kuan, T'ai Tsung declared himself against it; but in this matter he went too softly, and the evil has merely increased. As for me, after having read and weighed everything put before me upon this matter, after having maturely deliberated with prudent persons, my decision is made. It is an evil, and must be remedied. All my enlightened and zealous officials throughout the Province urge me to set about the task. According to them, it is to dry up the source of the errors that flood the Empire; it is the way by which to re-establish the government of our ancestors, it is for the common good, it is the very life of the peoples. How, after that, can I excuse myself?

Having given his reasons, the Emperor now proceeds to what is to be done. Another reason for suppression occurs to the reader, that the State will doubtless grow rich on the spoil.

This then is what I decree: first, that more than 4,600 monasteries (Bonzeries), which are spread here and there and everywhere throughout the Empire, be completely destroyed: consequently let the Bonzes, men or women, who inhabit those monasteries and who, in all, number 260,500, return to the world, and pay their proportion of the ordinary taxes. Secondly, let more than 40,000 monasteries also be destroyed, less numerous, which are spread in the country-side: consequently let the lands that were attached which amount to some thousand myriad square kilometres, be added to our domain and let 150,000 slaves belonging to the Bonzes be put under the rule of the Magistrates and be considered part of the people.

As for the foreign Bonzes (monks) who come here, to make known the Law which is current in their Kingdom, there are about 3,000 of them, both from Tachin and from Mu-hu-po.[1] My command is that they also return to the world so that in the customs of our Empire there be no mixture. Alas! it is only too long that people have delayed to put things back on their ancient footing! Why delay any longer? The thing is finished and done. In view of the present command, let it be put into execution. Such is our will.[2]

This was apparently done, if we are to believe a gloss on the text, and we have no reason to doubt it.

The last piece of documentary evidence is one which mentions Alopen. The *Chronicles of Ch'ang-an* say: 'The foreign monastery of Po-ssŭ was erected in the 12th year of chên-kuan by T'ai Tsung (638) for Ol-o-ssŭ a foreign monk from the kingdom of Tachin.'[3]

What happened to these Nestorian Christians, after the suppression in 841, is unknown. Many guesses have been made: they became Buddhists, they turned Mohammedan, they were absorbed into the Manichean Church.

The Manichean sect, called by St. Augustine a Christian heresy, was sufficiently near in faith to the Nestorian to make it possible for the latter to be absorbed. But in fact we do not know what happened to the many Nestorian Christians of those times. The ones found by Fr. Ricci in the seventeenth century, whose only knowledge of their faith was the sign of the Cross, are just as likely to have been Mongol infiltrations as a native remnant dating back to so remote a past.

[1] Perhaps foreign Zoroastrians.
[2] Havret, *op. cit.*, part II, pp. 244 ff. cf. also P. Léon Wiéger, *Textes historiques* (3rd edit., Hien-Hien, 1929), Vol. II, pp. 1491–3.
[3] Havret, *loc. cit.*

iv. The Technique of the Nestorians, Especially That of Adam, the Writer of the Tablet

As interesting as the final fate of the Nestorians in China is their missionary technique. They seem to have favoured much the same organization as did the Far Western Christians in Ireland. The unit was the monastery; it had a bishop attached, who was of course a monk. He operated from there. Their manner of presentation of the Christian truths is still topical for us. These they transposed into a Chinese idiom. There is no doubt that of all the attempts by foreign Christians to get inside the Chinese mind, the Nestorian was by far the most thorough. True, the Jesuits adopted Chinese customs and manners, and even made use of Confucian ideas. But here, if we are to go by the technique of the Nestorian Inscription, is a thorough-going trans-position of idiom, not only into a Confucian idiom, but into Buddhist and Taoist as well, to an extent that has never been attempted since. The only comparable example was that made by the early Christians in the Greco-Roman world.[1]

The writer of the Tablet by some happy chance is known by more than his name, which was Adam Ching-ching. He was an expert translator. On one occasion he did it once too often, and the Emperor himself intervened with a sharp rebuke. This Adam was boon companion, it seems, to a Buddhist monk, also a translator, who had come from India. Between them they set about translating a Buddhist work in seven volumes into Chinese, but as the Indian did not know the language from which they were translating and Adam did not know Sanskrit nor have real knowledge of Buddhism, according to the Emperor, 'they could not get half its gems'. The Emperor went on to make some searching remarks upon the two religions, the Christian and Buddhist, which were he said 'entirely opposed to each other'

[1] cf. Havret, op. cit., part II, p. 216, note 2. 'The two (native) Chinese cults gave place to Buddhism for hierarchic names and for ceremonial; whilst for abstract and metaphysical ideas the Taoist repertoire was more suitable. All the rest, moral principles as well as literary allusions, were derived from the Confucian canonical or historical books.'

in customs and doctrine. His advice was that these two monks should keep off each other's preserves: 'Adam ought to hand down the teaching of the Messiah' and the Indian Buddhist 'should propagate the sutras of the Buddha'.[1]

This rebuff from imperial headquarters came one year too late to prevent Adam from composing and writing the Nestorian Monument. If we are to go by modern critics, we must say that the Emperor was being hypercritical.

Fr. Havret goes on to explain in his copious notes to his translation, that Ching-ching, if not a scholar in Sanskrit, was certainly one in the Chinese language; indeed almost every line is reminiscent of some great work and not least the five classics of the Confucian canon.

> This list [of literary echoes] contains three or four hundred expressions: that is to say, that four hundred times a skilled *literatus* would, on reading our inscription, experience that satisfaction of the humanist, which every Chinese experiences when someone conjures up before him a recollection of past ages. More than thirty of those expressions are borrowed from the Book of Changes alone; almost as many come from the Book of Odes; twenty or so from the Annals. The Canonical Books alone furnish a total of about 150 allusions. The Historians provide more than a hundred others; the Philosophers about thirty; the remainder come from different collections.[2]

Professor Saeki notes innumerable uses of Buddhist and Taoist ideas. The Monument is quite orthodox in its terminology. It has, however, one strange omission, namely all mention of the Crucifixion and Death of Christ, although the passage on the Tablet, 'He hung up the shining sun in order to triumph over the empire of darkness', does contain the word *Hiu* 'hung up'

---

[1] All this is fully quoted in Col. Yule's *Cathay and the Way Thither*, Vol. I, pp. 112–13, note by H. Cordier.

Sir Henry Yule: *Cathay and the Way Thither*, 4 vols., ed. Henri Cordier, issued by Hakluyt Society, 2nd series, nos. 33, 37, 38, 41, in 1913, 1914, 1915, 1916, an invaluable work on the Franciscan Age in China. Cited in footnotes as Yule, *Cathay*, also Wyngaert, O.F.M., *Sinica Franciscana*, Vol. I, Florence, 1933.

[2] Havret, *op. cit.*, part II, p. 216, note 2.

and is an allusion, though no doubt very veiled, to the Crucifixion of Our Lord.

Besides, there is a cross at the head of the Tablet. Lastly, it is probable that the Chinese of the seventh century, as those of the sixteenth century and those of today, used the crucifix as a means of deriding the Christian religion. Therefore these early missionaries thought it right not to expose the most sacred truth to the mockery of the Gentiles.

But like the Emperor of Adam's day, we must give only a guarded approval to Adam in his work. He was a pioneer, and deserves full praise for breaking new ground, but there are dangers, and more especially in the East where religions tend to amalgamate. Did we not see in the very decree of the Emperor T'ai Tsung an eclectic point of view which, if followed, would have led to all loss of individuality in any religion?

This chapter peters out in the discussion of minutiae, with scraps and pieces, and so it should, for the Nestorian chapter of the Christian approach to China seems to have petered out in the same way. It was buried just as the Tablet surely was during the anti-foreign convulsions of the mid-ninth century. Never were the Christian missionaries again to start with so great an initial advantage, for their own outlook was Eastern. It was to have been the marriage of two like minds, but the marriage was not to take place.

v. The Second Nestorian Wave

As has been shown we are tolerably well informed on the Christian mission to China up to the suppression of foreign cults in A.D. 845. It is the next period which remains dark. This is all the more tantalizing in that at its end we are provided with a blaze of light. The thirteenth century gives us numerous accounts of bodies of Christians in many parts of China. The researches of the last fifty years and more have lifted the veil a little.

Where then did the Nestorians come from who were fairly numerous in the thirteenth century? Both Marco Polo and his

Franciscan contemporaries in China note the presence of numerous Christian groups.

On the edge of China to the north and to the north-west there existed, all these centuries, a ring of Turkish, Mongol and Tartar tribes, mostly nomadic, warlike and mobile, ready always to descend upon the rich sedentary population within the Wall. To the west were the Eastern and Western Turks, now dominated by the Chinese, now dominating them.

This is not the place to go into the labyrinth of Central Asian power politics in the dark ages of the tenth and eleventh centuries. One Turkish tribe followed another in achieving a precarious supremacy: Uighurs, Kirghiz, Kitans, Keraits. The interesting thing about them from our point of view is that very often, if they were not Manichean, they were Christian. For instance, a bishop of far-distant Merv wrote to his spiritual superior, the Nestorian Patriarch at Bagdad, in 1009, asking him to be lenient with the laws of fasting for the Keraits. He mentions the unlikely number of 2,000,000 converts.[1] The Keraits were to play an important part in the struggle for control of China and Central Asia in the thirteenth century. Genghis Khan, after having used them for his own purposes, defeated them in A.D. 1203, having already crushed the Uighurs—another partly Christian group. Then he crushed the Naimans (also Christian) in A.D. 1206. As these were more civilized than their conquerors, they became the indispensable scribes, administrators and doctors. The fact also that one of them had prophesied to the Great Khan a victory in a famous battle made them popular with Ghenghis Khan.

The khans married into the Kerait princely family, so that we find wives and mothers Christian, and even in the Persian Mongol dynasty a number of Christian khans.

When therefore China was overrun by the armies of Kublai Khan, and there was much moving of populations, much resettlement, it was inevitable that a number of Kerait, Naiman

[1] cf. Sir E. A. Wallis Budge, *The Monks of Kublai Khan, or . . . The Life and Travels of Rabban Sauma . . . and Markos who . . . became Patriarch of the Nestorian Church in Asia*, London, 1928, pp. 34–5.

and Uighur Christians should settle in China. An example of this is the story of the civil servant in the city of Chen-Chiang fu, now known as Chinkiang, on the south bank of the Yangtse where the grand canal crosses it. This man, Mar George, was a Nestorian. His maternal grandfather had cured Ghenghis Khan of a sickness by administering sherbet, and the secret recipe had been passed down in the family. Naturally enough he did a good trade in it. He was ending his honourable career in this city, when he had a dream that he should build seven monasteries. This he proceeded to do. He financed the venture with the proceeds of the sherbet business, and all went well, except when he built one of his new monasteries on the remains of a Buddhist one. He was ordered to hand it back. Whether he did or not is now immaterial, but the point is that, to populate these monasteries, there must have been a considerable number of Christians.

It is such sidelights as the above which give us an idea of the strength of the Nestorian Church in the Far East at this period. The death-knell for the whole Nestorian Church of Central and Eastern Asia was the rise of the bloodiest and most cruel of all medieval conquerors, Tamberlaine (Timur-i-Leng). He began his conquests in 1358 and once in control of the key position of Transoxania his armies went forth to the Volga and Damascus, to Delhi and to the Western borders of the Chinese Empire. Wherever he went he brought slaughter and devastation. It is said he was an assiduous reader of the Koran, but this, though it might save the Mohammedans, did not save the Christians. By the time of his death at Kesh, of his embalming and burial at Samarkand in 1405, the work of extermination was nearly complete.

In China itself the toleration extended to Christians by the Mongol overlords came to an end with the collapse of their dynasty in 1368.

The native Chinese dynasty, which followed, persecuted every foreign religion.

Chapter Three

THE FRANCISCANS IN CATHAY

Bird's-eye View

The Franciscan period, like the Nestorian, is self-contained. It is one of the greatest epics of distant travel in recorded history.

The Mongol threat to the survival of Christian Europe in the thirteenth century set popes and kings dispatching missionaries and ambassadors across Asia to the court of the Great Khan.

The Beginnings were thus the heroic journeys of two Friars, John of Pian di Carpina and William of Rubruck, who both blazed a trail and brought back news of China beyond. They were followed by Marco Polo. But meanwhile, in the reverse direction, there appeared in the West two Christian hermits from Peking on pilgrimage to the shrines of Jerusalem and Europe. Christian curiosity was much roused by them.

These feelers were followed by a period of Promise when Blessed John of Montecorvino became resident archbishop in Cambaluc or Peking. Colonies of Christians were established at other points in China.

The Decline set in very soon, and its causes must be described. The whole episode lasted scarcely one hundred years.

i. *The Mongol Threat*

THE story has reached the middle of the thirteenth century, the age of St. Francis and of St. Dominic; a great Council of the Church was in progress at Lyons in the year 1245. It had been convoked by Innocent IV in agreement with the Emperor. The chief business was how to counter the imminent threat to the safety of Europe caused by the sudden terrifying emergence of the Golden Horde on its eastern flank. The Golden Horde of Ghenghis Khan's successor, under the nominal command of Batu, grandson of Ghenghis, and Subotai the Mongol general, was advancing across the plains of Poland and Hungary. At that hour, Christendom's very existence seemed at stake. The Mongol victories both east in China and west in Europe had indeed been spectacular. The conquerors had taken Peking; Persia had been laid waste. Gibbon well remarks: 'five centuries have been insufficient to repair the ravages of four years'. Genghis Khan was dead, but his redoubtable son, Ogodei, after setting about the conquest of China, aimed at empire over the whole earth, from the Yellow Sea to the Atlantic. The arrival of the swift horsemen of Ogodei on the plains of Hungary should have been the signal for swift response.

The complacency and lassitude of Europe were shaken. Yet Europe might have been overrun, had not the Mongol Great Khan Ogodei died in 1241, three thousand miles east in the steppe. On news of the death reaching the Golden Horde, Batu, their general, ordered a general retreat. They vanished as suddenly and mysteriously as they had come. But this fact neither Pope nor Emperor knew.[1] The Council which met in 1245, accomplished little; but Innocent IV had not waited for the Council before setting on foot one of the most momentous expeditions of medieval times; an expedition to the Great Khan himself.

ii. The Beginnings
(a) John of Pian di Carpina

Innocent IV chose for this arduous and vital journey one of the first disciples of St. Francis himself, *Friar John of Pian di Carpina.*[2] How near the heart of any Franciscan such a task

[1] Mgr. Mann, *Lives of the Popes*, Vol. XIV, London, 1928, pp. 174-201. A good account of the contacts between the Papacy and the Mongols and numerous references to sources. Cited in footnotes as, Mann, *op. cit.* cf. also, Yule, *Cathay, op. cit.*

[2] This is the name of the village, fourteen miles from Perugia, as it was called in the Italian of his day, and from which he sprang. Yule, *Cathay*, Vol. I, p. 156.

would be can easily be understood if we remember St. Francis' own great longing to convert the infidel. When the story of his interview with the Sultan in Egypt is still vivid to us, eight hundred years later, how much more so to one who may have heard the account from the lips of the Saint himself? Thus, despite his age (he was sixty-three), Friar John, who was rather stout, did not murmur, but set out for Karakorum in 1245. He left Lyons on the 16th April, furnished with a letter from the Pope to the Great Khan.[1] This included the following request: 'Moreover we would wish you to tell, through these brothers, what has moved you to the extermination of other nations, and what are your further intentions.' Friar John was the first to bring news to the West of the distant world of China beyond the vast plains of Central Asia.

Friar John set off with a companion, Friar Stephen, a Bohemian, but was later joined by Friar Benedict, a Pole. These two circumstances, and the fact that he had relations in Poland and had done much work in northern Europe, combined to settle his route: Bohemia, Poland, Russia, Kiev, the Black Sea, the Caspian. By February he was on the Volga and on the 22nd July, the day of St. Mary Magdalene, they arrived at the court of Güyük, the Khan-elect, in the centre of the Asian steppe.

He had arrived at a most crucial moment, and but for his descriptions nothing would be known of the life of the Mongols in their mobile camps before they began to live in cities, nor of the election of a Great Khan. One thing is very striking, the vast concourse of representatives from almost all the tribes and races of Eurasia. There was a Russian duke, the two sons of the Christian King of Georgia, an ambassador from the Caliph of Bagdad, and, more to our purpose, 'many dukes of the Cathayans'.[2] In another chapter he describes the wars between the Mongols

[1] For the whole letter cf. Mann, *op. cit.*, pp. 184–6.

[2] The handiest work on Franciscan medieval travellers East is Manuel Komroff, *Contemporaries of Marco Polo*, London, 1929, cf. ch. 24, p. 61. The best account is P. Pelliot, 'Les Mongols et la Papauté', in *Revue de l'Orient Chrétien*, 3e série, Vol. III (22), Paris, 1923. See also, *The Mongol Mission*, ed. Christopher Dawson, London, 1955.

and the Cathayans, or Chinese, and then gives this information:

> The men of Cathay are pagans, having a special kind of writing by themselves, and, as it is said, the scriptures of the Old and New Testaments. They have also recorded in histories the lives of their forefathers: and they have monks[1] and certain houses made like our churches. They say that they have many saints also, and they worship one God. They adore and reverence Christ Jesus our Lord, and believe the article of eternal life, but are not baptized. They also do honourably esteem and reverence our Scriptures. They love Christians, and bestow much alms, and are a very courteous and gentle people. . . . In all occupations which men practise, there are none better craftsmen in the whole world. Their country is exceedingly rich in corn, wine, gold, silk, and other commodities.[2]

These scraps of information not only whetted the curiosity of Friar John, but also that of Western Europe.

Friar John's approach to the Mongols is made clear in his speech to Batu, whom he met on the Volga.

> We are the envoys of the Lord Pope, who is the father and lord of the Christians. He has sent us to your emperor, as well as to your princes, and to all other Tartars, for this purpose, because it is his pleasure that all Christians should be friends with the Tartars, and should have peace with them. It is also his desire that they should be mighty with God in heaven. Therefore he advises them through us as by his own letters, to become Christians, and to embrace the faith of our Lord Jesus Christ, because they cannot otherwise be saved.[3]

He went on to say that he was astonished at their monstrous slaughter and massacres of mankind, and especially of Christians, but most of all of Hungarians, Moravians and Poles, who were all his subjects and who had not injured them in any way, nor attempted to do them hurt. 'And because the Lord God is

---

[1] There is a certain confusion in this passage between Buddhist and Christian practices and belief. There were some Nestorians in China. Perhaps even there is a confusion between Manicheans and Christians.

[2] Komroff, *op. cit.*, ch. 7, p. 37.   [3] *ibid.*, ch. 18, p. 52.

grievously offended by this, he advises them from henceforth to beware of such dealings, and to repent of what they have done.'[1]

This approach was not likely to have the desired effect, and Güyük Khan, despite all the thousands of miles the missionaries had travelled to see him, never once spoke with them directly.[2] Indeed for weeks they were almost left to starve. But for a Russian goldsmith named Cosmas, a favourite of the Khan, who gave them food, their tale would never have been told. Far from making a friendly gesture, Güyük and his chiefs, even whilst Friar John was in the camp, 'erected a flag of defiance against the Church of God, and the Roman empire, and against all Christian kingdoms and nations of the West'.[3] Finally, however, the Emperor deigned to send a message to the Pope, a message far from encouraging.

> The strength of God, Güyük Khan, the ruler of all men, to the great Pope. . . . If you desire to have peace with us, you Pope, Emperors, all kings, all men powerful in cities, by no means delay to come to us to conclude peace, and you will hear our answer and our will. The series of your letters contained that we ought to be baptized and to become Christians; we briefly reply that we do not know why we ought to do so. As to what is mentioned in your letters that you wonder at the slaughter of men and chiefly of Christians, especially Hungarians, Poles and Moravians, we answer shortly that this too we do not understand. Nevertheless, lest we should seem to pass it over in silence, we think proper to reply as follows. It is because they have not obeyed the precept of God and of Genghis Khan, and holding bad counsel have slain our messengers,[4] wherefore God had ordered them to be destroyed, and delivered them into our hands. But if God had not done it, what could man have done to man! But you, inhabitants of the West, believe that you only are Christians, and despise others; but how do you know upon whom He may choose to bestow His favour? We adore God, and, in His strength, will overwhelm the whole world from the East to the

[1] Komroff, *op. cit.*, ch. 18, p. 52.

[2] This was the normal procedure, the barbarian outdoing the etiquette of the civilized man.

[3] Komroff, *op. cit.*, ch. 26, p. 64.   [4] These were the Persians.

West. But if we men were not strengthened by God, what could we do?[1]

Such was the ruler of Asia, no friend of the Christians, despite the Nestorian chapel that stood outside his tent, 'where the priests do sing publicly and openly, and ring bells at certain hours'. Members of his family were Nestorian, his mother especially, who later became the wife of Hulagu, the destroyer of Bagdad.

Friar John 'travelled all winter long, lying in the deserts oftentimes upon the snow. . . . And oftentimes in the morning we found ourselves all covered with snow driven over us by the wind. . . . The citizens of Kiev, hearing of our approach, all came forth to meet us, with great joy. For they rejoiced over us, as over men that had risen from death to life.'[3] They arrived at Kiev on 9th June 1247. He delivered the Khan's message to the Pope, apparently having accomplished little; but in fact, apart from having performed a feat of almost incredible endurance and fine courage, he had opened the eyes of the West to the Far East, pointed the way to a Marco Polo and a Blessed John of Montecorvino. With that we take our leave of this intrepid explorer, though it will be necessary to refer to certain aspects of his findings later.

(b) *William of Rubruck*

For the next ten years there were many embassies and missions of minor importance from either side, but we may justly pass on in this history to the next traveller to bring news of China, the yet more famous William of Rubruck, or Rubruquis as he is sometimes called. It was his fate too not to reach that kingdom, but his information upon it is more detailed than Friar John's, and his description of the Nestorians in those distant parts ample proof, if proof were needed, that that Christian body was melting away.

St. Louis, while on a Crusade, heard from messengers that

[1] Taken from Mann, *op. cit.*, pp. 193–4.
[2] Budge, *op. cit.*, p. 107.
[3] Komroff, *op. cit.*, ch. 31, p. 70.

Sartach, the commander of the Mongols on the Don, was a Christian. As a good Christian and a leader of a Crusade against the Saracens, he was inclined to get into touch with Sartach. It was the aim of both parties, then and later, to co-operate in order to vanquish the common enemy, the Sultan of Egypt. Consequently St. Louis chose *William of Rubruck*, a Franciscan like his predecessor, as messenger. He went, not as a political agent, but simply as a missionary with letters of recommendation from King Louis, visited Sartach but was disappointed of his hopes; Sartach was no Christian. He went on to Batu and finally reached the camp near Karakorum where Mangu was now the Great Khan. It seemed to be the *rendez-vous* of the whole world, Tanguts, Tibetans, Chinese, Saracens, Georgians, Keraits, Naimans, Alans, even a Frenchman, an Englishman and a woman of Metz named Paquette, who had been a prisoner in Hungary.[1] Master William Buchier, whose brother lived on the Grand Pont over the Seine in Paris,[2] was very kind to Friar William. On Palm Sunday:

> The Mass said, evening approached and Master William took us with him to his home for supper, in great joy. His wife was the daughter of one Lorraine, and born in Hungary, she spoke French well and a language spoken by the Mongols. We met there another European, named Basil, the son of an Englishman, and born in Hungary . . . the supper passed in real joy.[3]

He was in touch very soon with all the Christians there.[4] Holy Thursday and Easter were then approaching.

> I did not have my priestly vestments, and I was watching [observing] the manner of consecration of the Nestorians, and I was very anxious. Will I receive the Sacrament from them? There was a swarm of Christians there, Hungarians, Alans, Ruthenians, Georgians, Armenians, all of whom had been deprived of the Sacrament since their captivity, for the Nestorians would not admit them in their Church, unless they were baptized by them. However

---

[1] Komroff, *op. cit.*, ch. 34, p. 149. [2] *ibid.*, ch. 35, p. 150.
[3] *ibid.*, ch. 47, p. 172. [4] *ibid.*, ch. 48, p. 174.

these priests raised no objections to us in this regard. On the contrary, they recognized that the Roman Church was the head of all the churches, and that they themselves would have to receive their Patriarch from the Pope if the roads were open.

The end of it was that Master William the goldsmith fashioned an iron for making hosts:

> So I celebrated Mass on Holy Thursday with the Nestorian silver chalice and their paten . . . likewise on the day of Easter. And gave Communion to the people, with the blessing of God, I hope. More than sixty persons were baptized on the eve of Easter, in very good order, and the joy among the Christians was very great.[1]

Meanwhile Friar William had had an interview with Mangu Khan almost as soon as he arrived, immediately after the previous Christmas. The curtain of felt was raised to let him and his companion in. There sat Mangu on a couch, dressed in a spotted, glossy fur, with him a woman and a child, his daughter. The friars on entering began to sing:

> *A solis ortu cardine*
> *Et usque terre limitem*
> *Christum canamus principem*
> *Natum Maria Virgine.*[2]

This pious approach did not soften the suspicious Mongol, who took no chances. The missionaries were searched for knives; after which a strange conversation ensued, for two of the four participants were drunk. 'The Khan had his interpreter . . . we had ours, such as he was, though drunk. . . . Until now I had always understood my interpreter, but since his state of drunkenness, I could no longer. It seemed to me that Mangu Khan himself was staggering a bit.'[3] Under such circumstances important matters could not be discussed and Friar William became silent. Later Mangu came to the Nestorian Christian Church and examined curiously William's Bible and his Breviary, asking what the illuminations represented.[4] The Queen too was present and

---

[1] *ibid.*, pp. 174–5.
[2] *ibid.*, ch. 33, p. 146.
[3] *ibid.*, ch. 38, p. 155.
[4] *ibid.*

stayed on after Mangu retired. Wine was brought in. All drank. 'Everyone was a little drunk... so they passed the day till evening. And then the queen herself, tottering with drunkenness, mounted her chariot in the midst of the singing and the howling of the (Nestorian) priests, and went her way.'[1] Little wonder that the khans saw no profit in the religion of Christ as exemplified by these degraded descendants of the heresy of Nestorius, or that he could say, 'God has given you a testament, and you do not follow it.'

Meanwhile, Friar William, by keeping his eyes and ears open, had gleaned much information both instructive and amusing about the Cathayans or Chinese.

Beyond is the great Cathay, whose inhabitants are the same as the Seres of the ancients. . . . These inhabitants of Cathay are small in build and speak through their noses. Like all orientals they have small eyes. They are very skilled workers in all crafts, and their doctors know well the virtue of herbs, and understand diseases through the taking of the pulse; but they have no knowledge of urines; this at least is my observation. There are great numbers of these people at Karakorum; and it has ever been their habit that all sons should follow the trade of their father whatever it might be. . . .

Friar William now describes one of the greatest obstacles to the Catholic missionaries of that time in the Far East, the decadent Nestorian Church.

Among them there are Nestorians and Saracens who are considered as foreigners in Cathay. There are Nestorians in fifteen cities of Cathay and in a city called Hsianfu there is a Bishop. . . . If it is necessary to believe what I have heard, there are also hermits who live ascetic lives in the woods. Yet they recite their prayers and have their holy books in Syrian, and they do not understand them. The consequence is that they chant as do the monks in our country who are unversed in grammar.[2] They are above all usurers, drunkards

[1] Komroff, op. cit., chap. 38, p. 155.
[2] There certainly were Nestorian anchorites, as was proved visually to astonished Rome and Western Europe when a few years later one of them, Rabban Sauma, appeared having travelled from Peking, as will be recorded in its due place.

and some live with the Tartars and have like them several wives. . . . The bishop rarely visits their country, perhaps only once in fifty years. At that time all the little male children are ordained priests, even those still in the cradle. . . . They are very attentive to their wives and children, and so are more concerned to obtain money than to spread the faith. Those among them who educate the young noble Mongols, while teaching them the Gospel and the Faith, succeed in alienating them from the practice of Christian virtue, through the bad example of their lives.[1]

Finally, towards the end of June 1254, Mangu decided to send the friars back to King Louis with a message. It contained a menace: 'We, therefore, are sending you the written order of the word of the eternal God . . . and if you resist it, saying, "Our land is far away, our mountains are high and many, our sea big", the eternal God knows that we know what we can do.'[2] Once again an embassy to the Great Khan had failed.

Friar William prepared to depart, but his companion could not face the journey and remained: 'If I go with you, I see danger for my body and my soul, for I can no longer bear such hardships.'[3] Thus Friar William travelled alone and reached the Holy Land in the summer of 1255. As King Louis the saint had already left it, the two did not meet. The Provincial made Friar William stay at Acre, instead of proceeding to France. At Acre he wrote his report, and thus we have the written account. Friar William died in 1270 at the age of fifty-five.

The reports of Friar John and Friar William on the belligerent intentions of the Mongols were terribly verified three years later, when Hulagu, the Khan of Persia, attacked Bagdad. He utterly destroyed it and massacred its inhabitants, wrecking also the entire irrigation system of Iraq, a system of immemorial antiquity which has never since been repaired. Yet all was not black in the picture, for the Great Khan's wife was a Christian; so also was his general, Kit-Bugha.

The effect of these events was two-fold. The West turned to the Mongols, hoping to find in them allies against Islam. The

[1] Komroff, *op. cit.*, ch. 29, pp. 135–7.   [2] *ibid.*, ch. 54, p. 199.   [3] *ibid.*, p. 200.

peaceful possession of Central Asia by one victorious power opened up the caravan routes as never before. It was now possible to travel in safety across the great Central Asian plain from Rome to Peking. The first to seize the opportunity, after the Franciscans, were merchants: Marco Polo, his father and his uncle. Their rediscovery of China was as great a wonder to medieval Europe as was that of the New World to the Renaissance. Medieval men, who believed in wonders, would scarcely believe in this, so wonderful was it.

(c) *Marco Polo*

The feeling of security was such that Maffeo and Nicolo Polo set out as merchants to the Far East. In 1269 they returned with a letter to the Pope from the Great Khan of China asking him for a hundred men 'wise in the Christian law and acquainted with the seven arts'. The Great Khan of the time was Kublai who in 1257 had styled himself Emperor of China, thus founding the Yuan dynasty. The Pope, Clement IV, was dead (d. 1268) when the Polos reached Acre on their way back to Cathay, but they told their tale to the Papal Legate, Tedaldo Visconti. Finally, after much delay and a return to Acre, after they had already set out with Marco, the son of Nicolo, this same Legate, now Pope-elect, sent them off with, not a hundred, but two Dominicans and letters for Kublai Khan. Sad to relate the two Dominicans gave up; the three Polos therefore continued their journey alone, reaching Kublai Khan at Peking in 1275. The first eye-witness account, then, of China by a Western European is that of Marco Polo. The first missionary, Br. John of Montecorvino, reached Peking in 1292, a year after Marco Polo's departure from it.

Marco Polo's testimony to the presence of large numbers of Christians in China used to be entirely discounted as part of his supposed habit of exaggerating; but another explanation seems now more probable.

His evidence in full about the Christians existing in the south-east of China in his day has come to light in the recently discovered MS. of Marco Polo's travels, the famous Codex Z, a Latin document found in the Ambrosian Library at Milan by Professor Benedetto. According to this version, a Saracen in Foochow got in touch with the three Polos, telling them that in that city there was 'a race of people of whom no one knows what law they follow'. He suggested that they should all go and visit them to extract some information. At first these people were most suspicious, as they thought their visitors were spies sent by the Government intent on depriving them of their religion. By repeated visits, and by assuring them that there was no dark motive, barriers were broken down. 'And so at last we discovered that they followed the Law of Christ. For they had books.' These books were the Psalter. They said that they had received their religion seven hundred years before, but that now after so long a time they had forgotten what had been taught in the beginning. The only element of teaching that had been preserved was that they had to reverence three of the seventy who went preaching, three 'apostles'. They had a painting of them in one of their temples. The Polos jumped to the conclusion that they had found a distant Christendom, a relic of an ancient age. Their advice to these supposed Christians was to get in touch with the Great Khan, ruler of China, so that, being recognized as Christians, they would have permission to exercise their religion freely. This they did. But 'the head of the Idolaters', when their case was put, denied that they were Christians. There was a dispute. Finally the Khan commanded these people themselves to appear before him. He asked them whether they wished to be Christians or Idolaters. And they answered him that, if it pleased him and 'if it was not unbecoming to his majesty, they would fain be Christians, as their fathers had been'.[1]

The chapter ends with the remark, 'And it was found that, scattered here and there throughout South China, called Manzi, there were over 700,000 families who followed this Law.'

A minor point of interest in this account is that these people were advised by the Polos to get in touch with an official at the

[1] *Marco Polo's Travels*, ed. L. F. Benedetto, trans. Professor Aldo Ricci, pp. 261–3, London, 1939.

court whose business it was to concern himself with the rights of Christians in the Empire, a fact which implies a considerable number of them. But the point of major importance is whether these people really were Christians at all.

So long as the Manichean *diaspora* was not seriously considered, there seemed no other explanation of so great a number of families following this Law; but now that it has become abundantly clear that Manicheanism had spread with far greater force east than it did west, it is the opinion of several authorities, particularly Professor Paul Pelliot that these 'Christians', who did not know what they were until the Polos put it into their heads that they were Christians, were in fact descendants of Manicheans. At one time such a theory would have been scouted; but today, since the discovery of the works of Mani and his early disciples in a box in the Fayum district of Egypt, it becomes more than plausible and almost amounts to a certainty. For Manicheanism is not a new religion, it is an offshoot from Christianity by a man who attempted to create a syncretic religion from all religions, particularly Christianity, Buddhism and Zoroastrianism. This very 'Psalter', which the Chinese showed to the Polos, would have had hymns to Jesus. Mani called himself an apostle of Jesus. He was interpreting, so he maintained, the promise of Jesus that the Holy Spirit would come leading them into all truth. This truth was to be the sum of all religions, as discovered by Mani. It is a fact that Mani travelled in India *c.* A.D. 240. He then returned to Persia. From there he descended into Mesopotamia; he penetrated into Parthia, but expressly says that he never crossed over into the territory of the Roman Empire. He was put to death in A.D. 272. We know that the Uighurs were converted to Manicheanism early in the eighth century, but later seem to have become Nestorian; we know that the sect flourished in China about the same period, but that it was persecuted and its books destroyed in the general persecution of foreign religions in the ninth century. These Fukien 'Christians' must surely be precisely the remnant of that widespread Manichean Church, which had attracted and then repelled St. Augustine in the fourth century, that had appeared unexpectedly in Provence in the twelfth century, and whose scattered remains are today found from Fukien in China to the Fayum in Egypt. The theory here baldly stated cannot be proved absolutely, but it does seem best to fit the known facts.

From all this it is clear that some idea, however vague, of Christianity, still persisted in China in the thirteenth century. But most of the Christians would be soldiers of the invading armies now settled in the land, particularly the valiant Alans[1] from the Caucasus, subjugated by the Mongols and enlisted in their armies some years before.

Marco Polo was not concerned with the evangelizing of China and therefore his well-known narrative has small place in this work.

(d) *Rabban Sauma and Mark the Nestorian Patriarch*

Meanwhile in Europe interest had not flagged. A deputation from the Khan Abaga of the Western Mongols in Persia and Bagdad had been received at the next General Council of Lyons in 1274. Five Franciscans, headed by Gerard of Prato were sent to Abaga and told to pass on to China. This they did not succeed in doing. But again interest was stirred all over Western Europe, this time by the arrival in Rome of a Nestorian Christian monk whose home was Peking, and who had travelled all the way with a companion to venerate the Holy Places. From there he had passed on to Rome and Paris and Bordeaux. His name was Rabban Sauma. His arrival was so unforeseen, so novel, so mysterious, so opportune, that it roused the Church to action, and therefore some account of this amazing story should be given here.

In the Year of Our Lord 1278 there lived alone in a hermitage, not far from Peking, Bar Sauma, son of two pious Uighur

[1] For Alans, Asu or Asas of Chinese annals, cf. Yule, *The Book of Sir Marco Polo* with Henri Cordier's Notes and Addenda, 3 vols, London, 1920–29, Vol. II. ch. 74, note 2. It was the Alans in Cambaluc (Peking), who held high office there, who wrote to Benedict XII imploring him to send a successor to Archbishop John of Montecorvino.

Nestorian Christians of Peking.[1] He and a friend decided to visit the Holy Places at Jerusalem, a journey of many thousand miles. Neither returned, but that they could not know.

Many people tried to dissuade them from so hazardous an adventure, but they were firm and set off probably in the year 1278 or perhaps 1279. The route was the famous Central Asian highway: they first reached Su-chou, the gateway into China from the west, in the old province of Tangut where many Nestorians still lived. Marco Polo mentions three churches there. From there they were sent on to Khotan, where they had to remain six months owing to a war between Kublai Khan and Oko—a king not otherwise famous. The next stop was Kashgar, the junction for travellers of Asia from east and west and from India in the south. But it was then far from being a Christian centre, for it had been deserted by its inhabitants when the Chinese army had pillaged it. The next halts were at the city of Khorasan and at Tus in the same province. Bagdad was now the next immediate objective; once in that area they visited many monasteries and famous shrines throughout Mesopotamia and eastern Syria. Finally they settled at Tar'il, but the Patriarch of Bagdad, whom they had already met at Maraghah, called them to him at Bagdad. He sent them on some diplomatic mission to Abaga—successor to Hulagu—in which they were successful. They then felt justified in pushing on towards Jerusalem, via Armenia, but they were forced, owing to the dangerous condition of the roads, to return to Bagdad. The Patriarch thereupon informed them that he had a high design for them: Mark was to be Patriarch of China and Sauma his Vicar-General. Reluctantly they accepted and set off, but their road was barred by wars in Transoxiana, so they turned back to arrive at Bagdad just when the Patriarch died. At the ensuing election Mark was elected in his place, partly no doubt because he knew the Mongol language and was *persona grata* with the Mongol emperors.

Arghon, the Ilkhan, wished to attack the Mohammedan countries of Palestine and Syria, but knowing he could not succeed alone he

[1] cf. Budge, *op. cit.*

arranged for Sauma to be sent to the Christian West to work up a Crusade. Sauma went via the Black Sea and Constantinople and so on to Rome[1] (1287). Honorius IV, the Pope, had died in the same year, but the cardinals received the traveller cordially. One day he was officially interrogated by them:

A CARDINAL: It is a strange thing that you, a Christian, a deacon at the Throne of the Patriarch of the East, should come as ambassador from the Mongol king.

SAUMA: Know ye, O our fathers, that many of our Fathers have gone into the country of the Mongols, and Turks, and Chinese, and have taught them the Gospel, and now there are many Mongols Christian. For many of the sons of the Mongol kings and queens have been baptized and confess Christ. . . .

A CARDINAL: What is your profession of faith? To what 'way' are you attached? Is it one held by the Pope today or another?

SAUMA: No man has come to us Orientals from the Pope. The Holy Apostles, whose names I have mentioned, taught us the Gospel, and to what they delivered to us we have clung until this present day.[2]

A theological discussion followed in which the cardinals seemed to expect to find Monophysitism, though they ought to have expected Dyophysitism, i.e. Nestorianism; Sauma seemed serenely unaware that he might be considered a heretic. He cut short the argument by saying: 'I have not come from remote countries to discuss or to instruct any in matters of faith, but to get the blessing of the Pope and from the shrines of the saints, and to make known the words of King Arghon and the Catholicus.' Sauma then gave himself over to sight-seeing, and to making pilgrimage to the shrines at Rome. He passed through Lombardy and France; reaching Paris he spoke with Philip the Fair. He marvelled at the monastery of St. Denis. At Bordeaux he met

---

[1] At Naples he saw a battle between the armies of the kings of Naples and Aragon from a roof-top, and admired the way in which the Franks (i.e. Westerners) waged war; for they attacked none of the people except those actually combatant. cf. Budge, *op. cit.*, p. 171.

[2] *ibid.*, pp. 173 ff.

King Edward I of England, who received Holy Communion at his hands.[1]

We can scarcely exaggerate the impact that this strange, holy apparition from another world must have had upon the Western Christian world, as this pilgrim knelt at its shrines, demonstrating his Christian birthright. More than anything else, except doubtless the terror of the Mongol menace on one hand and on the other the old tales of Prester John, king and priest over some fabulous empire, like Melchisedek of old, this message of peace stirred the ancient embers of the apostolate to flame. There were worlds beyond the eastern horizon to win for Christ.

Sauma returned to Rome in the spring of 1288. He was received liberally by the new Pope, Nicholas IV, the first Franciscan to be elected Pope. He was sent back with many promises, letters to the Khan, presents, rich relics. He celebrated Mass in St. Peter's on Passion Sunday, and, at the sight, the people cried out: 'The language is different, but the use is the same.'

Whatever the differences between Sauma and the cardinals on his first visit to Rome, now, in his second visit, it seems certain that he had been personally reconciled to the Mother of all the Churches, for, after this Mass he received the Pope's blessing and pardon of his sins. But he went on: 'Besides the pardon of my transgressions and sins which I have received from thee, O our Father, I beseech thy Fatherhood, O our Holy Father, to let me receive the offering from thy hands, so that the remission of my sins may be complete.' And the Pope said: 'So let it be!' There is something greatly moving in this reconciliation of East and West in the persons of Sauma and the Pope Nicholas. It was a reconciliation, however, which had come too late.

It seems likely that on his return to Bagdad he recounted his experiences and thoughts to his younger friend Mark, and that

[1] King Edward made a fine reply to Sauma when the latter asked him to show him any church or shrine of note: 'You shall speak thus to Arghon and all Orientals: "We have seen a thing than which there is nought more wonderful, that is to say, that in the country of the Franks (the West) there are not two Confessions of Faith but only one . . . namely, that which confesseth Jesus Christ; and all the Christians confess it." ' Budge, *op. cit.*, pp. 186–7.

this influenced the latter in his turn to submit to the Pope. We have proof of this in the Latin version of his letter to Benedict XI in 1304. The section dealing with the Papacy runs as follows:

> We proclaim, besides, the holy Roman supreme Pontiff and universal father of all the faithful of Christ and we confess that he himself is the successor of S. Peter, the universal Vicar of Jesus Christ, over all the sons of the Church, from the East even to the West; whose love and affection is firmly established in our hearts, and we are under obedience to him, and we need and ask for his blessing and we are ready for any command from him.[1]

Sauma had died ten years before at Bagdad in 1294. Unfortunately the rise of Christianity in the new Mongol kingdom of Persia was short-lived. Arghon greatly favoured the Christians. He had his own son Kharbandi baptized by Mark, the Patriarch; he built many churches; Sauma followed his army until his health broke down. But, underneath, the Mohammedan masses, whose Christian ancestors had been forcibly converted to Islam, waited only for an opportunity to rise and shake off their Christian masters. Before long one of Arghon's sons, Kazan, turned Mohammedan, with the inevitable result; not only were the churches destroyed but the widespread Nestorian religion in his realms became almost extinct.

The very existence of these two remarkable men, Sauma and Mark, proves the extent of the Nestorian Church from China to Bagdad in the thirteenth century. It is difficult to reconcile this fact with Friar William's strictures recorded above. Sauma was well brought up in theological knowledge in Peking where a Nestorian Metropolitan, Mar George, reigned in a cathedral church. From him he had received the tonsure and had became door-keeper of the church. His fame must have spread far, for Mark came from Kawshang in Khorasan to join him. It is surmised that the powerful King George by his influence had re-instated the Nestorian Church of those parts, and that the King's submission and that of his tribe to Rome, effected by John of

[1] Budge, *op. cit.*, pp. 99–100.

Montecorvino at the end of the thirteenth century roused the Nestorians to violent action. On the King's death he was succeeded by an infant son, and his brother saw to it that the tribe returned to their old heresy.

We need not follow Rabban Sauma on his return. But it is worth stressing here, that these two Nestorians were very holy men, that they seem to have been unaware that they were in heresy, that probably both—but certainly the Patriarch— renounced their heresy, and that this journey spurred on Pope Nicholas to act. He acted quickly. In 1289 John of Montecorvino was sent to China to convert it. Here we must pause and recount fully the missionary endeavours of that great man. As Yule wrote: 'already nearly fifty years of age . . . he plunged alone into that great ocean of paganism'.[1]

iii. The Period of Promise

John of Montecorvino was born in 1247[2] perhaps at Pietra Montecorvino near Foggia in southern Italy. In 1272, already a Franciscan, he was in the East and was entrusted by the Emperor Michael Palaeologus with the delicate matter of the return of the Greek Church to union with Rome. In 1289 he was still in the East and his heart was there too, for he was aware of the movement towards the Church among many races in Western Asia, and he knew too the desire of princes and people to hear the word of God.

The itinerary of Friar John was different from that of the previous two friars who visited the Great Khan. To begin with he could not go via the Red Sea, as the Saracens were astride the marches of Asia and Africa; he did not go overland all the way, probably because of the appalling hardships and perhaps because of the then unsettled state of the Central Asian steppe. Consequently he went via the Black Sea, and then south of the Caucasus to Tabriz where he stayed till 1291; then down through Iraq, Arghon's country, to the entrance of the Persian Gulf and the

---

[1] cf. Yule, *Cathay*, Vol. I, p. 168.
[2] cf. his first letter, *ibid.*, Vol. III, p. 50.

great port of Ormuz where he took ship for India. He tarried on the coast of Malabar and visited the site of St. Thomas's tomb. The seas between India and China are still perilous, but they were certainly much more so in the days when Friar John ventured on them. The year he arrived sixty ships were lost.

Their ships in these parts are mighty frail and uncouth, with no iron in them, and no caulking. They are sewn like clothes with twine. And so if the twine breaks anywhere, there is a breach indeed! . . . And they have a frail and flimsy rudder like the top of a table, of a cubit in width, in the middle of the stern. . . . They have but one sail and one mast, and the sails are either of matting or of some miserable cloth.[1]

Friar John was thirteen months in India and then took one of these boats for China which he must have reached at long last in 1292 or 1293.

He reached China alone, the first Catholic priest to set foot on Chinese soil, for of his two companions, one, John of Palma, died before they left Europe, and the other, Brother Nicholas of Pistoia, a Dominican, died in India[2] and was buried in the church of St. Thomas.

On his arrival he presented his letters from the Pope to Kublai Khan,[3] now a very old man, and tried to persuade him to become a Catholic; but the Emperor, he writes, 'had grown too old in idolatry'. But he showed kindness to the Christians. Later John hoped to convert the Emperor Timur, but, as always, the evidence

[1] cf. Friar John's third letter. There are three extant. From the second letter, it appears that the first was addressed to the Vicar and Friars of the province of Gazaria; it is dated 'at the city of Cambaluc in the kingdom of Cathay in the year of the Lord 1305 and on the 8th day of January'. Cambaluc=Peking.

The second, dated Quinquagesima Sunday, 1306, from the same city (Peking), is addressed to the Vicar-General of the Order of Friars Minor, to the Vicar of the said Order, and to the Master of the Order of Preachers, and Friars of both Orders in Persia.

The third was written first, before he had reached China. The recipient is not known. It was dated 22nd December A.D. 1292 (or 1293) from Malabar.

[2] Yule, Cathay, Vol. III, p. 44.

[3] It is not clear that he is referring to Kublai Khan, it may be Timur (1295–1307).

for such conversions is conflicting; and in his case, in view of his known leanings towards the teaching of the Lamas of Tibet, improbable. Nevertheless Blessed John was allowed to build a church in the Emperor's own city of Peking, and later to build one by the gates of his palace, so that the Emperor could hear the chanting of the choir. The first church was probably completed in 1300.

But he had not been in China long before the Nestorians started spreading rumours that he was a spy and an impostor, even that he had robbed the real envoy of the Pope, murdered him and was now impersonating him. These reports were believed; and several times he was near death on account of them. At last someone confessed that these stories were lies, and these same Nestorians were themselves banished.

All this persecution lasted for five years. But he was not without his consolations. The King of Tatung, George, a Nestorian, of the family of Prester John, attached himself to Friar John on his arrival and was converted to the true Faith by him. He would assist Friar John at the celebration of Mass, dressed in his royal robes. He brought over with him a great part of his people. His zeal was boundless; he built a magnificent church[1] in his kingdom, to be called the Roman Church; had he lived he would have translated the whole Latin ritual into his own tongue. Friar John proceeds, 'and whilst he was alive I used to celebrate Mass in his church, according to the Latin rite, reading in that language and character the words of both the Preface and the Canon'. But in 1299 King George died. This was a signal for those who objected to the change to draw back to Nestorianism all those who had been brought into the Church. Alone as he was, and unable to

---

[1] According to the Dominican John di Cora, Archbishop of Soltania c. 1300 in his *The Book of the Estate of the Great Cann* (cf. Yule, *Cathay*, Vol. III, pp. 89 ff., esp. p. 101) 'When that archbishop (John of Montecorvino) of whom we have been speaking was building those abbeys of the Minor Friars, these Nestorians by night went out to destroy them, and did all the hurt they were able.' He goes on that there were 30,000 Nestorians in China in that period. John di Cora was appointed to succeed John of Montecorvino but seems never to have reached China.

leave the Great Khan, Friar John could not make the long journey to save the situation.

Steadily he was making converts. By 1305 he had baptized six thousand persons, and but for the action of the Nestorians he says the figure would have reached thirty thousand. One of his special cares was the *Opus Dei*, the celebration of the liturgical services. His own letter describes his methods admirably.

Also I have gradually brought one hundred and fifty boys, the children of pagan parents, and ages varying from seven to eleven, who had never learnt any religion. These boys I have baptized, and I have taught them Greek and Latin after our manner. Also I have written out Psalters for them, with thirty Hymnaries and two Breviaries. By the help of these, eleven of the boys already know our service, and form a choir and take their weekly turn of duties, as they do in monasteries, whether I am there or not. Many of the boys are also employed in writing out Psalters and other things suitable. His Majesty the Emperor, moreover delights much to hear them chanting. I have the bells rung at all the canonical hours, and with my congregation of babes and sucklings I perform the divine service, and the chanting we do by ear, because I have no service book with the notes.[1]

When he had two churches, he formed the boys into two communities and said Mass at each church in alternate weeks. He writes begging for an Antiphonal and Gradual and Psalter with musical notation. The only liturgical books he had with him were a little Missal and a pocket Breviary.

The year 1303 had an unpleasant surprise for him, in the person of a Lombard leech and surgeon, who must have wounded Friar John deeply by spreading the vilest rumours about the court of Rome, the condition of the Franciscan Order and the state of things in the West. Not only did this hurt, but it disquieted him, for how could he verify these statements or contradict them? Then, when he thought he had been completely forgotten, he was some few months later joined by Friar Arnold, a German of the province of Cologne.

[1] cf. Yule, *Cathay*, Vol. III, pp. 46–7.

He now set about building the second church already mentioned. This he was able to do the more easily as a certain Italian merchant, a devout man, who had shared the perils of the journey to China with Friar John, bought the land 'and gave it to me for the love of God'.[1] This was Master Peter of Lucolongo. Pictures, with writing in Latin, Uighur and Persian characters explaining them, were put up, reminding us of St. Benet Biscop's similar method of teaching the uncultured Saxons the Bible story and of the later similar experiments of the Jesuits in China. The church was opened on the Feast of St. Francis, 4th October (presumably 1306). But note, there were no explanations in the Chinese characters. Was this then a mission only for foreigners in China?

John of Montecorvino, though only fifty-eight, was feeling old and grey, 'more with toil and trouble than with years'.[2] Like Fr. Ricci and Fr. Verbiest after him he implores the Vicar-General to send more sharers in his work.

'Indeed if I had but two or three comrades to aid me, it is possible that the Emperor Cham would have been baptized by this time! I ask then for such brethren to come, if any are willing to come, such I mean as will make it their great business to lead exemplary lives and not make broad their phylacteries.'[3]

The itinerary he suggests was the overland route, taking five or six months, but he points out that for the time being, as when he himself had come, wars made that route impassable. To encourage them he says:

I have a place at the Cham's court, and a regular entrance and seat assigned to me as legate of Our Lord the Pope, and the Cham honours me above all the other prelates, whatever be their title. And although his majesty the Cham has heard much about the court of Rome, and the state of the Latin world, he desires greatly to see envoys arriving from these regions.[4]

When Pope Clement V at Avignon received this appeal for help he commanded the Minister-General of the Franciscans to choose seven brothers, zealous and learned in Holy Scriptures to

[1] cf. Yule, *Cathay*, Vol. III, p. 55.   [2] *ibid.*, p. 50.
[3] *ibid.*, p. 48.   [4] *ibid.*, p. 57.

be made bishops. They were to go to China where they would consecrate Friar John Archbishop and Patriarch of the whole East. He was to have almost Papal powers in those parts except that: *Tam ipse fr. Johannes quam omnes archiepiscopi Cambalenses futuri per saecula Romanae ecclesiae subjaceant in his pactis*, that is, he must acknowledge the supremacy of the Roman See and receive the pallium from it.[1]

The names of the seven selected for this missionary enterprise were, Gerard, Peregrine of Castello, Andrew of Perugia, Nicholas of Bantra, Andrutius of Assisi, Ulrich Sayfustordt and William of Villeneuve.[2] Only the first three reached their destination, the others, and many other friars, died from the heats of Lower India.[3] William, however, appears never to have started. Those that did, suffered the greatest privations, even to being robbed of their habits and tunics. But three ultimately reached Peking in 1308.

iv. Expansion

Now began the period of expansion. The helpers had arrived and foundations could be made in other towns than Peking. The Emperor being still very favourable, each friar received from the royal treasury a salary, which was used to good purpose, building friaries and churches.

Friar Andrew wrote a letter in A.D. 1326 to the Warden of his old friary in Perugia; and most of our information of this period is derived from this source.[4] The three suffragans proceeded immediately to Cambaluc (Peking) where Friar John of Montecorvino, who had been awaiting them fourteen years, was consecrated Archbishop of Peking. For five years they all lived together in the capital; but in 1313 a rich Armenian lady gave money for the building of a church in the great city of Zaiton (the port Ch'üan-chou). John of Montecorvino made it into a cathedral

---

[1] cf. Mann, *op. cit.*, Vol. XVII, p. 96.   [2] Yule, *Cathay*, Vol. III, pp. 9–10.

[3] Yule thinks Ormuz in the Persian Gulf. The names of places were still in hopeless confusion, China at times being called Upper India. cf. Blessed Oderic *passim*.

[4] Yule, *Cathay*, Vol. III, pp. 71 ff.

for Friar Gerard, and some friars were appointed to him. This apostolic lady also endowed the friary in her will. Its first bishop soon died; on which Archbishop John offered the see to Andrew of Perugia, but he refused it, and Peregrine was made Bishop of Zaiton. But he quickly followed his predecessor, dying on 7th July 1322. In 1318 Friar Andrew had already left Peking and joined the friars at Zaiton. With the moneys he had been receiving from the imperial treasury, he 'caused a convenient and handsome church to be built in a certain grove a quarter of a mile outside the city, with all the offices sufficient for twenty-two friars, and with four apartments such that any one of them is good enough for a church dignitary of any rank'.[1] In 1322 he was appointed to the see of Zaiton and divided his time between the friary in the city and the one he had built on the outskirts.

The community of Zaiton must have been surprised and moved to devotion on the arrival of a certain Friar Oderic who came with the mortal remains of four members of the Order who had been martyred in India in the city of Tana. They were Friar James of Padua, Friar Demetrius, a Georgian lay brother, Friar Peter of Siena,[2] and a fourth Friar Thomas of Tolentino.[3] This last had already been to Cathay on the mission which brought the three newly consecrated bishops in A.D. 1308. He it was who, while evangelizing Tartary in 1307 had heard of the great work being done by John of Montecorvino. He must have visited him, for he was the messenger who in 1307 gave Clement VI at Avignon these glowing accounts and who handed him the letter from John of Montecorvino.[4] Friar Oderic must have told the assembled friars in China the story of the martyrdoms—and no one told a story better than Friar Oderic.

[1] Yule, *Cathay*, Vol. III, p. 73.

[2] 'Travels of Friar Oderic', in Yule, *Cathay*, Vol. II, p. 117 ff.

[3] His skull was perhaps not taken by Friar Oderic, but was taken from India to Italy.

[4] There is no certain evidence that Friar Thomas went to Cathay though this seems probable. After all someone may have handed on to him in Tartary the letter from Peking. (The facts about his life are conveniently tabulated in Yule, *Cathay*, Vol. III, p. 118.)

These martyred friars had been staying in a house of a Nestorian and his wife in India. The husband took it into his head to beat his wife, and she complained to the Cadi—the chief Mohammedan—and to prove her point she produced the four friars to witness. A dispute arose about who Christ was. Friar Thomas was spokesman for the friars, and the Cadi was routed. This annoyed him and he said: 'What do you say of Mohammed?' Friar Thomas replied: 'Since you can only repeat, "What do I say of him", I should blush to refuse the reply you seek. I reply then, and tell you that Mohammed is the son of perdition and hath his place in hell with the devil his father, and not he only but all such as follow and keep his law, false as it is, and pestilent and accursed, hostile to God and the salvation of souls.' There was only one answer: 'Let him die.' The friars were all put in the broiling midday sun, but they praised God; then preparations were made to burn them in the great square. A vast crowd soon collected. Friar Thomas went forward to throw himself into the blaze. But he was prevented, for they thought he might have some device for not being burnt; they seized Friar James and threw him in. As they did so he protested saying: 'Suffer me and I will go of my own free-will.' He was lost to sight in the flames, but his voice could be heard calling on the Blessed Virgin Mary. The fire died down and there he was unscathed. . . . He was then stripped and covered with oil and a greater fire made; again he was thrown in: but again he emerged unscathed. The people by this time were amazed at the miracles and staggered between two minds, whether they should cast off their Mohammedan faith or no. So the authorities carried off the friars and that night sent four soldiers to kill them. They found three of them at Matins at midnight, these they killed; and the fourth was found next day; he was tortured, and slain by the sword. It was the relics of these men that Friar Oderic bore with him to the church at Zaiton, where they were preserved and venerated.

But Friar Oderic did not stay long, and, though he went to Peking, he makes no mention of the venerable Archbishop. In all his busy account of people and things he scarcely mentions the progress of the Church in those parts. He stayed in a friary at Cansay (Hangchow) where four friars were stationed and he mentions another at Jamzai or Yangchow. But at the very end of his account there is an addition that Friar Marchesino ordered Friar Henry of Glatz to write, for he said that he had heard it from the lips of Friar Oderic himself. It runs as follows:

> When the great Khan was once on his journey from Sandu to Cambalich, he [Friar Oderic], with four other Minor Friars, were sitting under the shade of a tree by the side of the road along which the Khan was about to pass. And one of the brethren was a bishop [presumably Friar John]. So when the Khan began to draw near, the bishop put on his episcopal robes and took a cross and fastened it to the end of a staff so as to raise it aloft; and then the four began to chaunt with loud voices the hymn, 'Veni Creator Spiritus!' And then the great Khan hearing the sound thereof, asked what it meant. And those four barons who go beside him replied that it was four of the Frankish Rabbans [i.e. monks]. So the Khan called them to him, and the bishop thereupon taking the cross from the staff presented it to the Khan to kiss. Now at the time he was lying down, but as soon as he saw the cross he sat up, and doffing the cap that he wore, kissed the cross in the most reverent and humble manner....
>
> Now it is clear enough from this that the Khan himself had some savour of our Catholic faith as he well might, through the Minor Friars who dwelt at his court continually.[1]

Friar Oderic and his companion, Friar James, an Irish Franciscan, passed on and reached Europe by the overland route, visiting Lhasa and the Old Man of the Mountains on the way. But his further adventures do not concern us. He died in the odour of sanctity in 1231 in the Friary of Udine on 14th January, and was later beatified. The shadows were lengthening.

v. The Decline

In 1311 Pope Clement V sent three more bishops to China, Thomas, Jerome and Peter of Florence. Peter, we know, reached

---

[1] Yule, *Cathay*, Vol. II, pp. 270-1, and note 2. Probably the great-grandson of Kublai Khan, Yisun Timur (*regnabat* 1323-8). Oderic certainly arrived in China after 1322, as in that year the four friars were martyed at Tana.

Cathay, for in *The Book of the Estate of the Great Caan* by John di Cora he is said to be ruling over one of the churches in Zaiton whilst Bishop Andrew presided over the other. It seems as if these were the only two bishops left in China. The great figure of John of Montecorvino had gone. He died in 1328. In the words of John di Cora:

That Friar John converted a multitude of people to the faith of Jesus Christ. He was a man of upright life, pleasing to God and men, and stood in high grace with the emperor . . . much was he beloved by all, pagans as well as Christians. And certes he would have converted that whole country to the Christian Catholic faith, if the Nestorians, those false Christians and real miscreants, had not hindered him and done him hurt.

The said archbishop took great pains with those Nestorians to bring them under obedience to our mother. the Holy Church of Rome, for without this obedience, he told them, they could not be saved. For this the Nestorians hated him greatly.

This archbishop, as it has pleased God, is lately passed from this world. To his obsequies and burial there came a very great multitude of people, both Christian and pagan. And those pagans rent their mourning garments as their manner is; and both Christians and pagans devoutly laid hold of pieces of the clothing of the archbishop and carried them off as relics with great reverence.

So in Peking he was buried with great honour, after the manner of faithful Christians. And they still visit the place of his interment with very great devotion.

As John de Marignolli observed, the Mongols and Alans venerated him as a saint, and saint he must truly have been.

Five years elapsed before the news of Friar John's death reached the Pope. John XXII in Avignon appointed his successor (1333); together with twenty other friars and six laymen he set out for Peking. But in 1338 they had got no farther than Turkistan, for Pope Benedict XII in that year wrote a letter which gives evidence that Nicholas and his party were busy building and repairing churches in those parts.[1] It is very doubtful if they got farther,

[1] Mann, *op. cit.*, Vol. XVII, p. 98.

unless we accept the hypothesis that a certain Nicholas, a merchant, and our Nicholas are the same.[1]

Meanwhile an embassy appeared in 1338 from the Great Khan and from some of his Alan chiefs with letters from both. The letter from the Khan was short and to the point.

In the strength of the omnipotent God! The Emperor of Emperors commandeth: We send our envoy Andrew the Frank, with fifteen others, to the Pope, the Lord of the Christians . . . to open a way for the frequent exchange of messengers between us and the Pope; and to request the Pope himself to send us his blessing, and always to remember us in his holy prayers: and to commend to him the Alans, our servants and his Christian sons. Also we desire that our messenger bring back to us horses and other rarities from the sun-setting. Written in Cambaluc, in the year of the Rat in the sixth month on the third day of the moon.[2]

The letter from the Alan chiefs reads—following Yule's Latin version which he quotes from Wadding.

We, Futim Joens Chaticen Tungii Gemboya Evenzi, Joannes Luchoy (and Rubens Pinzanus). . . .[3] Our heads bowed to earth, kissing his feet, we salute our holy Father the Pope, begging his blessing and grace and begging him to remember us in his holy prayers and never to forget us. Let this be known to your holiness, that now for a long time we have been instructed in the Catholic faith, and

[1] For a discussion of this cf. p. 69 below and Yule, *Cathay*, Vol. III, p. 12, and Mann, *op. cit.*, pp. 100–1.

[2] Yule, *Cathay*, Vol. III, pp. 180. Some authorities are doubtful as to the authenticity of this letter, though they agree that the accompanying one from the Christians was genuine. cf. Cordier, *Histoire Générale de la Chine*, Vol. III, p. 42. 'C. d'Ohsson regarde comme une supercherie et doute de l'authenticité des lettres; peut-être a-t-il raison pour la lettre du Grand Khan qui demande sa bénédiction au Saint-Père et lui recommande les Alains porteurs de sa lettre, mais il y a des raisons de croire a l'authenticité par les chefs alains.'

[3] These are weird names found by Prof. Pelliot in Yüan Shih the Chinese history of the Mongol dynasty. In parenthesis let it be said that the Alans were one of the races, members of which had been swept up by the Mongols to help them in their conquest of China. At this time their home was the Caucasus range, but even in Marco Polo's time there were settled groups of them in China and they, although at first Greek Orthodox Christians, were now Catholics.

sweetly governed and abundantly consoled by your Legate, Brother John, a worthy, holy and capable man, who is now dead these eight years, during which we have been without a ruler, without spiritual consolation. Although we have heard that you have despatched another legate, he has not yet arrived. Consequently we implore your Holiness to send us a good, capable and wise Legate who may have care of our souls, to send him quickly, for wretched are we without a head, without instruction, without consolation. We also request your Wisdom to give a gracious reply to our Emperor . . . for it has happened on several occasions, three or four times now there have come on your behalf to the aforesaid Emperor our Master, messengers who were graciously received by him, honoured and loaded with gifts; and yet from then on the said Emperor received no reply from you or the Apostolic See although each promised to bring a reply back. Therefore let your Holiness see to it that this time and henceforth there is a reply and envoy sent, for the Christians are put greatly to shame in these parts when they are found to tell lies. Written in Cambaluc in the year of the Rat, the sixth month, the third day of the moon.

This distant cry of distress was effective; the envoys were sent back by Benedict XII with letters. One of the Tartars was kept by him as sergeant-at-arms, and some months later a great mission was organized, Nicholas of Bonet, S.T.D. of Paris, Nicholas of Kolano, Gregory of Hungary with their leader or Legate John of Florence, better known as John Marignolli, together with fifty friars. Many gifts were sent including noble horses for the Emperor. The exact number of persons is doubtful; John Marignolli, however, says that they mustered thirty-two on reaching Cambaluc. No doubt some turned back for one reason or another; for example, Nicholas Bonet probably did; others may have died. These then are the nameless ones, many of whom must have remained in China after John returned. But their history is now known to God alone. It is reasonable to suppose that they survived some time and served the Christians of those parts; but there seems to have been no bishop among them. John Marignolli eventually returned, was made Bishop of Bisignano and settled down to a garrulous old age. For centuries it was thought that no more could be known of this mission, till last century a rambling chronicle of Bohemia was unearthed in a library. It was by this very Bishop John and proved to be more concerned with his travels in the East than with Bohemia.[1] The following is a summary.

They left Avignon in December 1338, were later joined by the envoys from China, and took the route round the north of the Black Sea and consequently the land—or commercial—route, on account of the horses, if for no other reason. Their progress was slow, for they only reached Peking in May or June of 1342. There John the Legate spent three or four years, visiting the houses of his Order in China. He sailed for home from Zaiton in the December of either 1346 or 1347, passing through Ceylon, Ormuz, Damascus and Jerusalem, and reaching Avignon in 1353. What happened during their stay in China? They reached Cambaluc and were duly impressed by its size, wealth and power. His story runs:

> But the Grand Kaan, when he beheld the great horses, and the Pope's presents with his letter, and King Robert's too, with their golden seals, and when he saw us also, rejoiced greatly . . . and treated us with greatest honour. And when I entered the Kaan's presence it was in full vestments, with a very fine cross carried before me, and candles and incense, whilst *Credo in Unum Deum* was chaunted in that glorious palace where he dwells. And when the chaunt was ended I bestowed a full benediction, which he received with all humility.

The Emperor lent them some of the imperial apartments; princes were detailed to wait upon them. 'And this they did in the most liberal manner, not merely as regards meat and drink, but even to such things as paper for lanterns.' This continued for four years. 'And I should add that they kept us and all our establishment clothed in costly raiment. . . . And we had many and glorious disputations with the Jews and other sectaries; and we reaped a great harvest of souls in that Empire.' But to the great distress of both Emperor and people John would not remain.

[1] The relevant passages are printed in Yule, *Cathay*, Vol. III, pp. 209 ff.

He left with a further letter from the Emperor to the Pope asking for a cardinal and bishop for Cambaluc. It seems incredible to us now, that he had not been given power to consecrate bishops or that he had not been made a bishop before starting. Perhaps the reason is that when in 1333 the news of John of Montecorvino's death reached Avignon a certain Nicholas of Paris was appointed in his place and set off with twenty friars and six lay brothers.[1] It is generally considered that these, like many others before and since, never reached their goal. But there is a strange story recorded in the famous Chinese history of the Ming dynasty (1368–1644), the Ming Shih, that the founder of the Ming dynasty, who supplanted the khans, heard of a certain trader,[2] Nicholas, and sent him with gifts and messages of peace to his King. The history goes on: 'But this embassy (i.e. from the West) was not repeated until, during the Wan-li period (1573–1620), a native[3] from the great Western Ocean came to the capital who said that the Lord of heaven, Ye-su, was born in Ju-te-a.'[4] So it is possible that Nicholas arrived, but only after the anti-foreign rule was in full swing, for we know that in 1338 he had not arrived and was presumed dead, as is shown from the letter of the Alans to Benedict XII quoted above.

Thus John Marignolli left China and the dusk settled into night. As far as we know no other bishop reached Cambaluc for nearly three hundred years. Cosmas was chosen to succeed the vanished Nicholas, then William di Prato, a noted theologian in Paris, then Joseph Dominic, Conrad, James, Leonard, Bartholomew, Bernard, Jean de Pelletz, Bartholomew II and finally, the fourteenth Alexander di Caffa who was captured by the Turks in 1475 but released seven years later. But why recite these names, for none of them saw China?

Not only were bishops appointed by the Holy See, but groups of missionary friars were sent out from time to time, to be

[1] Yule, *Cathay*, Vol. III, pp. 12–13.

[2] It is not unlikely that Nicholas was disguised as a trader. He must not be confused with Nicholas Bonet of John Marignolli's party, nor with Nicholas of Bantra (Yule, *Cathay*, Vol. III, pp. 13, 15).

[3] Father Ricci, S.J.   [4] Cordier's note in Yule, *Cathay*, Vol. III, p. 12.

swallowed up by the vastness of the East and not to be heard of again. A number were sent in 1371 with William di Prato. All these went their way east and were lost to view.[1]

Meanwhile the native Ming dynasty, enemy of the intruding Mongols, and of all their works and associates, had won its way to the imperial throne. (Chu Yüan-chang proclaimed himself King of Wu in 1367 and assumed the title of Emperor in 1368.) During the time of trouble that preceded the founding of the Ming dynasty, the Christian communities were persecuted, their churches destroyed. James of Florence, fifth Bishop of Zaiton, was killed by the Chinese. It was two hundred years before other Franciscans visited China; they were Fathers Pedro de Alfaro, John Baptist Lucarelli de Pesaro, Sebastian of Saint Francis, and Augustine de Tordesillas in 1579. But they did not remain.

vi. Conclusion

At this distance and with such meagre evidence it is difficult to judge why the Franciscan mission to China failed utterly in the end. When Fr. Ricci reached there towards the close of the sixteenth century, not a trace of it among the inhabitants remained, not even a memory. The following will be only a collection of probable causes. Obviously the distance of China from Rome made quick decision difficult, but the real failure seems to have been not giving a quasi-autonomy to some person on the spot. John of Montecorvino did, it is true, have wide powers, but the episcopate seems to have died out. Then, the dangers of the journey made survival difficult, so many missionaries never reaching their destination.[2] This continued to be a difficulty even in the great days of Portuguese expansion. But perhaps the chief cause of the collapse was that the rate of conversions was very slow, especially among the Chinese. In the missionary letters there are very few references to the native Chinese or to their specific problems; their ancestor worship, their family ties, their

[1] Henri Cordier, *Histoire Générale de la Chine*, Paris, 1920, Vol. II, pp. 425–6.

[2] Remember especially the mission of seven bishops sent by Pope Clement V, only three of whom reached China, the others having died on the way.

ideas of God. The Church (at that date) seems to have been very much a 'foreign mission' in China, a Church for occasional Europeans, for that flood of foreign mercenaries who came in the wake of the Mongol conquerors, to mention only the Alans. We may wonder whether these heroic and simple Franciscans could grapple with the Chinese language and writing as the Jesuits so brilliantly did later. The fact is that so long as a religion is 'foreign' for the Chinese, then for them—thinking themselves to be the most ancient race in the world and the wisest—that religion is inferior. Last but not least, the Nestorians, now a degraded fossil remnant of a great Church, made life and missionary success extremely difficult for the Catholic friars. Add to these a violent persecution and what little success they achieved was rapidly submerged. So ended the first and not the least glorious attempt of the Catholic Church to draw China to Christ.

The work of these heroic Franciscans was so utterly obliterated that Fr. Alvarez de Semedo of the Society of Jesus, one of the earliest Jesuits in China, and the historian of the mission[1] wrote that they could find no trace of the ancient Christians.

During these thirtie years, we have gone about all China and founded Churches in severall of the biggest towns, planting the Christian religion, and using all diligence to discover this truth, without having been able to obtain our purpose in the least. It is true we found a small Bell, such as is used at Mass, with Greek letters round about it, and a cross very handsomely graved.

All then that remained was the tinkling of a sacring bell.[2]

[1] Semedo, *The History of China*, London, 1655, Pt. I, ch. 31, p. 166.
[2] In all this work Fr. Semedo seems completely unaware that Franciscans ever trod the ground of China. He is dimly aware of the Nestorians. cf. also Fr. Ricci's letter to P. Claudio Aquaviva, S.J., dated 26th July 1605 where he mentions he had seen in 1595 'a little bell, very old and with a cross and Greek lettering in the hands of a Chinese', which bell apparently had come from the province of Honan. Ricci, *Opere Storiche del P. Matteo Ricci, S.J.*, ed. P. Pietro Tacchi Venturi, S.J., Vol. I, *I Commentari della Cina*, Macerata, 1911; Vol. II, *Le Lettere della Cina*, Macerata, 1913. *Lettere*, No. 35, p. 292. The Rome edition of the *Opere Storiche*, edited by P. D'Elia is in process of publication and will supersede the older edition.

One other scrap of evidence for this vanished Christian Church was recently unearthed. On the 22nd January 1952 during demolition work on the walls of Yangchow in Kiangsu was found the following inscription upon a stone:

In nomine Domini. Amen. Hic jacet Katerina de Viljonis quae obiit in anno Domini mileximo CCCXXXXII de mense Junii.

'In the name of the Lord. Amen. Here lies Catherine of *Viljonis* who died in the Year of the Lord 1342, in the month of June.'

Who might this intrepid woman be? The idea that she might be a nun has only to be stated to be set aside. No European nun went to China until the nineteenth century. She must have been the wife of some merchant like Marco Polo. He had been governor there in Yangchow three years. But considering the perils of the journey, the remoteness of the place, it is an astonishing discovery which makes one realize that the links between Far West and Far East were not so tenuous as one had previously supposed.[1]

And now news comes through that perhaps the Tomb of Andrew of Perugia has been unearthed at Zaiton.[2]

With that we take our leave of the Middle Ages and the medieval missionary endeavours.

[1] For the first news of this discovery see the *Osservatore Romano*, 26th April 1952, p. 3.
[2] *Illustrated London News*, 14th May 1955.

Chapter Four

THE JESUIT AGE

Bird's-eye View

This chapter naturally falls into four parts: the first arrivals, the consolidation of gains, the quarrel, the persecution.

(i) THE FIRST ARRIVALS

To understand the chapters some historical introduction is necessary: the Portuguese, the Spaniards, the French and their politics played a large part in the work of the Church in the mission field during this period. The period itself starts with the glorious and apparently fruitless effort of St. Francis Xavier. Though the chapter must be called the Jesuit Age, it was, apart from St. Francis, initiated by heroic Dominicans, Franciscans and Augustinians from the Philippines. But St. Francis' initiative was taken up in the Society of Jesus by a worthy successor, Fr. Matteo Ricci. So great a missionary was he that some space must be dedicated both to his life and to his method.

(ii) THE CONSOLIDATION OF GAINS

After Ricci's death in 1610 the Jesuits consolidated their gains. The friars got a footing, but the internal state of China was much hampering the missionaries; the collapse of the Ming and the rise of the Manchu dynasty have to be told in their relationship with the missionaries. All during this period the 'Patronage of Portugal' played an important part in the fortunes of the Church in the Far East. It needs studying in some detail.

This leads us to tell of the efforts made by the Holy See to extricate the mission fields from political influence, and to recount the noble life of Fr. Pallu and his founding of the Missions Étrangères of Paris. As a result of his activities two questions become uppermost: a Chinese clergy and the Chinese liturgy.

All these currents were stirring before 1685, date of the arrival of the French Jesuit mission to China.

(iii) THE QUARREL

The stage was set for the tragedy now to be enacted: the quarrel over the Chinese Rites.

(iv) THE PERSECUTION

The persecution which followed lasted well over a hundred years. During this period the Jesuits were finally suppressed by the Holy See and the Lazarists took their place in China. The story of the heroic lives of the missionaries during this period makes moving reading. An account of some of them is given.

i. *The First Arrivals*

FOR a century and a half, the West had no link with or news of the Far East, that is until the arrival of the Portuguese traders at the opening of the sixteenth century. During that period the Chinese had not approached any nearer to European ways, if anything they had become more remote, more bound up in their own peculiar customs. Certainly that was their wish, for they refused admittance to all foreigners, and should an ambassador be allowed as far as Peking he was escorted in a closed vehicle with the express purpose of his seeing nothing. The fact that the Emperor was never seen and did all his business through his eunuchs was symbolical of the whole spirit of the Ming period. The Ming dynasty stood for the reaction of the native Chinese against the Tartars and all other foreigners.

The Portuguese at the beginning of the sixteenth century suddenly appeared at the mouth of the Si-Kiang. They came not for conquest but for trade. They were not allowed to live on the mainland. At the mouth of the river there were several islands and on one of these, Shang ch'uan,[1] the Portuguese built themselves temporary huts. There they lived each summer for the time needed to do their trading, and then left. But, not long

[1] Sometimes spelt Sancian.

after, it was suggested by the peace-loving Chinese, that if they, the Portuguese, were willing to purge of pirates another and better island farther up the river, then the Chinese would allow them to build themselves a permanent city. This the Portuguese did very effectively; and that was the origin of the great sixteenth-century city of Macao.[1] They probably got this permission in 1557. The Portuguese were doing in that age what the English were to do in Hong Kong in the nineteenth century on the opposite side of the same estuary.

It may be asked why the Portuguese came to China.

Winter fare in Western Europe during the Middle Ages was very dull. The feeding of cattle on roots had not yet been discovered, and therefore fodder for this period of the year was lacking. Consequently farmers were forced to kill almost all their cattle in autumn, and salt the meat. There was thus a great scarcity of fresh meat in the winter months.

It was this domestic but universal problem which instigated the trade in spices, used as condiments with food in winter. The only known ways to the sources of spices in the Far East were overland, of which ways the two chief were via the Persian Gulf at whose entrance stood Ormuz, or via the Red Sea at whose entrance stood the Island of Socotra. Across these routes between the East and the West lay the Islamic States; the trade to and from India was itself organized by these same Mohammedans, too lucrative a trade to be shared with Christians.

Europeans had long dreamed of finding some safe way to the Far East, but it was not until the indefatigable labours and confidence of Prince Henry the Navigator, of Portugal, that these dreams were turned into a reality. By his time the compass was known, astronomy was more scientific, mathematics a science—all of which aids came to him and his master mariners as unintentional gifts from his natural enemies the Moors. Prince Henry was born in 1394.

[1] Semedo: *op. cit.*, p. 168. For all versions of the story, cf., Cordier, *op. cit.*, Vol. III, pp. 129–32. The most recent account is in *South China in the XVI Century*, edited by C. R. Boxer, London, 1953.

In 1420 Zarco rediscovered Madeira; in 1484 Diego Cam reached the Congo river and found himself beyond the Mohammedan power. In 1487 Bartholomew Dias was swept on beyond the Cape of Good Hope and found to his joy that, although he was heading north, the coast was on his left and running north and south.

But the great epoch-making journey was to be undertaken by Vasco da Gama, who, setting sail in the *San Gabriel* from Lisbon on Saturday, 8th July 1497, had by the 20th May 1498 dropped anchor in the harbour of Calicut on the Malabar coast of India. He had edged up the east of Africa from the Cape to Malindi, where the Arabs gave him a pilot; and from there he had sailed straight across the Indian Ocean to Calicut.

After this it was only a matter of time before the Sultan of Egypt and the Arab traders should come into conflict with the Portuguese; for the latter began trading and making commercial agreements with the native chiefs, and by so doing deprived the Moors of very much of their European trade and profit. The rivalry reached its climax in the historic battle off the Island of Diu in 1509 near the mouth of the Indus river, in which the great fleet of the Egyptian Sultan, which he had constructed at Suez from wood brought down from Asia Minor, was utterly destroyed; and a mere handful of survivors lived to tell the tale. This is one of the decisive battles of the world, laying open Eastern seas to Western ships, Eastern riches to Western merchants and Eastern minds to Western thought, Eastern souls to Western religion. First the Portuguese, then the Spanish, later the Dutch and the English and then the French were to go through the breach.

The Portuguese, in order to safeguard their commercial interests, finally built forts at Cochin and other places and seized Goa. Their tentacles were groping even farther east. In 1511 the great soldier and administrator, Albuquerque, took Malacca in the Malay Straits. It was now but a step to China. According to a letter from Andrew Corsali, a Florentine, dated 6th January 1515 from Cochin, addressed to Julian de' Medici, 'Last year our Portuguese went to China, yet the inhabitants refused to let them land, saying it was against their habits to allow any stranger in their houses.'[1] This is the earliest recorded contact of the Portuguese with the Empire of China.

Though these Portuguese adventurers and traders had reached the gates of the Celestial Kingdom, all they were allowed to do was to present their wares at Canton during the three months trading season of the year. They did not cross the threshold, or if they did it was to be tortured and killed. The Moslems, the defeated foe of the Portuguese, had already poisoned the mind of the Emperor and his advisers against the newcomers; but worse, the very brother of a European envoy behaved abominably to the Chinese, thus confirming their worst suspicions. The Chinese consequently suspected every pacific move on their part as being merely 'peaceful penetration' which would end, as it had done on the African and Indian coasts, and in Malacca, as conquest and subjugation. The Chinese pulled down an iron curtain. It was the Catholic missionary who was to be the first to enter China, and to rediscover it.

(a) *St. Francis*

No account of the relationship between Christ and China after 1500 can begin except with a retelling of the story of St. Francis Xavier and his final sacrifice on the Island of Sancian[2] off the south coast of China.

In 1534 on the Feast of the Assumption St. Ignatius and his friends, whom he had gathered round him at the University of Paris, made a vow to dedicate their lives to God. Among his friends was one Francis of the castle of Xavier, a Basque like Ignatius. Ignatius' first idea was to convert the Mohammedan, as St. Francis of Assisi had striven to do; but already in 1538 he and his disciples were preaching in Rome against the Reformers. Yet he knew that preaching was not enough. They must restore to God and his Church the numbers fallen away; and here to

[1] Quoted by Cordier, *op. cit.*, Vol. III, p. 118. Much else for this section has been found there.

[2] Chinese form Shang-ch'uan or Shang-chwan; Portuguese Samchoao; Latin, Sancianum. cf. J. Brodrick, *St. Francis*, p. 513.

hand were the new worlds, both East and West, disclosed by the explorers sailing the high seas.

On the 14th March 1540 Ignatius, the 'General' of the new Order called the Society of Jesus, commanded Francis to set sail for the conversion of India, that vague, half-mythical kingdom to the east, only reached by travelling the full circle of Africa.

English readers may be put out by this appearance of Jesuits cast in the role of heroes. To them the name Jesuit may signify, though unjustly, everything that is underhand and foreign. They must put away these prejudices especially when dealing with the Jesuit chapter of Christ's coming to China. It is the noblest chapter; and, though not entirely a Jesuit one, may without exaggeration be called Jesuit-inspired. The inspiration came from St. Francis Xavier himself.

Naturally Francis sailed from Lisbon, but that act was fraught with far-reaching effects. The Church, in order to fulfil its missionary office, was obliged to ask the secular State to give it material aid. Thus, in order to reach their objective, the only method for missionaries was to take a Portuguese ship, for no other was allowed along the route, and at that date (1541) no other nation had knowledge of the currents or the winds, or the landfalls in those distant regions of the earth. The way to India was still a secret jealously guarded by the Portuguese.[1] The result was that the missions in the East were linked with the power of Portugal, and its crown claimed rights in the appointment of bishops, a claim which in later years seriously hindered the progress of the Church in Asia.

St. Francis reached Goa on 6th May 1542; it had taken him a year and a month. These journeys were not only tediously long, they were unhealthy, and many missionaries died on the way. Later they were sometimes to be dangerous, when the English or the Dutch piratical ships prowled the India Ocean and captured or sank their Portuguese or Spanish enemies. That journey was to be one of the chief obstacles to success.

[1] cf. François Caron, *A True Description of the Mighty Kingdoms of Japan and Siam*, 1935, for the story of how the secret was wrested from them.

Goa was to India what Macao was to be for China. Merchants had arrived first. Goa was a thriving entrepôt, full of adventurers. They were the despair of St. Francis, as similar types were to be at Macao. Their example was not such as to inspire among the non-Christians admiration for the religion they professed to follow. If that was the effect of practising the Christian religion, so said the pagans, it was not a religion to be embraced.

St. Francis did not reach Japan until 1549. His journeys there were important in two ways for the later missionary developments in China. He made two excursions through Japan. The first he performed in poverty, dressed in his Western ecclesiastical clothes. He found that thus attired, he could not impress the Japanese, who despised him for his poverty, and suspected him for his foreign appearance. Knowing that such externals were not essential, he decided that on his second expedition he would wear Japanese dress. He therefore donned silk, the clothes of a Japanese sage. At one bound he had leapt the barriers of contempt and suspicion, and could now get in touch with the human beings whom he wanted to convert. His justification for this change of dress was the cry of St. Paul that he would be 'all things to all men'. What did it matter wearing silk? Holiness did not consist in a garment, but in striving to do the will of God and loving one's neighbour.

Though Francis had abolished two barriers, there remained still one, and that unsuspected. To all his efforts at conversion, the Japanese replied that they had received their wisdom from the West, from China, and China was not Christian, therefore it followed that the Christian way of life was worthless. It was evident to Francis that there was only one thing to do and that was to convert their mentors, the Chinese.

He went back to Goa to plan and act. By 1552 he was ready to attempt single-handed the beginning of the conversion of the ancient civilization that is China.

In the year 1552 the Portuguese had only just established relations with China; the method of trading was so complicated that it could, one feels, only have arisen in the Far East. The great port of Macao on the mainland with its factories, huge churches and seminaries had not yet been founded; the merchants could only use a desolate, uninhabited island, some miles off the mouth of the west river, the Si-Kiang, where Canton is situated. Each year for three months the Portuguese merchant ships would cast anchor at that inhospitable place, the traders would be allowed into Canton but not to live there, and then off the fleet would sail. It was St. Francis' plan to be taken by one of those rich galleons and to be left upon the mainland. He little realized that the merchants were loath to risk their whole trade by having a share in such a venture. The Chinese, made suspicious by the Mohammedans, who had told them stories of the conquering guile of the Westerns, and also by the behaviour of the earliest Portuguese to approach their shores, would at no price admit one of them into their Empire. Their rules against it were strict. Any infringement by the Portuguese of that prohibition might wipe out in a day the concessions which the Chinese had so slowly and grudgingly granted in the course of many years. Francis, therefore, was not popular.

For several months he found it impossible to persuade the Viceroy, Don Alvaro, to allow the ship carrying him to proceed. In the end they set sail and St. Francis went, accompanied by Fr. Gago, Br. Alvaro Fereira, Christopher his Malabar servant and a Chinese servant Antonio. On arrival at the island off the estuary they were obliged—like everyone else—to build themselves huts on the hillside. It was one thing to reach Sancian but quite another to enter Canton. All the merchants were against it. Why, at that moment there were Portuguese sailors languishing in the prison of that one gateway to China. The thing was an impossibility. That, however, was not the conviction of St. Francis, for whom nothing was impossible with God. Meanwhile he fretted a little, wrote some of the most moving letters and then fell ill of a fever.

At first he was transferred to the *Santa Cruz*, but the rocking of the ship made him worse; so he was carried once again to the island—China land—where in the end he was left, the Chinese servant alone remaining with him. After three days of delirium, during which his mind wandered back through the years to his childhood days in the Basque mountains, he passed away to God in the year of Christ 1552, 3rd December,[1] a Saturday, in the bitter cold of dawn, as the sun was about to rise over the dark China sea. So we pass from that heroic and symbolic act to the second wherein Christ, in the person of St. Francis' successors, was received in China. Francis Xavier had not succeeded; he had not even landed on the shores of the Middle Kingdom; his mission was a failure. More, he had died in the attempt. It was a calamity for the whole missionary effort. But, in truth, this is not so. The death of St. Francis outside the gate to China was a great victory. By his life he had renewed the wonder of the Apostolic Age, travelling half the earth to bring souls to Christ, the coast of Africa, the Cape Comorin, Meliapur, Malacca, the islands of the East Indies, the kingdom of Japan, Cochin. His name was already a legend in the East. It still is. It can truly be said of him that in his generation he *was* the missionary effort in the Eastern hemisphere. It had seemed to him necessary and wise to attempt single-handed this supreme problem of the Far East, the conversion of China, and this was enough to make it the business of his successors to carry on where he had left off. Thus the China mission has been the greatest endeavour in the missionary field for four centuries and it is not yet concluded.

(b) *Dominicans, Franciscans, Augustinians*[2]

Before proceeding to the main attack, which begins with the sublime death of St. Francis within sight of the mainland, some

[1] Mrs. Yeo's dates, but Cordier in work previously cited (Vol. III, p. 144) says St. Francis died 27th November 1552 at 2 a.m. (cf. Cros, P. L., *S. François Xavier: sa vie et ses lettres*, 2 vols, Paris, 1900; Vol. II, p. 349). In his life of St. Francis, p. 526, Fr. Brodrick quotes the letter of his faithful Chinese companion, Antonio, and concludes for 3rd December.

[2] For the sake of completeness it should be stated that the first missionary to land in China at this period was a Jesuit, Fr. Melchior Nuñez Barreto, who spent two months in Canton in 1555; in the same year a Spanish Dominican, Gaspar de la Cruz, may have penetrated into the same city. Martin de Herrada, an Augustinian, in 1575 was in Fukien, having reached there from the Philippines. But all these attempts, though heroic, were not permanent.

account of the Spanish approach from the other side of the world, from the Philippine Islands, must be given.

Whilst the Portuguese were approaching China from the west, the Spaniards were spreading their power from the east, via Mexico, the Marianas or Ladrones; and in 1565 they colonized the Philippines, so called after Philip II, King of Spain. The Spaniards had sighted and landed on these islands previously, under the leadership of Magellan; but this new landing was occupation and not merely discovery or trading. In this they differed from the Portuguese, who had been content, on the whole, to trade and settle only to the extent required for defending their trading rights.

The Spaniards found many Chinese not only trading with the natives but settled among them, particularly in the north. It is not surprising therefore to find that the Church of the Philippines —perhaps the most successful missionary venture of modern times—was considering the evangelization of the mainland and that the Spanish authorities were hoping to use the missionaries as spearheads. So it was that the Spaniards were among the first to land in China.

The Dominicans, the Franciscans and the Augustinians do not figure largely in this early period, not because they showed no interest, but rather because their efforts were thwarted, even more than were those of the Jesuits. It so happened that their base was usually the Philippines, and they worked under the sovereignty of Spain. The Franciscans and Dominicans added to the difficulties of their apostolate by going headlong at it, without any of the slow precision of their contemporary, the Jesuit Fr. Ricci. Some account of the Franciscan beginnings will give a typical picture of these ventures.

A small party of friars of St. Francis advanced beyond the Philippine Islands on to the mainland of China. On 19th June 1579 they disembarked at Canton after thirty days of buffeting by gales; their names were, Pedro de Alfaro, Agustín de Tordesillas, Juan Bautista Lucarelli de Pesaro and Sebastián de Baeza, all priests; two sailors accompanied them, both Franciscan tertiaries, one of them later to become a member of the First Order, and to be the first Franciscan to set foot in Japan, Friar Juan Pobre.

The leader of the expedition took possession of China in the name of Christ by offering Mass on the 24th June in Canton. But the devil, using as his instruments the Portuguese merchants, nervous for their trade and suspicious of the simple friars whom they imagined might be the forerunners of a Spanish infiltration, whispered into the ears of the Chinese that it would be wise to expel these newcomers. Might they not be spies sent by the Spanish conquerors of the Philippines? The result was that this little band was cast into prison forthwith, where they suffered many privations; then after about two months they were hustled back to Manila, an ignominious ending to a brave beginning.

Alfaro and Lucarelli, however, could not be persuaded to abandon the enterprise so easily. They clung to Macao like limpets, despite the unfriendly attitude of all the authorities in that precarious bridgehead on the Chinese shore. Against almost universal opposition they succeeded in founding a friary, *mirabile dictu*, and a church dedicated, in true Franciscan tradition, to Our Lady of the Angels. Their sufferings and their heroism made an impression on some of the local youths, and five of the local nobility joined the Order. This really alarmed their rivals and the persecution increased. Pedro de Alfaro therefore made up his mind that only one thing could be done, to appeal personally to the Archbishop of Goa, and to the Viceroy of the East Indies. So he took ship for Goa in 1580, only to meet death at sea in a terrible storm.

This left Juan Bautista Lucarelli alone with his five neophytes. The contemptuous treatment meted out to him forced him now to withdraw to Malacca. But there a new Captain-General of the colony proved friendly, with the result that he was sent back to Macao with strong recommendations. Forthwith, courageous and trusting as a saint, he founded a seminary or apostolic college for native catechists. He had twenty young men from many countries; they included Japanese, Chinese,

Indo-Chinese. But it was born out of due time, was strongly opposed by the Portuguese, and was finally abandoned.

Meanwhile a great party of thirty, all members of the Franciscan Reform of St. Peter of Alcantara, which left Sanlucar in 1581, had now reached Manila. One of their number, Martín Ignacio de Loyola, a relation of the founder of the Society of Jesus, set off for China. He disembarked on the coast of the province of Fukien with six others of his Order, and, strange coincidence, it was in the very same year that Ricci made his discreet entry via Canton.

Father Loyola was not kindly received. He was put in chains, sent from one city of the Empire to another, and finally escorted to Canton. One of the party died of the ill-treatment, but the remainder were rescued by the skilful diplomacy of the civil governor of Macao, the same Captain-General, Arias Gonzalez de Miranda. There in Macao the liberated Franciscans met to their joy Lucarelli in charge of his seminary. Consulting with one another they decided that the only way to survive in Macao and in China would be to sever their connection with Manila and establish an independent *Custodia* or province, thus allaying, so they hoped, the suspicions of the Portuguese lay and clerical authorities. They now set up two houses, one in Macao and the other at Malacca.

When Ignacio and Lucarelli reached Malacca their reception was so unfriendly that they resolved to continue their journey to Lisbon. By reaching Lisbon, Martín Ignacio was doubtless the first friar to circumnavigate the world. He then went on to Rome where Gregory XIII gave him a Bull 'Exposuisti nobis', dated 8th December 1584, encouraging him in his missionary endeavours in China. This encouragement being noted by the Spanish Council for the Indies, the return journey was made easy. And as the crowns of Portugal and Spain had been united in Philip II, since 1580, on his way back the great missionary traveller set off from Portugal. He was not alone. He sailed with a party of twenty missionaries. His story had fired the imagination and apostolic zeal of the peninsula.

On his arrival at Macao, a second time he entered Canton with two other Franciscans, but once again the malevolence of some Portuguese put the Chinese on their guard. He was beaten, insulted, imprisoned. And once again the Portuguese authorities had to extricate him, which they did, but only on condition that he remained in Macao and did not again attempt entry into Canton. Nevertheless in 1588 he was again at large in the city. To the relief of the authorities he left the same year for Spain via the Pacific. His later apostolate in America does not concern us.

The Franciscan venture now fades from the picture till 1633. Philip II, in order not to offend his Portuguese subjects, forbade Spaniards to interfere in China. The Spanish Franciscan foundations, whose short history we have just sketched, were handed over to the Portuguese province; the Holy See gave the exclusive right of evangelizing China to the Jesuits (1585). Not until the next century were other Orders allowed to share this immense task.

Apart from the extremely useful information published by several of these friars on what they saw in China, the story just recorded had little influence on the turn of events;[1] it is a sample of the influences at work and shows how the various rivalries bedevilled the conversion of China. There was the rivalry between the Orders, between the nations; there was the characteristic fear of foreigners among the Chinese. But when we judge the Jesuits or the merchants we must remember that the Franciscans in their evangelizing did not believe in the discreet methods of Fr. Ricci, rather would they march openly through the streets dressed in their outlandish habit, cross in hand. Nor would they mince their words in their references to the idolatry that they found. Both the Jesuits and the merchants, as time went on, saw their patient labour destroyed by what they thought indiscreet and impatient activity.

[1] For these accounts see *South China in the XVI Century, being the narratives of Galeoto Pereira, Fr. Gaspar da Cruz, Fr. Martin de Rada* (1550–75). Edited by C. R. Boxer, London, 1953.

(c) *Father Matteo Ricci*

By a strange coincidence the very year, 1552, that St. Francis died, abandoned on Sancian, Fr. Matteo Ricci, his greatest successor, was born in Italy.

The example of St. Francis bore fruit. In 1555 Father Melchior Nuñez Barreto, as Provincial of the Jesuits for the Indies and Japan, called in at Macao on his way to Japan and spent two months in Canton attempting to ransom six Christians, three of whom were Portuguese.[1] There he held disputations with one of the *literati*, but, though victorious, got nought for his pains but to be spat at.

There were other fruitless efforts, but the first move towards a concerted attack was the early establishment of a house at Macao for the Jesuit Fathers. This was done by Fr. Francis Perez. From tiny beginnings, this residence became a large seminary and college with as many as sixty to eighty Jesuits living there together, studying theology and these new, strange and most difficult languages. Besides, the local children, both Portuguese and Chinese, were taught in its school. Semedo tells us that there were as many as ninety pupils in the lowest class.[2]

Fr. Alexander Valignano arrived at Macao from Lisbon where he had embarked with thirty-eight other missionaries in 1574. He had been appointed Visitor and Vicar-General of the Jesuits for the Orient, and he was on his way to Japan. In the full flush of his enthusiasm he determined that the evangelization should begin. He asked for help and was sent Fr. Michael Ruggieri, a Neapolitan like himself, Fr. Francis Pasio of Bologna and greatest of them all, Fr. Matteo Ricci, who arrived in Macao in 1582.

As Fr. Ricci is the most justly famous and the model for all those missionaries in the sixteenth, seventeenth and eighteenth centuries, a short sketch of his life is opportune. In the words of Fr. de Chavagnac, S.J., to Fr. le Gobien, S.J., when writing from Chuchow (30th December 1701): 'I advise all who feel called to China to read and re-read the life of Father Ricci . . .

[1] Cordier, *op. cit.*, Vol. III, p. 246.   [2] Semedo, *op. cit.*, p. 170.

and to study at leisure the character of that great man, who is considered with reason as the founder of that flourishing mission.'[1]

Matteo Ricci was born on 6th October 1552 in Macerata in the March of Ancona; he went to the local Jesuit school towards the end of 1561, and in 1568 he was in Rome studying law. On 15th August three years later he joined the Jesuit novitiate where he was trained in the spirit of the Order by Fr. Fabio di Fabj. Before he had finished his theological studies or been ordained, he was sent to the Far East, leaving Rome in 1577 for Lisbon. He studied theology for a time in Coimbra setting sail, in March 1578, in company with Michael Ruggieri and others. On his arrival at Goa he continued his theological studies and taught Humanities.

On 15th April 1582 he was called to Macao and on his arrival on the 7th August, he set about studying Chinese, not the local dialect but Mandarin, and learning to write it. There is a delightful letter written to a friend at home in which he tries to account for and discount his astonishing reputation in China. It is full of humour but also very revealing, not only of the difficulties he encountered, but also of the character and attainments of the man.

The second reason [he writes] is that one day I was with some *literati* at a party, and I made them write a great number of letters—now with them a letter stands for a word—and reading them once through I recited them to the assembly (from beginning to end by memory). They were all so dumbfounded that it got about that I could remember a book by heart on reading it once through, and had therefore no need to read it again. Consequently it was said that I had the power to teach this memory work. . . . The third reason was that Chiusiancou spread about my mathematical powers, there being no one in the world my equal, so it was said. Indeed if China were the whole world undoubtedly I could call myself the greatest mathematician and scientist, for their opinions are just ridiculous; and it is amazing how little they know, for they are concerned entirely with moralizing and the elegance with which they say it, or rather write it. . . . They think me a monstrosity of

[1] *Lettres édifiantes*, Tome XVII, éd. Paris, 1781, p. 85.

learning and that nothing like me has ever left our shores. All this makes me laugh heartily. . . .[1]

Whether he was a monstrosity of learning or not, he set to work with a will and within a year could read, understand and speak some Chinese.

Meanwhile Fr. Ruggieri was attempting to penetrate beyond Canton where he went with the traders. But every attempt was frustrated and the Fathers were expelled from Canton and sent back to Macao. So despondent did Fr. Valignano become that he was for abandoning the enterprise. He is said to have gazed, from his window in the residence at Macao, across the water towards China crying out 'with a loud voice and the most intimate affection of his heart, "Ah, Rock, Rock, when wilt thou open, Rock!"'[2]

The time was at hand. The Fathers had scarcely been sent back to Macao and publicly reproved when a message arrived from the district magistrate of the city of Chao-ch'ing inviting them to his city. They reached that city in the autumn of 1583. Before long they were ejected, as the viceroy who had invited them retired. But once again they were allowed to return. Ricci's description of their reception by the populace is both comic and tragic. The people threw stones at their house; they did so especially from a neighbouring tower and to such effect that the building nearly collapsed. All kinds of slanderous tales were spread; that they maltreated the son of a citizen, that Ruggieri had committed adultery, when in fact he had been miles away. But the Fathers remained, trusting in God. They proceeded with their studies and at this time translated the Ten Commandments into Chinese.

The technique used in Chao-ch'ing will serve as a sample of what was done by all Ricci's Jesuit successors. He describes it himself in his *Commentari*.[3]

The Fathers had hung up in their hall a map of the whole world, with the names in Arabic characters. When the Chinese understood

[1] Ricci, *Lettere*, No. 22, p. 206.   [2] Semedo, *op. cit.*, p. 172.
[3] *Op. cit.*, pp. 141 ff. (1911 ed.).

what it was, never having seen or imagined such a thing before, all the more serious minded of them wanted to see it printed with Chinese characters, so as to understand its contents better. . . . So the Father (i.e. Matteo Ricci, who wrote always in the third person) who knew something of mathematics, having been a disciple of Fr. Christopher Claver when in Rome, set about the task, helped by one of the *literati*, a friend of his; and before long he had made a map of the world, bigger than the one in the house. . . . And it was the best and most useful work that could be done at that time, to dispose the Chinese to give credit to the things of the Faith. For, up to then, the Chinese had printed many maps of the world with titles such as 'Description of the whole world' in which China was all, occupying the field with its fifteen provinces, and round the edge they depicted a little sea where a few islets were dotted about, on which they wrote the names of all the kingdoms of which they had ever heard; and these all put together would not have equalled in size one of the provinces of China. . . . When they saw the world so large and China in a corner of it, so small to their way of thinking, the more ignorant began to make fun of such a description, but the more intelligent, seeing such an orderly arrangement of parallel lines of latitude and longitude . . . could not resist believing the whole thing true . . . it was printed again and again and all China was flooded with copies.[1]

The printed copy, according to Fr. Bartoli,[2] did have China in the middle, but in its right proportion to the rest of the world. That Ricci placed China in the centre is an example of his delicate perception, for he did not wish to hurt the susceptibilities of the Chinese.

Then a little further on:

Many were drawn by the big clock and the little one; others by the fine oil paintings and other prints; others by the various mathematical instruments, the maps of the world and the manufactured articles which came from Europe.

The books also made them all marvel on account of their different

---

[1] I give these long extracts because as far as I know this book, which is a masterpiece, has not been translated into English.

[2] Daniello Bartoli, *Dell' Istoria della Compagnia di Gesù, La Cina, Terza parte, dell' Asia*, Bk. II, p. 302.

bindings with much gold and other ornamentation, besides the books on Geography and Architecture in which they could see so many countries and provinces all over the earth, the beautiful and celebrated cities of Europe and elsewhere, the great buildings, palaces, towers, theatres, bridges and churches. Later, musical instruments arrived which were much to their taste ... very gradually they came to realize that our country, our savants, our people, were quite different from what up to that time they had thought all foreign countries to be, namely, barbarous and in no way comparable to their own.

On such occasions the father began to speak of our holy Faith.

Consequently the house was full all day of grave personages and the street full of their litters, the river bank in front of our house full of boats belonging to the mandarins.[1]

And, as Fr. Ruggieri wrote:

The Jesuits could scarcely go into the streets but a vast crowd collected to look at them. This happened in all the towns they visited.[2]

After endless petty persecutions, expulsions, bodily assaults, and with small profit in number of conversions, but with the approval of the Chinese authorities, Ricci moved to Shao-chou in 1589, a city in the same province.

In 1594, after the Fathers had been at Shao-chou five years, they decided to adopt the dress of the *literati*. Up to then they had been given the name of bonzes, this being the generic name for all monks in China, of whatever religion. As the Fathers had gone about with shaven chins and with short hair, the Chinese could not be persuaded they were anything else than bonzes: they did not marry, they recited Office and stayed in church just as the bonzes did. The bonzes' reputation for holiness was by no means great. For these reasons Fr. Valignano decided it was absolutely necessary to let beards grow—and Ricci wrote that whereas the Chinese had not more than eight or ten hairs to a beard, his was a monster—and the hair of the head also was allowed to grow. The bonzes alone among the Chinese shaved hair and beard, and were of very low reputation indeed.

[1] Bartoli, *op. cit.*, p. 179.   [2] *ibid.*, p. 271.

Fr. Valignano also decided that the Fathers should have a distinctive dress of silk for special occasions and also a special biretta. Finally they took the manners of the *literati*, with their bowings and honorific titles. This was readily accepted among the Chinese, especially in the North, where the Jesuits were put in a grade of some eminence, namely that of 'preaching *literati*'.[1] Near Canton it was more difficult, for all the priests, regular and secular, of Macao still went by the old name of bonzes.

It now became the central aim of Ricci to stabilize the Chinese missionary venture by getting recognition from the Emperor himself; for, so long as this was not obtained, the whole undertaking was at the mercy of any timid or hostile official who happened to report the presence of strangers in the Empire. And for this he had to reach Peking.

Ricci made two attempts, both minutely recorded in his own great work, the *Commentari*, the first in 1599 and the second in 1601. The first, made in company with Fr. Lazare Cattaneo and two lay brothers, failed because at that time the Japanese were invading Korea and the presence of a foreigner—and all foreigners were alike to the Chinese—in the heart of the Empire was inopportune; so after a dismal and isolated wait of a month, they withdrew, bringing back with them their 'curiosities from Europe', two paintings on linen cloth, a harpsichord, a striking clock, and some 'triangular glasses', that is to say, some prisms.

At Nanking, where they had friends, they bought a house, and now at last made great progress. An old friend of Canton days, a *literatus*, introduced Ricci to the learned society of this second city of the realm and here he instructed Hsü Kuang-ch'i[2] known to the Catholic world as Paul Hsü, the father of the Zi-ka-wei mission at Shanghai. His daughter Candida, a young widow, financed the translation and printing of the *Summa Theologica* of St. Thomas in Chinese. He himself, when later the Chief Secretary of the kingdom, was put in charge of the reform of the calendar, a task which he completed with the assistance of

[1] cf. Ricci, *Commentari*, Bk. III, ch. 9, pp. 241, 242.
[2] Baptized by Fr. da Rocha in 1603.

Fathers Longobardi, Schreck and finally Adam Schall and James Rho.

In 1600 Fr. Ricci set off again for Peking, laden with presents for the Emperor; after imprisonment and after being despoiled of his presents and even of his chalice and reliquaries in the prison of Tientsin, after fruitless journeyings of the lay brother to Peking and when all seemed hopeless, the Emperor suddenly sent for them. Ricci describes it thus:

> All that our Fathers ever discovered was that the king, being one day alone, remembered a memorandum which said that certain foreigners wished to give him a bell which rang of itself; and he began to cry out 'Why have they not given me this bell that rings of itself?' Then the eunuch in attendance replied: 'If your majesty does not command the carrying out of the memorandum how can these foreigners dare come to court without licences?' Then the king wrote the necessary permit on the memorandum.[1]

The Fathers arrived at Peking on 4th January 1601. This was a major victory, and may be called the turning-point in the whole story of the Jesuit mission in China up to the end in 1814, when the last Jesuit in Peking died.

The opposition was soon roused; but the Emperor refused even to acknowledge the remonstrances and decisions of the Board of Rites; this was equivalent to an approval and so the Jesuits stayed. But there was also a very practical reason why the Fathers remained. The eunuchs in charge of the great striking clock, which the Fathers had presented to the Emperor, were terrified that, if the good Fathers left, no one would know how to make the clock go. Consequently they used all their considerable influence to keep the Jesuits where they were. The Emperor was as fascinated as a child would be with this new-fangled machine, and had a fine tower built for it. He wanted to see these strangers, but this was not allowed by the appropriate Board of Rites, so instead he had large portraits painted of them.

Before long the Fathers had a house of their own and a pension

[1] Ricci, *Commentari*, Bk. IV, pp. 363 f.

from the Emperor, but no written official approval; and this kept them for years in a permanent state of anxiety.

The work of evangelization however flourished; there were many conversions, the most important being that of Li Chih-tsao, a great mandarin, learned in Chinese literature. Like so many others of his class he could not be baptized because of his many wives, but he had his family christened and he himself followed their footsteps some time later. Now known as Leo, he was the founder of a church in Hangchow, where he went to live. Together with Paul Hsü he aided the Fathers in translating European works into Chinese; books of philosophy, mathematics, astronomy and theology flowed from their pens. Ricci himself, with their aid, wrote more than a dozen works, very few of which, unfortunately, have survived even in one copy.

Once Ricci had arrived in Peking, he never left it. His reputation grew immensely especially among the learned, so that all day *literati* were in the house to visit him. His continual labours wore him out and at the age of fifty-one he died, surrounded by his brethren.

After much difficulty the Emperor gave permission for the Jesuits to have a burying-ground; this was situated in the old Tartar city, and with reverent ceremonial—the many Christians carrying lighted candles—Fr. Matteo was buried, later to be joined by some of his famous successors. It is fitting to end this notice of so great a man with his own words, from a letter to his General Fr. Claudio Aquaviva on 22nd August 1608.

The Christians up to now in these four provinces number more than 2000. In that of Peking there are a little over 300 persons, but many of them are *literati* and good Christians. We have four houses, thirteen priests and four brothers; these, with other novices who have entered this year, make eight; there are another four or five boys studying in the house, and they help like the brothers.[1]

In another letter:

As to what you ask, hoping to hear news from China of some great conversion, I tell you that I and all the others who are here, dream

[1] Ricci, *Lettere*, No. 40, p. 358.

of nothing else night or day; and for this purpose are we dressed and shod in Chinese fashion, and we neither speak nor eat nor drink, nor live in our house except in the Chinese manner . . . the time in which we live in China is not one of harvest.[1]

He is recorded as having said on his death-bed: 'I leave you the gate open to great victories, which nevertheless are only to be obtained with great pains and combats.'[2]

The methods of evangelization devised by Ricci are in themselves so interesting and important and in their later effects so sadly a failure, that a full examination of them is imperative.

This meeting of Ricci with the Chinese was the first true encounter of the Far East and West; the Church had once been faced with the Greco-Roman civilization and now she was to be confronted with a new and very old civilization, that of China. It was Ricci's task so to present the Faith that he neither abandoned any part of it for the sake of an immediate result, nor forced upon his hearers elements which were more Hellenic than Christian.

In fact Ricci was a very adequate representative of the West of his day. He had imbibed the spirit both of the ancient humanism, being a Greek and Latin scholar, and the new scientific interests, astronomy, cartography, clock-making and architecture.

It was not Ricci who *rediscovered* the Chinese civilization, but the Augustinians who in 1575 entered Fukien and stayed there one month. When they left they took with them three hundred Chinese volumes. Fr. de Rada in the Philippines produced a report on China based on this information. Ricci would almost certainly have knowledge of this from the Franciscans at Malacca. 'Certain Spaniards have come here from the new world . . . they experienced many dangers, but the Portuguese have managed to set them free.'[3]

Nor was it Ricci who was the first among the Jesuits to examine the problem. Valignano made the decision that the missionaries had to know Cantonese as well as Mandarin. Ruggieri, Ricci's companion in the early days, attracted the Chinese by the mechanical novelties; he too was the originator

[1] Ricci, *Lettere*, No. 28, p. 246.   [2] Semedo, *op. cit.*, p. 197.
[3] Ricci, *Lettere*, No. 2b, p. 31.

of the idea of wearing the dress of the *literati*. But, as soon as Ricci had mastered the language, he took the leadership. He transposed Ruggieri's catechism into Mandarin style; he adapted Ortelius's *mappa mundi*, made a pendulum clock, worked out a Chinese-Portuguese vocabulary, the first ever made between Chinese and any European language. It was in three columns: the first Portuguese, the second an Italian phonetization of the Chinese and then the Chinese character.

Meanwhile he was learning to appreciate China. His first account of it may be found in Valignano's life of St. Francis Xavier. He is not uncritical of the Chinese. While praising their discipline and the antiquity of their culture, he condemns their morals, greed and cowardice.

Ricci's second account of China is known to us only through Hakluyt, where the Latin dialogue in which form it is written was translated into English.

China, he realized, was exceedingly rich, but the legend that war, pestilence and famine never occurred, Ricci affirms to be a fabrication.

He notes the enormous quantity of gold, the silk, the porcelain. In passing he observes that the Emperor may be seen only once a year when he holds the plough and the Empress the mulberry tree. The olive, he writes, is not known, nor the vine, though this latter is obtainable. He notes the orderliness of life but the cowardice and effeminacy of the people. Their education is literary.

'Although it is generally said that many of the liberal sciences, especially natural and moral philosophy, are studied in China; and that there are universities, it is "hear-say" more than reality; belles-lettres are especially cultivated there.'[1]

Finally he asserts that China had hitherto never heard of the true religion. At this time he was unaware of the earlier Nestorian or Franciscan efforts in preceding centuries—as were indeed the Franciscans themselves—or was not yet convinced that ancient Cathay was none other than China. Confucius he had not yet

[1] cf. Hakluyt's *Principal Navigations*, Vol. IV, pp. 210–19 (Everyman ed.).

read, but he gathered from his Chinese friends that he was a 'notable philosopher'. 'The sum of his doctrine is that men should follow the light of nature. . . . If Confucius had made any mention of Almighty God or of the life to come and had not ascribed so much to the heavens, and to fatal necessity, nor yet . . . intreated of the worshipping the idols of the forefathers', Confucius would have been very praiseworthy. As for the Buddhists, he thought they had some inkling of the life to come. He has a poor picture of Taoists and was never closely in touch with their literature. The priests of both these sects, he wrote, 'lead a base and most servile life'.

Two events in the early days at Shao-chou influenced Ricci's life profoundly. The first was his associating with a delightful Chinese humanist Ch'ü T'ai-su whom he first met in 1590 at Shao-chou, and who was very clever but too rich to bother to pass examinations, and the other event was the arrival of Fr. Lazare Cattaneo. The first opened his eyes to the Chinese mind and culture and the second gave him an opportunity to resume serious study, a thing he had had to abandon for six or seven years owing to the great load of work.

Ch'ü T'ai-su first approached Ricci because he thought the latter had the secret of the philosopher's stone. That was the poor man's weak point. Ricci was already aware of this dangerous association of ideas: he was clever, he must therefore be an alchemist. He had, consequently, to put away his silver chalice for one of *calaim* (copper, zinc, nickel?). Ch'ü T'ai-su was gradually weaned from such fancies and set his excellent mind to the study of mathematics under the expert guidance of his Jesuit master. He read Euclid, studied the spheres of Fr. Claver— Ricci's old master—he made sun-dials, manipulated sextants and astrolabes. In fact he was the door through which Western scientific inventions and study re-entered China after a lapse of centuries. His enthusiasm was immense; it led him to set out these wonders in clear and elegant Chinese, propagating them among all his friends.

The moment came when Ch'ü T'ai-su wanted to be informed

of the religion of these astonishing, charming, unselfish travellers. Ricci described the incident in his *Commentari*.

> Once he stopped the classes for three or four days and wished to speak of this subject, and he did so very much to the point. For, in order to do so to the best advantage, he had made a book of the difficulties he had found in our Catholic faith in order to put underneath the answer and solution the Fathers would give to each.[1]

Ricci answered them all to the complete satisfaction of the young man. But these conversations were for the immediate future of more profit to the Jesuit than to the Chinese student, for the latter had a marriage entanglement and for the time being did nothing; but Ricci thus entered more fully than ever into the Chinese mentality.

In 1594 the arrival of Lazare Cattaneo to replace Fr. de Petris, who had died, gave Ricci the opportunity, as we have already said, to take up once again the serious study of Chinese. He therefore turned to the five Canonical Books. He had supposed that Confucius, for all his high morality, was a materialist and fatalist. It was the current and official view. He wrote about this time: 'I have noted in the Canonical Books many passages which are favourable to the things of the faith, such as the unity of God, the immortality of the soul, the glory of the blessed.'[2] This was a revolution, as it gave him and his companions something Chinese to build on in the conversion of the country. In no country would this be so important as it was in the Middle Kingdom, for nothing that was not old had in the eyes of its inhabitants any value whatsoever. It was, besides, the first serious return in modern times to the sources in Chinese literature, and as such is a great event in the world's history, and the beginning of Chinese scholarship.

Ricci now saw reasonable grounds for optimism. Brother Sebastian Martinez used to say to him 'Better go off to Japan, where there is more hope'. 'Be quiet', Ricci would answer, 'you do not know what you are talking about . . . our enterprise is not

[1] Bk. III, p. 211.   [2] *Lettere*, No. 22, p. 207.

so hopeless as you think. One day you will see me sitting in familiar conversation with the chief ministers of the land.'[1]

Ricci had realized that the door of entry was not so much clocks and astrolabes as Confucianism. He proposed to make himself all things to all men and to begin by turning himself into a *literatus*, not a Chinese mandarin, not a Chinese *literatus*, but one from the Great West.

Cattaneo had brought with him from the Jesuit authorities the permission for the Fathers to change their dress of bonzes into that of a *literatus*. Ricci's first writing in this character was his little treatise on Friendship.[2] This gave him a great reputation for learning. But he began to approach the religious question with greater caution than ever. He would start by laying the foundations of natural religion.

> Although we do not at present [he wrote] explain to them all the mysteries of our holy faith, we advance nevertheless by laying the first foundations: there is a God, creator of heaven and earth; the soul is immortal; good is recompensed, evil punished . . . it seems best to start by explanations founded on reason.[3]

The Chinese at that time were either Confucianists, Buddhists or Taoists, and the more sophisticated were an amalgam of all three. For the second and third sects Ricci had little sympathy, as we shall see, but for the first, while being very fully aware of its shortcomings—its hazy dogmatic content—he had increasing respect; and he intended to make it serve as a bridge between the Chinese people and Christ, much as Platonism served as a bridge between the Greek world and Christ in the earliest age of the Church.

> Although the sect of the *literati* (Confucianists) refuses to speak of supernatural realities it is in almost complete agreement with us in moral teaching; that is why . . . I began by making use of it to

[1] Henri Bernard, *Le Père Matthieu Ricci et la Société Chinoise de son temps*, Vol. I, 1937, p. 193.

[2] There were many great difficulties in the way of writing books for the benefit of Chinese and not least was the necessity of sending everything to Goa in India for an *imprimatur* before publication.

[3] *Lettere*, cf. pp. 220–5, 230.

attack the other (sects of idolaters) without refuting it, but interpreting the passages which appear contrary to our holy faith. . . .[1]

We can see the gradual *rapprochement* growing between the great missionary and the tradition of China, a *rapprochement* which to us reads like a Greek tragedy, for it was to end in fateful quarrel over the Chinese Rites and the destruction of nearly all that he had worked for and foreseen.

'The Chinese have always worshipped a supreme divinity whom they call Lord of Heaven, or Heaven and Earth, for it seems to them that perhaps Heaven and Earth were a live thing and were one single living thing, of which the divinity were the soul.'[2]

Thus we see that Ricci did not hide the truth from himself or from others, but believed in 'interpreting in our favour some texts which were ambiguous'.[3]

In the words of Fr. Henri Bernard, 'Ricci, in thus placing himself resolutely upon the plane of the philosophy of Confucius, seems to us simply to have renewed upon the borders of the Pacific Ocean what St. Justin, Athenagoras, and Clement of Alexandria had attempted in the Hellenic world.'[4]

Ricci saw Confucius as a moralist, an historian perhaps, but in religion no more than a rubrician. He believed that the veneration paid to Confucius was not different from that paid to ancestors. In the *Commentari*[5] he asserts that here there was no whiff of idolatry, and even 'one might be allowed to assert that there was no superstition either'.[6]

As for Confucianism as such he affirmed that 'since it neither commanded nor forbad anything to be believed concerning the next life, it was not formally a religion but only an academy'.[7]

---

[1] Letter of 15th February 1609. *Lettere*, No. 43, p. 387.

[2] *Commentari*, Bk. I, pp. 85–6. [3] *Lettere*, No. 43, p. 385.

[4] Bernard, *op. cit.*, Vol. I, p. 336. [5] Bk. I, p. 50.

[6] 'Fr. Ricci and . . . his superiors at Macao . . . did not deny at all that certain Chinese rites had at least the appearance of superstition and that others were really superstitious; but they thought that after carefully eliminating all the Buddhist and Taoist accretions (elements which were certainly superstitious) they would find it possible by stages to laicise completely the rites which were purely Confucian.' Bernard, *op. cit.*, Vol. II, p. 143.

[7] Ricci, *Commentari*, Bk. I, pp. 91 ff.

Unfortunately some replies to the missionaries of Nanchang which Ricci wrote and the 'Instructions' which he composed on how missionaries in China should behave, have disappeared. They were taken to Macao by Diaz for Valignano to read in 1603, but have not been seen since. However, his Catechism for neophytes and his 'Christian Doctrine' for those approaching the end of the catechumens' instruction give us a clear idea of his method. The first alone would make one imagine that he was preaching a pure Deism. But Ricci realized the difficulties of the Chinese and began by giving them the milk and not the strong meat. For instance the sight of the Crucifix horrified them, unless first they had been well instructed. A nude figure in art was forbidden by law; the sight of Christ on the cross was easily mistaken for magic, and as the ideas of the majesty and love of God were totally lacking to the Chinese of his day, he eliminated all mention of them in the Catechism, though, in the first one that he had translated, they had all been there.

An incident which occurred when he was making his way for the second time to Peking confirmed him in this opinion. He and his companions were held prisoners by a governor of a castle on the approaches to the capital. Towards the end of their captivity this eunuch, Ma T'ang, examined the Fathers' baggage.

> The thing that astonished them all most and gave us greatest pain, was the discovery among our effects of a very beautiful crucifix made in wood, the blood painted on so that it seemed alive. On seeing this, the cruel eunuch began to exclaim: 'so this is the sorcery you have made in order to threaten our king with. This cannot be a good or kindly person who goes about with such works of art.'[1]

If the Catechism was very discreet, the 'Christian Doctrine', written for those who truly wanted to become Christians, was completely explicit. The Our Father, Hail Mary, the Commandments, the Creed, the Sign of the Cross and all the rest were explained.

The business of the Calendar was inefficiently managed and hopelessly inaccurate. Ricci realized that, by showing the

[1] Ricci, *Commentari*, Bk. IV, pp. 357 ff.

Father Matteo Ricci

Father Ricci's Mappa Mundi made in 1602

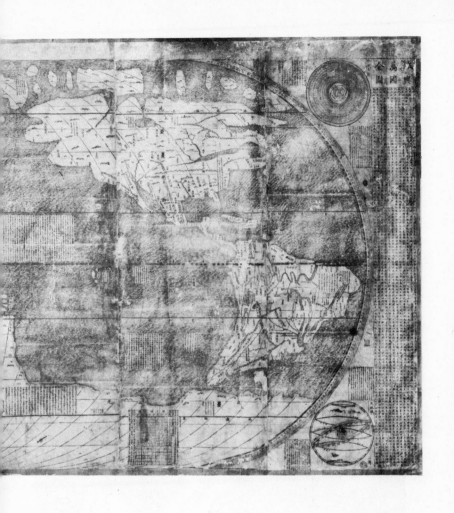

Father Alexandre Rhodes

Chinese how wrong they were even in purely material matters, he might find less difficulty in demonstrating how wrong they must be in spiritual teaching. Yet Ricci's own science was none too far 'advanced'; he believed in a solid heaven and the four elements. But he had been trained by Claver. He wrote home to Europe imploring the authorities to send him out an astronomer; meanwhile, much to the discomfiture of the two hundred imperial astronomers who haunted the royal precincts at Peking, he used to predict eclipses, which in fact occurred.

Of the ancient grandeur of Taoist thought, Ricci, and for that matter the Chinese, were unaware. Ricci met Taoist monks, particularly at the monastery near Nanking, where the great temple of heaven stood. He had not been impressed; Mo-Ti,[1] with his doctrine of universal love, was not well known in China at this time.

But Ricci did not have his own way without a struggle within the Society itself. The very man he chose to succeed him on his death, Fr. Longobardi, was far from sharing his belief in the method of 'grafting'. Longobardi admitted that the original texts might be interpreted in a manner favourable to Christian doctrine, but pointed out that the Commentators, whose views were almost as sacred as the originals, all interpreted the texts in an atheistic, material sense. Consequently, he went on, in the first place the Chinese would consider it impertinence on the part of foreigners to teach the *literati* their business and in the second place this very teaching would land them in a morass of merely verbal and fruitless discussion. It is well to remember the question of method was present to the minds of the missionaries from the start. And we must realize that Ricci's approach was far more cautious and balanced than has usually been admitted.

His was a subtle and delicate mind capable of an unceasing patience and a profound comprehension of another's soul. When he was dying he made a typical remark to one of his fellow missionaries, Fr. de Pantoja; the latter had probably asked him

[1] Henri Bernard, S.J., *Sagesse Chinoise et Philosophie chrétienne*, Tientsin, 1935, pp. 42–8.

how best he could thank him, Ricci answered: 'By showing always an exquisite kindness to the Fathers who come out from Europe; for these have renounced the charity of the colleges of the Society to emigrate to this desert of gentility.'[1]

(d) *Note on Blessed Benedict Goes*

No account of the life and labours of Fr. Matteo Ricci would be complete without some mention of the heroic journey of his fellow Jesuit, Benedict Goes, from Agra in India to Su-chou at the western end of the Great Wall of China. Yet it must be admitted that, from the point of view of the conversion of the Celestial Kingdom, the expedition would seem to have had little or no importance. Its chief interest lies, firstly in that once and for all the ambiguities regarding Cathay and China were settled, secondly in the endurance and apostolic zeal of this servant of God and thirdly in demonstrating once again the exemplary tenderness and care of the already heavily burdened Fr. Ricci.

The medieval travellers who reached China, Marco Polo, Blessed John of Montecorvino and the rest, always referred to it as Cathay. They never called it China. The descriptions they gave usually included mention of numbers of Christians to be found there, as we have already remarked. On the other hand, the travellers of the sixteenth century arriving at the sea frontier of China, the Jesuits who penetrated into the interior and the merchants who at least visited Canton, found no Christians or only the last vestiges of them. It was therefore generally agreed that these two countries were not the same.[2] It followed that there was general eagerness to discover where 'Cathay' really was! Add to this the complete lack of reliable maps, and one can understand the utter confusion all were in—except Ricci, who very soon came to the conclusion that the two were after all the same.

Ricci had been a disciple in Rome of Fr. Claver, the best astronomer the Society of Jesus had at that time. Therefore when

---

[1] Henri Bernard, *Le Père Matthieu Ricci*, Vol. II, p. 371.
[2] South China was not called Cathay by the medieval travellers but Manzi. Cathay was their name for the northern part.

his superior, Fr. Valignano, asked him to write some account of the geography of the country, he set about it not only with a good will but with technical ability. It was this survey and the map he made with the help of the Chinese cartographers that first convinced him that China was Cathay and that Peking was Cambaluc.

Another fact clinched the argument in his own mind. Merchants in Peking from across Asia, who had travelled the Silk road, in search of that precious material, all told him that in the countries they came from, Persia and the rest, China was still called Cathay. He wrote off this information to his superiors; but it appears that they were not yet ready to believe him.

Meanwhile, as Ricci had penetrated to the heart of pagan China, so were other Jesuits firmly established at the centre of the Mogul Empire in India. In Agra Fr. Jerome Xavier—not to be confused with St. Francis—also spoke with the merchants recently returned from their trek over the mountains of Central Asia in search of silk. They spoke of Cathay and of the many Christians that they knew were there. (These men were either deceiving Fr. Xavier for their own ends or mistook Buddhists for Christians.) It was determined therefore to send a trusty member of the Society with these merchants in order to solve the mystery and find these Christians. The man chosen was Br. Benedict Goes. It is Ricci who gives us almost all we know of his antecedents.

This blessed brother was a native of Villafranca in the island of St. Miguel [one of the islands in the Azores]. He was a member of the Order for nineteen years. . . . When a young man, and while serving as a soldier in India, he was sent with the fleet to the coast of Malabar. . . . He had hitherto lived a life of pleasure, devoting himself to gambling and various other follies to which youth is prone; but at that time he was seized with such bitter remorse that he lost all hope of salvation. However on landing near Coleche he came to the foot of an altar in a church and there he was vouchsaved a touching miracle in which he and his companions saw the child Jesus weeping in the arms of his Mother. This changed his life, as was to be expected. He joined the Society of Jesus forthwith.[1]

[1] cf. P. du Jarric, *Jahangir and the Jesuits*, ed. C. H. Payne, London, 1926, p. 158.

It is not our intention to retell the story of Benedict Goes' journey which has been told with such skill especially by Fr. Felix Alfred Plattner in *Jesuits Go East*. Suffice it to say that he set off from Lahore in 1603 at the express command of his superiors and with material support from the Emperor, Akbar, to discover, if it was humanly possible, the country called Cathay. He therefore joined a party of merchants, disguised as an Armenian in Moorish dress, but not hiding the fact that he was a Christian. He wore a cross on his breast. His route was up the Khyber Pass to Afghanistan, on to Yarkand and eastern Turkistan, then through the desert lands of the Tarim Basin to Turfan, Hami and, finally, Su-chou. He reached this gateway to China in December 1605, having achieved a feat never yet performed by a European and having proved beyond doubt that the Cathay of the merchants was the China of the Portuguese traders and of the Jesuits.

It was supposed by Ricci in his account that his Mohammedan companions, who were making him give them forced loans, poisoned him, so that he sickened and was near death. However, Benedict Goes managed to send a messenger secretly to Peking with a letter to Ricci. Immediately on receiving it, the latter sent a trusty lay brother, John Fernandez, to find him. But this was ten months after Blessed Benedict's arrival at Su-chou, and when Br. John reached him in May 1607, the traveller was little more than a skeleton. In ten days he was dead. This was the signal for the Mohammedan merchants, who had borrowed his money, to rush in and tear up the diary which, besides containing the precious account of this great journey, also contained the amounts that they owed him. The faithful Fernandez, however, collected these fragments and carried them to the Peking mission. Ricci, in spite of all his other immense labours, set about piecing together that priceless relic of the journey. He transcribed it and it was finally edited by Fr. Trigault. Thus did Blessed Benedict once and for all settle the age-long dispute and uncertainty about the location of old Cathay and modern China.

ii. *The Consolidation of Gains*

(a) *The Jesuits*

The period between the death of Fr. Ricci and the fall of the Ming dynasty is one of the most fruitful and most heroic in the history of the Chinese Church. It may be divided into two parts, the first, one of intermittent persecution and alarms, from 1610 to 1622; the second, one of peaceful progress, dating from the end of the persecution in 1622 to the end of the Ming dynasty in 1644.

At his death Ricci left the mission flourishing. In 1594 there were ninety youths destined for the priesthood, in 1602 the Jesuit Fathers had built their church in Peking. Fr. di Rocha had been made superior of Nan-ch'ang; Fr. Vagnoni was in Nanking, the most flourishing mission, and in 1616 he had with him Fr. Semedo, the historian of the early days and two lay brothers, Sebastian and John Fernandez. The three great mandarin converts Leo, Michael and Paul, were each established in their own home towns: Paul Hsü in Shanghai, Michael Yang in Chekiang and Leo Li in Hangchow. Each set up a mission station in his home country and also helped to teach the Fathers Chinese. They even hoped to arrange for one of the Jesuit astronomers to be on the Bureau of Astronomy, but persecution was to cut short all their schemes.

The chief cause of the ensuing disturbance was as usual the fear of foreigners. The Chinese had heard how these barbarians had seized ports in India and the Malay peninsula, how fortifications were going up at Macao, which was a fact and did not help good relations, even though they were being constructed under the inspiration of the Fathers and against the hated heretic Dutch. The smallest thing would set off the explosion. The actual circumstance was the appearance of one of the Fathers as he travelled north. Cattaneo was very stout and, as soldiers were well fed, was therefore taken for a military person. The Chinese suspected the worst: invasion, war. The Chinese of Canton threatened to starve out Macao. It was only after a friendly mandarin had been invited to inspect Macao that suspicions were laid to rest. This scare was only the beginning of sorrow.

A really serious persecution, which lasted eight years, broke out in 1615. The immediate cause was the jealousy of a noted Confucianist, whose name was Shen Ts'ui of Nanking. Fr. Vagnoni had perhaps been indiscreet, not keeping to the advice of Ricci. At all events, on 20th August this man obtained a decree from the Board of Rites in Peking ordering the arrest and expulsion of the Fathers. At Nanking Vagnoni and two servants were imprisoned on the 31st; the following day Fr. Semedo, Br. Fernandez and thirteen Christians were also seized. The great mandarin Christians tried to have the decree reversed; but in 1617 the Emperor by decree expelled all missionaries. Longobardi, the head of the Peking house, went into hiding. Vagnoni and Semedo were put in cages and conducted to Canton; their residence and church were destroyed. The facts are known because the jealous and triumphant Shen Ts'ui proudly published them to the world. But Shen Ts'ui's turn came in 1617 when he fell into disgrace. The Jesuits thereupon returned. But in 1621, four years later, he was back in favour and the Jesuits went into hiding once again. The following year twenty-two Christians of Nanking were tortured.

Gradually the persecution died down, the Fathers returned secretly, and finally were reinstated in their residences owing to the help of their most zealous convert, Paul Hsü.

Meanwhile Fr. Trigault, who had arrived in China a few weeks after Ricci's death, had been sent in 1613 by Longobardi, the new superior, to Rome via Ormuz, Persia, Syria. In Rome he saw Paul IV and many cardinals including the great Jesuit—Cardinal Bellarmine. He translated Ricci's *Commentari* into Latin and had it published at Augusta in 1615. On 25th January 1615 a brief of Paul V appeared which 'granted to the Chinese priests the faculty of reciting the divine Office, of celebrating Mass and of administering the sacraments in their own language'.[1]

---

[1] Fr. Servière in *Les Anciennes missions de la Compagnie de Jésus en Chine (1552–1814)*, Shanghai, 1924, p. 50, remarks that Fr. Buglio had already translated the Missal and Ritual into Chinese. It was the missionaries in Japan who stopped it.

In 1618, Trigault was ready to return. He sailed from Lisbon with sixteen Fathers and Brothers. Five of them died on the way, and of the whole number only two were finally directed to China—but they were worth an army—the Fathers Terrenz and Schall. They arrived at Macao in July 1619.

After the terror and disappointment of the years of persecution, the Jesuits reverted to the Riccian technique, that of not exciting the mob or the bonzes by any imprudent acts of proselytism. The addition, therefore, of these two notable men was an important event. It had been the wish of Ricci before he died that astronomers should be dispatched from Europe to share his burden and destroy the bogus scientific reputation of the Buddhists in the Bureau of Astronomy.

As soon as Terrenz and Schall could start work they did. In 1623 and 1624 Schall prophesied an eclipse and the mandarins failed to do so. Naturally this gave him a great reputation.

It is a pleasant thought that the noble Paul Hsü on his return to Peking after the trials of the persecution should find for his old age a true counsellor in the person of Schall. Now came the first golden age of the Church in China. Paul Hsü became Vice-President of the Board of Rites (1628), President in 1631, and received the honorific title of Kê-Lao; he also became a member of the Council of State, while Leo, his friend, was now in command of part of the capital and in control of the army. The knowledge that two such notable men had joined the new religion gave added weight to the words of the missionaries.

As early as 1620 Paul Hsü had imported some Portuguese cannon founders from Macao, and as these had been expelled in the persecution, he reverted to the idea in 1630, when he had the daring to introduce a Portuguese captain, Gonzalve Texeira Correa, with the duty of organizing a little army of his countrymen who would instruct the Chinese. Four hundred men with ten pieces of cannon got as far as Nan-ch'ang. But at this juncture the Emperor took fright and ordered them back. Texeira himself and a few companions reached Peking, where he was killed in a skirmish.

Schall meanwhile had become chaplain in the imperial palace

where a chapel was installed. Many eunuchs were converted, five hundred and forty baptisms took place in a few months, one of the Emperor's wives and her child being among the number.

In 1633 the life of Paul Hsü was drawing to its end; he was assisted in his last days by his friend Schall and the other Fathers of the Peking mission. One of Paul Hsü's last acts was to present two memorials to the Emperor; the first requesting that the Fathers should be maintained at the Bureau of Astronomy; the second that his successor as President of the Board of Rites should be a Christian, Peter Li T'en-chung, a Judge. Both these requests were granted and, shortly after, he died. The Emperor paid the expenses of his funeral; his body was taken to Shanghai by mandarins and then transferred to the village of Zi-ka-wei, later famous in the annals of the Catholic Church in China.

The reform of the calendar inaugurated by Paul Hsü and originally conceived by Ricci was now undertaken by Longobardi and Terrenz, then, after Terrenz's death in 1630, by Schall and Rho, who were attached to the Bureau of Astronomy. This link between the Church and the Bureau went on until the nineteenth century. The story of the Chinese calendar goes back to the very earliest days of Chinese history. The first civilization known to have existed was one which came in from the south and was agricultural in character and therefore matriarchal. The whole religious life of these peoples was intertwined with the fertility of the soil and the cycle of the year. A calendar was therefore of no little importance. The Chinese had made some miscalculations in judging the times of the seasons of the year. The astronomers of the Mongol dynasty had made improvements, but confusion still reigned, and, since the calendar was misunderstood by the ignorant bonzes of the Ming period, it got into worse confusion and created agricultural chaos. The ploughing, the sowing, the reaping were all ritual acts performed upon days appointed by the Astronomer Royal; and as he and his associates were utterly incompetent to decide when midsummer, midwinter, or the equinoxes occurred, the farming community, for the best religious motives, repeatedly ruined their crops.

It was this situation that the Jesuit astronomers were attempting to rectify when once again they were thwarted, this time by the collapse of the Ming dynasty.

(b) The Friars get a Foothold

As the Dominicans played an integral part in the story of the Chinese missions particularly in the seventeenth century, some account of their activities and methods and personnel is required.[1] Fr. Gaspar de la Cruz, as we have already mentioned, had gone from the province of Cambodia in Indo-China to China in 1556. His method was to be that of all the early Dominicans and Franciscans, much to the discomfiture of the later Jesuits, that is he set about overthrowing idols wherever he could lay his hands on them. The mandarins soon laid their hands on him and he was speedily ejected. He ended his days as a missionary at Ormuz at the entrance to the Persian Gulf, but retired to Lisbon before he died.

The first Provincial of the Order of Preachers in the Philippines, Fr. John de Castro, in the newly erected province of the Holy Rosary, together with Fr. Michael de Benavides—a true Chinese scholar—were imprisoned on their arrival in China in 1590 and then sent back to Manila because they were suspected of being spies for the King of Spain. Many other attempts were made, but, as their success was no greater than those recorded, it is futile to enumerate them. However a more important move was made in 1587 when Fr. Barthelemi Lopez—not to be confused with Fr. Gregory Lopez the future Dominican bishop—and two others succeeded in the face of the Portuguese and the Jesuit opposition in establishing a house for Dominicans in Macao itself.

Rome in 1633 finally opened the gates of China to all religious Orders. Fr. Juan Baptista Morales that year went there from Formosa, which had been partly controlled by the Spaniards since 1625. He, a Dominican, was accompanied by a Franciscan, Antonio de Santa Maria Caballero. Both these men made history

[1] Constantino Bayle, S.J., *La Expansión misional de España*, Barcelona, 1946.

in the Chinese mission. The former was about thirty-six when he reached China; he had joined the Order in Spain, his native country, and had now been in the Philippines eleven years. Morales has the dubious distinction of being the missionary to open the dispute concerning Chinese Rites, and we shall hear more of him later. He went to Rome with his complaints in 1643.

The statistics of converts and of missionaries are not always accurate, but one account tells us that by 1664 the Dominicans had churches in five cities, three towns, and three villages of Fukien, Chekiang and Kwangtung. This was not achieved without much perseverance and some martyrs. In 1648 a Dominican, Francis Capellas, was martyred in Fukien.

This proto-martyr of the Chinese mission deserves a special mention. Francis or John Fernandez Capellas was born at Bacquerín in Spain in 1607. He joined the Dominican Order in his youth, went through his studies at Valladolid, from there, after some time working for Christ in Spain, he was sent to the Philippines and finally to China in the year 1642. The area of his apostolate was round Fu-an in the province of Fukien. He soon learned the language and travelled everywhere on foot, carrying with him nothing but his Breviary and his crucifix, for in his preaching 'he relied solely on the virtue of the Cross'.[1]

A persecution soon broke out in Fukien, but an official was sent down to inquire into the disturbance, and was ordered to listen not only to the accusations against the Christians but also to their replies. One of Fr. Capellas' converts defended the Christian cause so ably that for the time the persecution ceased. However, before very long, it began again, and Fr. Capellas himself was captured, put in chains and cast into prison (November 1647). When questioned as to whose house he used for his lodging, he replied: "I have no other house than the wide world, no other bed than the ground, no other food than what Providence provides from day to day, and no occupation other than that of

---

[1] Huc, *Christianity in China, Tartary and Thibet*, London, 1858, Vol. III, p. 14.

labouring and suffering for the glory of Jesus Christ and the eternal happiness of those who believe in Him.'[1]

His eloquence, his serenity and his courage in prison brought him many converts. Sentence of death was passed. He was executed, 15th November 1648, before an immense crowd including some of his own Dominican brethren who had just arrived from Europe. At Macao, in the Philippines, in Spain, the news was not received with mourning but with great joy. Masses of thanksgiving were offered, Te Deums sung, and the populace gave itself over to fireworks displays.[2]

Among the recently arrived missionaries, who witnessed the martyrdom of the Blessed Fernandez Capellas was Fr. Morales returned from Rome. Fr. Capellas had roused the anger of the literati and others by his refusal to pay homage to the tablet of Confucius; Morales was to turn this into the policy of the Dominican province.

We shall deal with the Rites Question at length later, but it must be remarked in passing that Morales forbade his converts to practise any ceremony before the tablets of Confucius. When he was a prisoner in Canton he had leisure to study the matter even more closely and he came to the conclusion that the Portuguese missionary endeavour was unsound on these matters.

Morales' companion was a notable apostle, a Valencian, born at Baltanas in 1602; on his entry into China he was barely thirty-one. In his youth Antonio de Santa Maria Caballero had been to the University of Salamanca, but at the age of sixteen he became a Franciscan. Ten years later he was sent to the Philippines with twenty-nine companions. He had learnt Japanese from some lepers he nursed, and, full of zeal, hoped to be sent to Japan; but a companion of his, Fr. Cocchi, who had been sent to China in 1631, being left alone because his companion had died, needed a helper. The superiors therefore ordered Fr. Antonio to join him, consequently he went to Formosa where the Dominicans had

---

[1] ibid., p. 16.
[2] For a bibliography see Dictionnaire d'Histoire et de Géographie ecclésiastiques, Vol. XI, col. 857.

a station and where they taught him Chinese. On their arrival on the mainland they got in touch with a Jesuit Father, who told them they could not remain without the permission of Fr. Emmanuel Diaz, then Vice-Provincial of the Society in those parts. Fr. Antonio set off to find him. It was Christmas, and he was well received; but the advice given him was that he should go elsewhere. The next part of the story is obscure, but it appears that his servant was taken from him and another provided, who conducted him to Nanking, where he was seized and locked up in a house, outside the city, belonging to a Christian; there he was kept some months; but they finally carried him away by boat, tied hand and foot, back to where they had come from, all under the supervision of the servants of the Jesuits. This high-handed action could not fail to increase the tension between the Orders. But the strange thing is that, not long after, it was a Jesuit, the famous and holy Adam Schall, who greatly helped Fr. Antonio.

Meanwhile Angelo Cocchi, the Italian Dominican had died in the arms of Fr. Morales. When two more missionaries arrived, one Dominican and one Franciscan, they decided between them to leave Fukien to the former and make the Franciscans move elsewhere.

Soon Fr. Antonio was sent to Manila on the question of the Rites. He never reached it because the ship was wrecked in a storm. He and the crew were captured by the Dutch. For eight months he was imprisoned at Batavia not far from Malacca where he had great disputations with a Protestant *episcopus belgensis totius Indiae*—it is interesting that the Dutch had such a person in the Far East. They pressed him to read Spanish books, which he found 'full of heresy and blasphemies against the Mass'. Finally he reached Malacca and returned to Manila. There he and Morales were ordered to repair to Rome. At Macao, however, news spread that the Dutch were on the war-path, so Fr. Antonio's journey was put off. Four years later he was still at Macao; he left, however, when the Viceroy of the Indies in 1644 ordered all Spaniards to leave the city. In 1640 the two kingdoms of Spain and Portugal had disentangled themselves from their uneasy unity and most Spaniards had already left. Very shortly after Fr. Antonio's departure those who remained were massacred. He escaped with some Poor Clare nuns for whom he had been acting as chaplain. These political incidents, the expulsion and the massacre, are but two of many which endlessly interfered with the action of the Church.

After some years of frustration in the Philippines Fr. Morales reappeared armed with letters from the cardinals and Propaganda. He had also a personal letter from Pope Urban VIII giving him permission to go and preach the Gospel to the Chinese and to take with him companions of his own Order. In the year 1649 Antonio and Morales and some other friars once again set sail for the Middle Kingdom. Antonio, for some reason not given, bethought himself of the Koreans and attempted to reach them by land. When he arrived at the Great Wall he was prevented from passing it by the soldiers on guard, and ignominiously sent back to Peking. There he was most hospitably received by Fr. Adam Schall, now all alone. The friendship between these two great apostles grew with the years, in spite of their being on opposite sides in the fierce discussions over the Chinese Rites. Schall treated his guest with great courtesy and presented him with a letter of introduction to a mandarin of the city of Tsinan in Shantung; confident of success on account of this, and bearing presents—two knives, a pair of scissors, a bottle of amber, four pieces of Castilian paper, fifteen needles and the like—he reached Tsinan; the letters and the presents did their work. He was soon housed and writing to his superior that he had converted one hundred and fifty Chinese. This was the beginning of one of the most important Franciscan missions in China. Fr. Schall never forgot this new Christian community, and when supplies did not arrive from home for them he would himself make up the deficiencies.

But these kindnesses did not prevent Antonio from being extremely critical of Adam Schall's way of behaving in the capital. We hear in his letters the first distant thunder of the storm which was almost to destroy the Catholic missions in China.

On the 15th October 1649 he wrote a *relatio*, it does not record to whom; in it he says the following:

> Fr. John Adam Schall has for many years been a minister at the court of Peking, where he has been held always as a most learned man, especially in matters of astrology [*sic*!], on account of which the late king and the present one, because they are Tartars, have given him the title of Master of Astrologers;[1] and as they give him a salary for his livelihood, he has brought out for a number of years a calendar in Chinese lettering, wherein the moon and its eclipses and its mutations are treated of, and other natural things which may be known through the stars. This calendar is printed with the name, seal and signature of the said Father, making it clear who the author is. [But now begins the criticism.] Other matters are contained in this calendar more abstruse and foreign to Catholicism, for instance: not only are the suitable days for sowing seed and for cutting wood given, etc., which are things to be expected, but even things which are *superstitious and clearly diabolical*, such as: which day is good for getting married on, which for buying, which for selling, which for going out of the house, for going on a journey, for offering sacrifice.[2]

Fr. Schall replied that others had put those details in to the calendar. This did not satisfy Antonio, in spite of all the veneration he had for Schall's holiness. Antonio tells the story of how Schall, in order to reach a Christian viceroy, falsely put in prison and in danger of death, went disguised as a charcoal-burner, in order to hear his confession in which he succeeded. The calendar he still could not stomach.

In the fierce and general persecution of 1664, which broke out during the minority of the great K'ang-hsi Emperor—it was the third year of his reign—Antonio was put in prison and cruelly treated. By 1666 he and almost all the missionaries were in prison in the old Jesuit house at Canton. There, after three years of sickness and suffering patiently borne, he died. On the epitaph Bishop Gregory Lopez erected some years later over the grave

[1] It was not fair to call either Fr. Schall or the Mongols astrologers. They were astronomers.
[2] *Sinica Franciscana*, Florence, 1933, Vol. II, p. 376.

of his spiritual father, the priest who had poured the waters of
Baptism upon him, we read as follows:

A.R.P.F. ANTONIO A.S. MARIA
ORDINIS MINORUM, MINISTRO ET PRAEFECTO VERE APOSTOLICO
AB EXILIO CANTONENSI AD COELESTEM PATRIAM EVOCATO
ANNO M . D . C . L . XIX.
DECIMO TERTIO KALENDAS IUNII
FR. GREGORIUS LOPEZ, EPISCOPUS BASILITANUS
ET VICARIUS APOSTOLICUS NANKINI,
PATRI SUO SPIRITUALI, RESTAURATO SEPULCRO,
LAPIDEM HUNC
GRATITUDINIS MONUMENTUM EREXIT.[1]

Another Dominican figure who, towards the end of the seventeenth century, would become important, was one of Fr.
Antonio's and Fr. Morales' faithful followers, Gregory Lopez or
A-Lou, to give him his Chinese name. He was born in 1611 at
Lokjahuang. From his earliest youth he was brought up by
Antonio, who baptized this Chinese child and noticed in him
real intelligence and piety. This seems to have created in the
youth's breast a strong zeal to be an apostle; first his family were
catechized, but without success, then the neophytes in Peking
where he had followed the missionaries. But a persecution arose
and he went with some Franciscans to Cochin-China. Not long
after, he found his way to Manila, where in the College of St.
Thomas he learnt both Latin and Spanish. After having acted
as messenger between various missionaries and their headquarters
in Manila, especially during the persecution of 1664, Gregory
finally became a Dominican in 1650 at Manila, and four years
later he was ordained priest. His fame reached Rome, and
Clement X in 1674 decided to raise him to the episcopate. Fr.
Gregory refused from humility, but Innocent XI reaffirmed the
will of the Holy See, and in the end he was created Bishop of
Basilea. His territory included six provinces of China. Strangely
and significantly he was provided with a 'tame' theologian to

[1] *ibid.*, p. 329.

see that he did not stray from the truth in his theological pro-
nouncements.

It is worthy of record that he was in favour of the Christians
being allowed to perform the customary rites for the dead and
before the tablet of Confucius. He died full of honour and much
loved in 1687 at Nanking.[1]

The Augustinians made several efforts to establish themselves in
China from their base in the Philippines between 1572 and 1680
when they were finally successful. It was in the year 1572 while
they were holding their second Chapter of the Province that
some Chinese merchants landed at Manila from their junks. The
account they gave of themselves and of their country decided the
assembled Fathers to *pasar a la China*. It was easier said than
done. Apart from the journey of Fr. Martin de Herrada and Fr.
Jerome Marin, who went on an embassy to Peking in 1575
and whose account of their adventures was incorporated in the
famous history of Fray Gaspar de San Agustín, they had no
success until Fathers Alvaro de Benavente and Juan de Rivera
landed secretly from a fishing-boat in 1680; these two hid in
cottages, learnt the language and succeeded in settling at various
times in Kwangtung, Kiangsi and Kwangsi.

Thus we may end this short account of the restoration of the
Missions of the Friars in the seventeenth century after a lapse of
three hundred years. So long as Portugal controlled entry into
China, the efforts from the Philippines would remain impeded,
indeed any interference by another Power was strongly resented.

(c) *Collapse of the Ming*

As the seventeenth century wore on, a very delicate situation
arose for the missionaries. The Ming dynasty, which had come
into power with Chu Yüan-chang in 1368, was ending in
ignominy.

The first warning of impending collapse occurred in 1622 when
the intermittent revolts of the Manchu Tartars broke out again.
This was followed by a spell of quiet, followed again by a bout

[1] cf. Huc, *op. cit.*, Vol. III, pp. 18 ff., and 136 ff.

of fighting in 1629. Meanwhile the Portuguese had been called in to help and an Emperor, Hsi-Tsung, had died (1627). But jealousy of foreigners forced the Portuguese, under the leadership of Texeira, to retire. After an ineffectual attempt to patch up a peace, Abahai, the leader of the Manchu horde, held a council to concert the attack on the Chinese Empire.

In 1634, as a matter of form, he again offered terms of peace; again no reply; in 1635 he took the title of Emperor.

By 1640 there was civil war as well as the Manchu menace; a general, Li Tzü-ch'êng, took the name of Emperor in 1643. He marched on the capital, Peking, with an army of 300,000. The ineffectual Emperor attempted flight (1644). After a eunuch had treacherously delivered one of the city gates to the rebel chief, the Empress hanged herself, her women were massacred and the Emperor, finding flight impossible, hanged himself from a plum tree and thus ended the Ming dynasty. A general sent word to the Manchus, who had been waiting patiently, to pluck the ripening fruit. They came and they stayed until the twentieth century.

Abahai had died in 1643 and the Manchus had been governed by a Council of State, but on entering the capital city they proclaimed Abahai's nephew as the Shun-chih Emperor. Meanwhile the Ming dynasty wandered south, at first establishing itself at Nanking, then at Canton.

It was difficult for the Jesuits or any other missionaries to establish themselves in these shifting and perilous circumstances. In 1644 soldiers killed the Fathers Grassetti and Almeida and Gomez at Nanking. Fathers Buglio and de Magalhaens were made prisoners at Chengtu and only escaped with their lives because it was discovered that they were 'brothers' of the great Adam Schall of Peking.

At the siege of Kaifeng, Fr. de Figueiredo was drowned with 200,000 inhabitants, when the defending general broke the banks of the river in order to drown the besiegers. Fr. Walta died of wounds at the assault on P'u-chou in Shansi. Yung-li, the last of the Ming, desperately took refuge on the Burmese border. The collapse was complete. Meanwhile the missionaries carried on their religious activities as best they could. Some remained behind, others kept with the fleeing Emperor and his entourage; thus Fr. Köffler had converted the Emperor's mother —she was baptized Helena. His wife, son and daughter were also received into the Church. Fittingly enough the son was christened Constantine, but history did not repeat itself, the Ming dynasty fell, and China was not converted. A Christian general retook Canton in 1648 for the Ming, but it was only a flash in the pan. The Manchu finally captured Canton in 1651. In 1662 Yung-li was taken prisoner by his rivals and hanged himself at Yunnanfu. The young Constantine was killed and the princesses were taken to Peking. The Ming dynasty no longer existed.

(d) The Missionaries and the Manchu Dynasty

In Peking itself Fr. Adam Schall had been persuaded against his desire to set up a foundry for the making of cannon to help to save the Ming dynasty. This he was most unwilling to do, but as the request was really an imperial command, in the end he felt impelled to fulfil it. But no amount of cannon could save the rotten government of the Ming. The insurgents, when they captured the city, looted it, but by some providential intervention the house and books and astronomical instruments of Adam Schall were spared. When in a frenzy of rage the capital was fired, and the palace of lacquer came crashing to the ground and the city was nothing but charred remains, Adam Schall's house stood unharmed. He himself went about the city restoring some measure of calm and bringing hope. The Tartars, in alliance with the imperialist general, finally entered the city; but soon they showed themselves not as allies but as conquerors, and they ordered Peking's evacuation by the inhabitants within three days. Adam Schall went to the Great Council with a memorial printed by himself in the most perfect Chinese at his command, saying that his life work, the reform of the calendar, would be ruined; further, that the propagation of the True Religion would be hindered if he had to leave his house and sanctuary and the books and the wood blocks. When it was heard who he was and that he was working at the reform of the calendar, he was treated with the utmost deference, given protection and presented with a decree to hang out at his front door. He proceeded with the reform of the calendar.

The old party, not to be outdone, produced their calendar, following their antiquated technique. But a general cry went up that it was full of errors. A convenient eclipse of the sun was to occur in September 1645 which Schall predicted and the mathematicians could not. This eclipse was the final blow at the prestige of the old astronomers, and Adam Schall was appointed President of the Board (1645), which gave him control of this august body and the chance to complete his great work. This appointment was confirmed by the young Emperor when he took over the government, and, as was the way, Schall's father and grandfather and grandmother were ennobled.

It was the momentary glory of the noble Adam Schall. Ricci's church, the Nan T'ang, was enlarged, embellished and provided with an inscription by the Emperor in 1653. Meanwhile another church was being built in Peking by Fathers Buglio and Magalhaens. Schall, who had the ear of the wretched Shun-chih Emperor, got permission for other Jesuits to enter the provinces of China.

But the enemies of Schall were not idle. The great six Boards of the Central Government in Peking were at that time all controlled by Confucian *literati*, envious of the Jesuits both from the scientific and religious point of view, and at the death of the Shun-chih Emperor (in 1662) the attack began. A Jewish or Mohammedan astronomer in 1658 had published a pamphlet against the Jesuit missionaries, accusing them, according to a long-established custom, of being the advance guard of a Portuguese invasion. A refutation appeared, written by Fathers Buglio and Magalhaens, with a preface by Basil Hsü the son of the famous Paul Hsü. But in 1664 Yang Kuang-hsien went a step further by presenting his accusation to the Board of Rites.[1] Schall was old

---

[1] The Protocol Section of the Board of Rites had general charge of tribute-bearing missions from foreign countries to the imperial court. By a natural extension it came to have jurisdiction over all foreigners resident at the capital.

and paralysed, in his seventy-fourth year, and could not appear to defend himself. But the fate of the whole Jesuit enterprise in China depended upon the decision of this unfriendly Board. Verbiest, Schall's right-hand man, undertook the defence, but to no purpose. The first sentence condemned the Christian 'Law' as immoral, favouring rebellion and foreign invasion. Schall was condemned to strangulation, the three other Fathers to forty strokes with bamboo rods and to exile in Tartary.

The following year, 1665, the sentence was confirmed by the Council of Ministers of State; European science was condemned as bad, and Schall with five Christian assessors was condemned to be cut to pieces. Fr. Verbiest, as he was not in China when the 'wicked' calendar was concocted, was acquitted. This all occurred in January.

In April an earthquake took place which so frightened the court that the Queen Mother, who had affection for the Jesuits, interceded for them. The result was an amnesty. Schall, now truly a confessor of the Faith, returned from his captivity to the Nan-t'ang and died there on the Feast of the Assumption, 1666. But the five assessors had been killed.

Meanwhile in January the four Regents had issued a decree proscribing the Christian religion in China. All priests were to be brought to Peking and then conducted to Canton. There were thirty-eight in all China, eleven Dominicans and one Franciscan; all the rest were of the Society of Jesus. Four Jesuits remained in Peking, thirty priests set off from Peking for Canton. The convergence of most of them in the prison of Canton, where they could discuss the problems of the propagation of the Faith, was to have momentous results. The Rites dispute had already begun.

In the year 1669 the young Emperor reached his majority. Both his mother and grandmother were friendly towards the missionaries; and, as the date of his emancipation approached, the chances of their liberation increased.

Yang Kuang-hsien, now proudly settled in Adam Schall's famous house with his thousand books, and installed as President of the Board of Astronomy, had the effrontery to publish a calendar for 1669. It reached Verbiest's hands on Christmas Day of 1668. Noting, as was to be expected, a number of errors, he wrote a memorial to the young Emperor, challenging Yang Kuang-hsien to verify certain points by experiment. He was granted from 27th December till 1st February 1669 to prove his points. Verbiest, in this battle of wits, was completely successful, and by a reversal of fortunes typical of China of that time, he was given the post of his rival, that of President of the Board of Astronomy.

This is the beginning of the finest period of the Jesuit mission in China, the greatest missionary, after Ricci, collaborating with the greatest of the Emperors, Fr. Verbiest with K'ang-hsi. But progress was slow, there was so much prejudice to overcome, so many fears to be allayed. Schall was given a solemn funeral in 1669 and the Emperor himself sent a marble slab for the tomb with praise of the heroic missionary. The Nan-t'ang church was reopened. Relations between Macao and the mainland were once again free. In 1670 the Fathers petitioned for their re-entry at Canton; an edict of 1671 granted this. But there was no permit either for new missionaries to enter or for new churches to be built. There were thus twenty missionaries for 100,000 Christians, spread over eleven provinces.

There were now at court the Fathers Verbiest, Grimaldi, Pereira, and Thomas. Twice the Emperor visited them in their residence—such a thing would have been unheard of in the time of the previous dynasty—he sent them honorific inscriptions for their churches. Meanwhile the Fathers made instruments for the observatory and hydraulic contrivances for the imperial gardens; they founded cannon to conquer Turkistan, drew up plans for improving the canal system, wrote works of science, philosophy and religion. Verbiest became President of the Board of Astronomy, Vice-President of the Board of Public Works and a mandarin of the second class; his ancestors were ennobled.

The culmination of the good work done by the Fathers of the Peking mission came when the Emperor signed the Decree of the

Board of Rites granting protection to the Catholic missions and missionaries. This occurred in 1692, and the text is of sufficient importance to merit inclusion of its main features here.

> We have seriously considered this question of the Europeans, who, attracted from the extremity of the world by the renown of your remarkable prudence . . . have crossed the . . . seas. . . . Since they have been living among us they have merited our esteem and gratitude, by the great services they have rendered us in the civil and foreign wars, by their diligence in composing useful and curious books, their integrity, and their sincere regard for the public welfare. Besides this the Europeans are very quiet; they do not excite any disturbances in the provinces, they do no harm to anyone, they commit no crimes, and their doctrine has nothing in common with that of the false sects in the empire, nor has it any tendency to excite sedition.
>
> Since, then, we do not hinder either the Lamas of Tartary or the Bonzes of China from building temples, and offering in them incense to their gods, much less can we forbid these Europeans, who teach only good laws, from having also their churches and preaching their religion publicly in them.
>
> We decide therefore that all temples dedicated to the Lord of Heaven, in whatever place they may be found, ought to be preserved, and that it may be permitted to all who wish to worship this God to enter these temples, offer Him incense, and perform the ceremonies practised according to ancient custom by the Christians. Therefore let no one henceforth offer them any opposition.
> Given in the thirty-first year of the reign of K'ang-hsi. . . . (22nd March 1692).[1]

Verbiest was convinced that the future of the Chinese mission lay in the hands of a Chinese clergy, with a seminary at Peking, a school for boys. The best of these should be made priests, and that without Latin. Pope Paul V had already granted to Trigault a Chinese liturgy; and Buglio had translated the Missal and liturgy into Chinese. But political hindrances were beginning to be felt. Not least among them was the control by Portugal herself.

[1] Huc, *op. cit.*, Vol. III, pp. 202–3.

(e) *The Patronage of Portugal, Propaganda*[1] *and Fr. Rhodes*

Behind all this lies a story intimately connected with the progress of the Chinese mission. It must therefore be told here, though some of its incidents fall well before the arrival of the Jesuits and the other sixteenth-century missionaries and some well on into the eighteenth century.

So long as Portugal was alone in the Far East and so long as she could adequately supply the missionaries and the money to keep the missions going, it was unnecessary to inquire too closely into the rights and duties of that pioneer missionary country. When, however, the Spaniards and the Dutch and the English began to close in on her extensive dominions and spheres of influence, and when her power and capacity to produce missionaries and money dwindled almost to nothingness, it is time for the historian of these events to cast his mind back to see how that power over the Church exerted by Portugal came to be granted, and how the grave difficulties to which this power gave rise, were overcome. The Church in China, like that in all the countries under the care of Portugal, suffered grievous harm from the anomaly of the Patronage of Portugal.

Prince Henry the Navigator had captured Ceuta for Portugal from the Moors on 21st August 1415. This was to be the first move in the astonishing rise to power and influence of that little country. Ceuta, standing as it does opposite Gibraltar, was the key to the Mediterranean from the west. Pope Martin V three years later gave it a bishop, suffragan to that of Braga. In the Bull of institution, '*Romanus Pontifex*', he encouraged bishops and monks in Portugal to help in the expedition the King was about to make to Africa. The Pope was so enthusiastic that he ordered a Crusade to be preached, and in another Bull, '*Sane charissimus*', in the same year gave the King of Portugal all rights over future conquests.

The expedition prospered; and when the Portuguese got beyond the Guinea coast, Pope Nicholas V, besides confirming Bulls of previous Popes, went a step further in 1455 by giving the King

[1] The Roman Congregation whose special concern is the Propagation of the Faith and whose field therefore is the missions.

the sole right to send priests, secular or regular, to those regions. Looking back on that Bull, we may be tempted to think it rash, for who was to say that the successors in the Portuguese royal line would always have the like zeal for the Cross? But it is well to remember that the Western World looked a stable place in those days, more so than it has ever done since the Reformation.

Callixtus III in 1456 handed over all ecclesiastical jurisdiction in Portuguese territories outside Europe to the military Order of monk-soldiers called Knights of Christ. But as the head of it was Henry the Navigator, it was well under royal control. Julius III accepted this situation by granting its Grand Mastership as a hereditary title to the Portuguese crown in 1550. Its Grand Master acted as a kind of bishop over all these vast territories.

The Bull of Leo X confirmed all previous arrangements, especially Callixtus's Bull, and may be called the charter of the Portuguese Patronage. This Bull, '*Dum fidei constantiam*', was published 4th June 1514 and runs as follows, in that apparently inevitable ecclesiastical legal jargon:

> And nevertheless, to thee and to thy successors, kings of Portugal and Algarby, we grant the right of patronage and of presenting suitable persons to whatever churches and ecclesiastical benefices of whatever kind these may be, in these same provinces, lands and places, as aforesaid, which being acquired or regained from the infidels within the last two years, have been set up, and also in those places that, having been acquired or regained, will be set up in the future, whenever the living falls vacant.

According to an earlier Bull, that of Callixtus III, '*Inter caetera*', the provinces, etc., spoken of above refer to islands, towns, ports, lands, places from Bojador-Nam as far as the whole of Guinea and, beyond that southern shore, as far as the Indies already won and to be won, '*acquisitis et acquirendis*'.

All this vast area was at first organized as one diocese under a bishop residing at Funchal in Madeira. The Grand Prior of the Order of Christ became the first bishop. The King obtained the right of patronage over this bishopric—all he had to do was to present him to the Pope for investiture.

At first it was the Order and not the King which was responsible for the finances; but in 1534 this unwieldy diocese was dismembered. Goa was made a bishopric, and the King, while having right of patronage, was also financially responsible. The first bishop to reign was John d'Albuquerque, who reached Goa in 1538. Twenty years later Goa was a metropolitan see with suffragans in Cochin and Malacca. Macao became an episcopal see in 1576.

So far all these places were in Portuguese hands. But in 1588 a bishop was installed in Funay. Now Funay is in Japan and therefore is not and never was part of Portuguese territory. Yet in all these places, including Funay, the King of Portugal claimed and exercised right of patronage, and he was also responsible for financial support—a business of no mean proportions, particularly as the Church grew in those parts.

According to Monsignor Chappoulie, who has studied this particular matter in great detail:

> Apart from the Bishop of Funchal, whose money came from the Knights of Christ, the king had to keep in repair the churches, chapels, monasteries, places of worship, and provide them with all the necessaries: mitres, croziers, ornaments, sacred emblems, chalices, patens, thuribles, dishes, books, lights, organs, clocks. . . . To all ecclesiastics and lay folk also employed in the Church's service the king gave an income. The Bishop of Goa received 500 gold ducats, the Dean of the Chapter 100, Canons 30 only.[1]

In order to keep control, the Portuguese Government made every missionary going East take an oath of fidelity to the King of Portugal; each was carefully 'screened'; all had to sail via Lisbon in Portuguese ships and go via Goa. All this was of course a great waste of time and of money. The strain on Portuguese manpower was tremendous because she was unwilling to allow foreigners to co-operate. It is amazing that the supply lasted as long as it did. The well-known historian of Jesuit missions, Fr. Brucker, has summed up his finding for the Jesuits in Portugal

[1] H. Chappoulie, *Aux origines d'une église: Rome et les missions d'Indochine au XVIIe siècle*, Paris, 1943, Tome I, pp. 48, 49.

itself: in 1584 there were 510 Jesuits; in 1600 there were 631; in 1616, 680. At the same time, overseas, in 1584 there were 492; in 1616, 740; in 1626 there were 860, and almost all of these Portuguese.[1] Obviously this could not go on, and it did not.

By 1600 there were so few missionaries in China and Japan that Clement VIII allowed the Mendicant Orders to go to the Far East—up to then it had been a Jesuit monopoly—but to pacify Portugal he agreed that they should go from Lisbon, and all attempts via Manila in the Philippines would meet with an *ipso facto* excommunication. Eight years later Paul V took a step back; he allowed the Mendicant Friars to go East without starting from Lisbon. In 1633 Urban VIII opened the doors even wider, laying down that all the Orders could go on any route they chose and work anywhere in those parts except those directly under Portuguese control.[2] In other cases that might be satisfactory, but in the case of China there was but one way in, via Macao, firmly in the hands of the Portuguese.

Meanwhile the collapse of Portuguese power continued and accelerated. The Dutch were blockading Goa, sinking, capturing or burning ships that tried to run the blockade. Between the years 1636 and 1639 Goa was completely cut off by the Dutch from sea communication with the motherland, indeed with anyone. No great caravel sailed in those years. By the year 1648 many of the great families were in penury, although the palaces, the churches, the religious houses were filled with rich ornaments and hangings, and the people living and feasting as though the world was still theirs. All the time the Dutch were besieging them from the sea, and ruin was in the air.

Malacca, the Singapore of the age and the only safe way to the Far East, fell to the Dutch in 1641. Fr. Rhodes passed that way six years later, only to find even the great cathedral where St. Francis had preached all profaned and stripped of Catholic symbols.

[1] Brucker, *La Compagnie de Jésus, Esquisse de son institut et de son histoire*, p. 217, 2nd ed.
[2] cf. the Bull '*Ex debite Pastoralis*'.

The Portuguese had now lost the monopoly of the eastern trade. As no profits were being made, the missionaries were among the first to suffer. They took to trading on their own account.

Francis Ingoli, to be for twenty-seven years Secretary of the Roman Congregation of Propaganda, after an exhaustive inquiry, sent a report on the situation to the Holy Father in 1625, wherein he maintained that two obstacles impeded the success of the missions, one the quarrels between secular and regulars and between bishops and their clergy, the other the insatiable greed of the clergy for money.

This is the political background to the problem facing the progress of the Church in China: the *Padroado* of Portugal was a stranglehold on the missions for centuries. It was not the only problem. One closely associated with it was the question of Chinese clergy. Not only was it difficult to train them, it was difficult to persuade some that they were necessary. It was against these and a number of other vested interests that Fr. Alexandre Rhodes and Fr. Pallu and his friends struggled and finally won.

(f) *Fr. Pallu and the Founding of the Missions Étrangères de Paris*

This part of the story must begin with the life and labours of a Jesuit missionary, Fr. Alexandre Rhodes, a Frenchman born at Avignon in 1591. He was sent by his superiors, after the completion of his training in the Jesuit Order, to Cochin-China, then to Tonkin where he arrived in 1627. His success was immediate and startling. By 1631 he had already made 10,000 Christians, but five years later local opposition forced him into exile. These two facts caused him great distress: on the one hand that there were all these Christians and a great field ready, on the other that, if he were expelled, he could not help being a foreigner. There was but one solution: a native clergy. Now to have a native clergy it is necessary to have a resident bishop. But there were no bishops.

Another point struck him. The Orders had their centre not in a parish nor even in the diocese, but perhaps on another continent.

A persecution might start, the superior would withdraw his subjects. Neither he nor they had, after all, any intimate and necessary
relation with the place, nothing compared with the link that the
secular clergy would naturally have. Rhodes therefore became
convinced of three things, the need of a Chinese clergy, a secular
clergy and local bishops.

The Church in the Far East, besides being tied hand and foot
to Portugal, was peculiar in that it was entirely organized by
religious, and in the main by Jesuits; secondly it had few bishops.
India had one archbishop and three bishops; China one bishop;
the Church of Indo-China had one bishop in Malacca. Bishops
are essential for the establishment of a live Church, for a bishop
is fixed to a place; his first loyalty is to his diocese and he needs
clergy subject to him and local in origin.

Fr. Alexandre Rhodes was not the first to realize the dire need,
but he seems to have been the first to appreciate it to the point of
getting something done. The Jesuit Provincial for the Far East
at the end of the sixteenth century, Fr. Valignano, had written
to the Holy See asking for bishops. Another, Fr. Soleto, speaking
for Japan, wrote in 1624, 'Religious without bishops are like
nerves without bones.'

Rhodes, his mind made up and with the encouragement of his
superiors, set off for Rome in 1645, on fire with the idea of what
he wanted. He informed the Cardinals of Propaganda that there
were 300,000 Christians in Annam with an annual increase of
15,000. There was need for 300 priests and 500 crowns for the
journey of each missionary. How could anyone expect to provide
them or the money? In any case, would the King of Annam
tolerate so great an influx of foreigners? On the other hand it
was easy to find native priests. But they would need bishops.
Was not the Church in Japan also in jeopardy simply because the
foreign missionaries had been cast out? A similar thing had
happened to Fr. Rhodes himself and his mission in 1643. He had
been expelled. This gave poignancy and urgency to his requests.

It was this story that Rhodes told the Congregation of Propaganda on his arrival in Rome in 1650. His suggestion was that

bishops *in partibus infidelium* should be created. But that would have interfered with the right of Portugal to appoint bishops. The idea of Vicars Apostolic had not yet emerged in the discussion, in spite of the fact that this would prove the legal way round that impasse, because a Vicar Apostolic owes immediate obedience to the Apostolic See and yet could work in an area already subject to another jurisdiction.

The year after Rhodes made his suggestions, the authorities in the Congregation of Propaganda themselves proposed to Innocent X that a Patriarch should be created for Indo-China, with two or three archbishops and twelve bishops. This shows that the mind of Propaganda was quite open to suggestions. Innocent vacillated. He did not want to offend Portugal.

The Congregation of Propaganda had always been, even since its foundation in 1622, eager to rectify the anomalies in the Far East. In 1630 it had issued its famous decree, 'It is urgent to discover who are the most intelligent among the Christians or pagans recently converted, and having carefully instructed them, after having examined their behaviour over a period of several years, and having practised them in the Christian life, it will be well to raise them to Holy Orders, up to and including the Priesthood.' As we have already noted, three years later Propaganda proposed to the Holy See that archbishops should be made for Japan, China, Tonkin and Siam, if necessary without titles or salaries, to be nominated by the Holy See. They might be either secular or regular, and should be sent direct from Rome. This too would have gone contrary to all agreements with Portugal.

Why no one mentioned in this connection Vicars Apostolic at that time is difficult to understand, as already in 1637, thirteen years previously, the Holy See had appointed two Vicars Apostolic in the Far East, Antonio de Santo Felice, a Franciscan, and Matthew de Castro, a converted Brahmin.

Innocent X was so taken with Fr. Rhodes that he wanted to consecrate him bishop there and then; the latter, however, like the good Jesuit he was, refused. Whereupon the Pope told him to go off and find some clergy who were *episcopabiles*. Rhodes therefore set off for Paris in search of likely candidates for the episcopate. He was happy. He wrote that his superiors had asked him to procure three things: bishops, Chinese clergy and money. 'Mes supérieurs me donnèrent ces trois commissions dont je me suis chargé très volontiers.'[1]

In 1652, when Rhodes reached Paris it was a young Louis XIV who was reigning; it seemed the springtime of France's greatness. A spiritual renaissance was in progress. There was in Paris a fervent association called *La Compagnie du saint Sacrement* and within that body an inner circle called *les bons amis*. Fr. Rhodes soon found himself talking over his projects with them. This was natural as their chaplain was a zealous Jesuit, Fr. Bagot. These good people lived together in a house, in the rue Copeaux in Paris, under a rule. They were both priests and lay folk.

The upshot of his talk was a great enthusiasm, and five bishops wrote to Innocent X in 1653 pleading for bishops for the Far East. Three names were proposed, Montigny-Laval, Picques and Pallu. Rome made no move.

The schemes seemed to have come to nothing. Rhodes was sent off upon a forlorn mission to Persia. He enters no more into the story. However, *les bons amis*, not to be disheartened, set off on a pilgrimage to Rome, with the intention of asking permission to go to China, Tonkin or Tartary. Pallu was of the party and he persuaded Pierre Lambert de la Motte to join them.

In 1658 Propaganda proposed that Pallu should be made Vicar Apostolic with jurisdiction over Tonkin and administration of Yunnan, Kweichow, Hukwang, Kwangsi and Szechwan, in other words over Central and South-western China. De la Motte was appointed Vicar Apostolic for Cochin-China with the administration of the provinces of Chekiang, Fukien, Kwangtung, Kiangsi and the Island of Hainan. The same year Propaganda authorized the foundation of a seminary for Chinese clergy. A third Vicar Apostolic was appointed some months later, Cotolendi,

---

[1] *Archives of Propaganda*, Vol. 193, fol. 371 (the volume concerning India, China, Japan, 1654).

for Nanking, and for the administration of the provinces of Peking, Shansi, Shensi, Shantung and Tartary. He died before he reached his destination. These three administrative units were of the greatest importance. They wrested from Portugal great areas which that country was now quite incapable of manning. The bishopric of Macao was left intact but shorn of its exclusive powers. In fact after its bishop withdrew to Rome in 1623 no other was appointed until 1702. The difficulty now was to reach these areas without passing through 'enemy' or Portuguese territory.

The first scheme of Pallu and his party for avoiding the Portuguese was to build their own ships. They decided with the financial aid of the Compagnie du saint Sacrement to equip two ships. A subscription was started to collect the necessary 120,000 livres. Everyone subscribed, even the great Mazarin. A *vieux loup de mer* was engaged as captain; Louis XIV himself took a hand in the arrangements by writing to his ambassador in Holland, where the ships were being fitted out. Finally the *St. Louis* was built at Amsterdam, a frigate of 300 tons with twenty pieces of cannon and the King's flag flying. This was in 1660. But fate decreed that a great storm should blow; the boat struck a mud bank; then another storm swept down upon them all, in which a hundred ships sank. The *St. Louis* with all it stood for was abandoned.

As usual a staunch friend, this time the Duchesse d'Aiguillon, came to the financial rescue, and the arrangements for the journey went forward, now by a land route. De la Motte set off the year of disaster, travelling via Syria, Mesopotamia, Persia, Gomeron and Surat a hundred and fifty miles north of Bombay, and then he reached Juthia in Siam, his goal, in August of 1662. He wrote to his friend the Duchess:

> There is not a single missionary, I mean not a single one worthy of the name. All think of nothing but their own interests. . . . Is it not strange that the Jesuits of these parts (i.e. the Portuguese Jesuits) have shops in their houses at Macao full of all kinds of merchandise, and they have sea-going vessels of their own.

The journeys of de la Motte were lengthy but nothing compared to the tireless wanderings of Pallu before he reached his journey's end. Pallu left Marseilles in January 1662. He had received the following enlightened instructions from Propaganda before starting. The first necessity was secrecy. 'Avoid Portugal or the countries which depend upon her . . . do not disclose your dignities nor your plans, nor the purpose of your journey, nor your nationality, nor your name.' Then it goes on with reference to his missionary activities, 'With regard to the local customs, so long as they are not very evidently contrary to religion and good morals, respect them.' It went on, they were 'to go to the East to give the Faith and not European customs'.

Pallu also took the land route. His party included seven ecclesiastics and two laymen. They went via Malta, Crete, Alexandretta, Aleppo. There they bought Turkish clothes and passed through Armenia to Ispahan and down to Ormuz at the mouth of the Persian Gulf, so to Surat in India, across it overland, by sea to Siam and so to Juthia its capital (spelt variously Ayudhia, Ayouthia, Ayuthia), fifty miles north of Bangkok. He arrived in January 1664 exactly two years after starting.

Meanwhile the house in the Rue du Bac was bought, and Bossuet was specially invited to preach at the opening. Pallu found that de la Motte had returned to Juthia, having been roughly handled by the ecclesiastical authorities in Macao. He had been refused entry into Canton because he had not come provided with a Portuguese permit, and in spite of his authorization from the Holy See. None the less these two improved the none too shining hour by founding what came to be a famous seminary, le Collège Général.

The opposition at Macao is not to be wondered at when we remember that Clement XIII, on creating the see, decreed as follows:

To that church thus established, which will have for its see the town or place called Macao hereby made a city, we give in perpetuity the whole province of China, as also the islands of Japan and of Macao together with the other islands adjacent, the strong places, villages, distant localities and districts, as it shall be specified and ordained by King Sebastian himself, either by himself or those he shall appoint in the matter.[1]

The only reason—and a good one—the Papacy could put forward for qualifying the words 'in perpetuity' was that the Portuguese were no longer fulfilling their part of the bargain.

As a result of the treatment given to de la Motte in Macao, Pallu resolved to retrace his steps to Rome in order to procure more explicit authority. He travelled in a French ship via the Cape of Good Hope. The two Clements, IX and X, were mostly friendly. The latter signed a brief freeing the Vicars Apostolic from the jurisdiction of the Archbishop of Goa and from that of its Inquisition. (Lambert de la Motte had been excommunicated by the latter.) Pallu was back in Juthia in 1673. But still the opposition held firm, and on this occasion it was clearly the Jesuits on the spot who objected to his position. Once again the indefatigable globe-trotter hastened to Rome. On this his third journey he went via the Pacific, thus making the circuit of the earth.

For four years Pallu remained in Rome, winning his points one by one against the Society by sweet reasonableness. He objected to missionaries being traders. Thus for example he objected to the two trading ships of the Society, the *St. Francis Xavier* and the *Vera Cruz*.[2] He required the Jesuits in the mission field to submit to the orders of the Vicars Apostolic. He carried his points.

Having won in Rome Pallu set off on his last journey in 1681. It ended with his death in the province of Fukien five years later. Being refused entry into China by the Tartars who had just conquered China, he went on to Hanoi and so into Fukien. The Dominicans were already at work in that province. But Pallu did not live to meet them, for he died of his excessive labours in 1684, having given the right of succession to Mgr. Charles Maigrot, the prelate who was later to take so strong a part in the Rites controversy. Three days after Pallu's death there arrived at the house where he had died Gregory Lopez, the first Chinese priest and later the first Chinese bishop.

[1] A. Launay, *Histoire des Missions de la Chine, Mission du Kouang-si*, p. 1.
[2] Archives, *Missions Étrangères*, Vol. 650, pp. 313, 345, 377, Paris.

The next stage in the slow weaning of China from Portuguese influence was made after Pallu's death but may be attributed to his previous efforts. In 1690 Alexander VIII dismembered the diocese of Macao to create two bishoprics within China proper, one at Peking, the other at Nanking. The situation remained thus till the nineteenth century.

The only Chinese bishop to be consecrated until the nineteenth century was this same Lopez. When he just missed meeting Pallu, as recorded above, he was returning from Manila, where he had been refused consecration as, so he was told, Papal Bulls had no currency in Spanish dominions. Maigrot[1] wrote of him at this time that he was a man of about seventy years, vigorous and strong, speaking Castilian fluently but not Italian, mediocre in theology, while versed *plus quam satis* in Chinese literature. It pained Maigrot that there were not more of his kind.

(g) *The Chinese Liturgy*

Intimately connected with the idea of a Chinese clergy and the whole endeavour of Pallu and his friends was the question of a Chinese liturgy. It has remained a debated point almost to the present day. So long as the clergy were European, Latin was not an insuperable difficulty. But if the clergy was to be Chinese— and this seemed the only real solution—Latin appeared to some a grave obstacle. The problem was hotly debated at the time among the missionaries, as it still is among us. Their experiments may be of interest to us today.

Pope Paul V on 26th March 1615 granted a number of 'permissions', for example the right to say Mass with the head covered if this conformed to local etiquette. He allowed the translation of the Bible into Mandarin, and most remarkable of all, allowed Chinese clergy to use Chinese as their liturgical language. He wished, however, that local ordinaries should have the final word in this matter.

[1] Archives, *Missions Étrangères*, Vol. 403, letter no. 193. cf. also no. 192, pp. 177–95.

The Jesuits immediately started translating the liturgical books. The work was entrusted to and accomplished by Fr. Buglio. Meanwhile, independently, Alexandre Rhodes, while in Rome, also asked that a Chinese liturgy be allowed. A commission, set up there in 1658, favoured the idea, but the cardinals concerned thought that conditions were not yet ripe for the experiment. In 1660 Fr. Fabri, S.J., also put in a plea, but on this occasion the consulters of the Propaganda dispersed without coming to a decision. All this when forty years earlier the Holy Father, Pope Paul V, had given his fiat! Meanwhile in 1660 Cardinal Barberini wrote to the Vicars Apostolic to be cautious in these matters and to institute a local inquiry and then report back to Rome.

The missionaries on the spot were divided in opinion. Those in Macao believed in training Chinese youths at the local *petit séminaire* at Macao, and having them drilled in Latin. The Peking missionaries on the other hand believed in ordaining older converts and in using Chinese both as the educational and the liturgical language for them. By the time that the whole matter was debated along with so much else by the imprisoned missionaries at Canton in 1666, Fr. Buglio had already completed his translation of the Missal, the Breviary, the ritual and a moral theology, and indeed, *mirabile dictu*, the *Summa theologica* of St. Thomas Aquinas.

The indecisive conclusions of the Canton meetings were taken by Fr. Intorcetta to Rome. Paul V's brief was once again examined by Propaganda, but no decision was arrived at, except this, that all should await the entry of the Vicars Apostolic into China—for Pallu was on his way—and should hear their views before taking one side or the other. Meanwhile another twist was given to the knot, as the General of the Jesuits gave permission for Chinese to enter the novitiate of the Order (1672). This made the question an urgent one for the Society; and when Fr. Couplet, S.J., made further efforts in 1684 in Rome, saying how Latin was a waste of time, he was met by the usual delaying tactics and by the remark: Why did no one at the time take advantage of the brief of Paul V? Today, looking back, we can see what an immense difference this would have made to the Church in China.

Innocent XI was in favour. But as the question had been raised over and over again, it remained in suspense. The question became not merely one of theory but of practice when Gregory Lo, or Lopez, ordained the three Chinese converts already referred to. Liu, called Verbiest, was already fifty-six and had retired from his post of second President of the Tribunal of Mathematics. Paul Wan, called Bañez, was fifty-four, and Simon Xavier Wu, called a Cunha, a widower aged fifty-seven with two daughters, were hardly in the first flower of their youth. To learn Latin at that age would be a great strain. What then were they to do? Should they use Fr. Buglio's Chinese translations? Should they read the Latin without understanding it? Lopez himself used the permission of Paul V, the other three said Mass in Latin.

'I have assisted at Mass said by one of these,' wrote Fr. Philippuci, 'He sweated, was in an agony of mind, and those present were equally put out and irritated. God knows how many faults and mistakes he made, all hot and bothered as he was, reciting parrot-like what he could not understand.' (9th October 1688.) They always said a Requiem Mass, even when it was Easter Day. During Paschal time the Alleluia would be liberally sprinkled throughout.[1]

This problem of the language to be used by Chinese priests is closely connected with that of seminaries for Chinese clergy, their locality, their methods. Non-Latin-speaking Chinese were still being ordained in the eighteenth century, Mgr. Pottier was still ordaining them at its end; but he was an exception, and his successor Mgr. Dufresse abandoned the practice. Normally, Chinese wishing to be priests had to be put in an atmosphere where Latin could be learned, and it seems it was difficult to do that in China. The Jesuits, particularly the great head of the Peking mission, Fr. Verbiest, were unwilling to mix European and Chinese novices. Their outlooks were so different. As Fr. Verbiest remarked, *Novitius . . . est animal facile scandalizabile.*

[1] cf. article by Fr. Brou in *Revue d'histoire des Missions*, 1926, p. 519.

Nevertheless we find Chinese Jesuit scholastics spending two years at the French house of La Flèche as late as the mid-eighteenth century.

(h) *The Séminaire Général*

Of all the efforts to solve the problem of Chinese clergy, the most justly famous is the Collège or Séminaire Général of the Missions Étrangères. It was so essential to the survival of the Church in China during the dark days of persecution that some notice of it is necessary.

The Vicars Apostolic, whom we have already met in their peregrinations, sent out by the Holy See at the instigation of Fr. Rhodes, established, as the very first duty of their office, a Collège Général at Juthia in Siam, with the specific purpose of forming a native priesthood, not only for China but for the whole of the Far East. We must not imagine it as a makeshift affair, a few mud huts and a handful of unqualified professors. The historian of the institute, once a professor in it (and now archivist at Rue du Bac) remarked to the present writer when the latter was working in their archives, 'while the seminary in Paris remained for two centuries a rudimentary organization, this *collège général* was a true school of philosophy and theology'. The professors were almost all Doctors of the Sorbonne.

The embassy of Louis XIV, visiting Siam in 1685, was astounded at the standard reached in the seminary; it is not surprising therefore that the party should carry off to France with it one of the students. He defended a thesis before the Sorbonne to the delight and satisfaction of all. This youth, Pinto, went from Paris to Rome. Innocent XI was so enchanted with his intelligence and goodness that he was in favour of ordaining him priest, even before the canonical age. He would indeed have had him consecrated bishop, but the young man died in 1696.

Youths from all over the Far East were sent to Juthia to be trained: from Siam, of course, and from Cochin. There were Tonkinese, Chinese, and later, Koreans, Japanese, Burmese and Indians. The seminary was more than once destroyed only to be rebuilt or to rise elsewhere. In this college the common language was and is the Latin tongue. Thus we can account for the nine hundred pages of Latin diary of the Chinese priest Fr. Ly which we shall have occasion to mention later. To date it has trained more than one thousand priests and yet more catechists. It has the glory of having a hundred martyrs among its alumni, twenty-five of whom have been beatified.

This is perhaps the place to mention yet another attempt to grapple with the problem of training Chinese for the priesthood which was made by Fr. Matthew Ripa, though it took place in the next century, the eighteenth. He had been sent to China by Propaganda with the little deputation to carry the cardinal's hat to Tournon, one of the Papal Legates sent out during the Chinese Rites controversy. As Ripa was an artist he succeeded, in spite of the unpropitious times, in establishing himself as imperial artist in Peking. There he remained until 1724. He was saddened by the scarcity of missionaries, and the lack of local vocations. His first effort was to found a seminary in China itself. In 1719 he set one up at Jehol beyond the Great Wall and about 125 miles north-east of Peking. But owing to a number of difficulties it had to be abandoned. In 1724 therefore he made his way back to Europe taking with him four of his students. After further delay Rome finally in 1732 allowed him to start his College and Congregation of the Holy Family at Naples, whose express purpose was the training of Chinese clergy.[1]

(i) *The French Jesuit Mission*

While the activity of the Church in China was all one, it is impossible to pass over in silence the remarkable French contribution to that great enterprise in the seventeenth and eighteenth centuries. Most of the work was conducted during and after the

---

[1] It lasted until 1888 when it was suppressed by the Italian Government. But it had done its work. It must be admitted, however, that the idea had certain objections to it, such as the excessive distance from the field of operations. It had trained one hundred and six Chinese priests in the hundred and fifty years of its existence.

Rites controversy, a tragic incident which almost destroyed the endeavour and which we shall treat separately in the next section.

The holy missionary, Fr. Ferdinand Verbiest, had early realized that the Portuguese source was inadequate to meet the needs of the country and had written letters, since famous, to the Fathers in Europe. One of these letters came to the knowledge of King Louis XIV, doubtless through Fr. de la Chaise, his confessor; and its zeal so influenced the King that he decided to act upon it.

It happened that France, at that time under the financial régime of Colbert, was for commercial reasons interested in a thorough revision of the geographical knowledge of the day. Considering the immense enlargement of view, the sudden expansion of trade, Colbert was right. The English long before had appreciated the importance of accurate information about the eastern seaboards:

> It is to the English that one must turn if one wishes to have a more precise knowledge of these waters; for three years ago they made a general map of them. They have everywhere visited all the islands; they know which are inhabited, those where water is to be found. It took them six months and is a work worthy of the thoroughness and curiosity of those gentlemen[1] [so wrote Fr. de Fontenoy, the first superior of the French mission].

Colbert sponsored the scheme. But his death in 1680 put a stop to the plans for a time. 'Two years later, the King having decided to send an embassy to Siam, M. de Pouvois, successor to Colbert . . . asked of our superior that six Jesuits, good at Mathematics should be sent there.'[2]

They reached Peking via the port of Ningpo on the 7th February 1688, and not via Macao, because the Portuguese were hostile, and in an English ship, because English ships were safer and more hygienic. Of the original party of six sent out from France, only five arrived in China. They were Fr. Jean de Fontenoy, the superior, the Fathers Gerbillon, le Compte, de Visdelou and

---

[1] Letter of Fr. de Fontenoy, S.J., to Fr. de la Chaise 15th February 1703, from *Lettres édifiantes et curieuses écrites des missions étrangères, nouvelle édition*, Paris, 1781, Tome XVII, p. 231.

[2] *Ibid.*, Letter of Fr. de Fontenoy, S.J., p. 209.

Bouvet. Fr. Tachard, the sixth, got as far as Siam but was sent back to collect more members of the Order to help to evangelize that country.

The moment of their arrival was one of great sorrow for the Christians: the noble Fr. Verbiest had just died. Fr. de Fontenoy describes his funeral. The description is so revealing of the situation of Christians at that time in China that it is given here at some length.

The obsequies of Fr. Verbiest took place, 11th March 1688. We assisted and this was the arrangement of the ceremony. The Mandarins, whom the Emperor sent to honour the illustrious departed, having arrived about 7 a.m., we went to the room where the Father's body was enclosed in its coffin. Chinese coffins are big, made of wood 3-4 inches thick, varnished and gilded outside, but closed with exceptional care to prevent the air getting in. The coffin was carried into the street and put on a stretcher under a kind of richly covered dome, and held up by four columns. The columns were decked in white satin hangings (i.e. the Chinese colour for mourning), and from one column to the other hung several festoons of silk in various other colours. The stretcher was tied on to two poles a foot in diameter, and of proportionate length, which sixty to eighty men, lined up on both sides, were to carry on their shoulders. The Father Superior with all the Jesuits of Peking went on their knees before the coffin in the middle of the street. We made three profound bows to the ground, whilst the Christians who were present at that sad ceremony burst into tears, and cried out enough to melt the hardest hearts. The procession then set off in the following order.

In front there was a picture twenty-five feet high and four across, adorned with silk streamers made of red taffeta on which was embroidered the name and dignity of Fr. Verbiest, written in great Chinese letters of gold. This, which several men held in the air, was preceded by a troop of instrumentalists and followed by another carrying flags, festoons, banderoles and streamers. Then came the cross in a fine niche adorned with columns and various banners made of silk. Several Christians followed, some with flags like the first, others with candles in their hands. Then came the picture of our Blessed Lady and the Infant Jesus in a niche, holding the globe of the world in his hand. The Christians who came next also had flags or candles like the previous ones.

A picture of the Guardian Angel came next, accompanied in the same manner, and followed by a portrait of Fr. Verbiest, which was carried with all the symbols of the offices with which the Emperor had honoured him. We came immediately behind in our mourning clothes, which are white in the Chinese manner, as I have said; and from time to time we showed our sadness by repeated sobs, according to the custom of the country. The bc   ﬞf Fr. Verbiest followed, accompanied by the Mandarins whom the Emperor had named to honour the memory of that celebrated missionary. They were all on horseback; the first was the Emperor's father-in-law, the second his first captain of the guard, the third one of his gentlemen, and others less distinguished. This whole procession, which was done in fine order and great modesty, was closed by fifty horsemen: the streets were lined on both sides by an immense crowd, who preserved a profound silence as they watched us pass.

Our cemetery is outside the town in a garden which one of the last Chinese Emperors gave to the first missionaries of our Society. This garden is enclosed by a high wall; and a chapel and some small apartments have been built there.

When we arrived at the door we went on our knees in the middle of the road before the body and we then again bowed three times. The tears of the assistants began again. The body was carried to near where it was to be buried; an altar had been prepared there, on which stood a cross and candles. Fr. Superior then put on a surplice, recited the prayers and did the usual incensings according to the Ritual. We prostrated ourselves again three times before the coffin, which was taken off the stretcher to be put into the ground. Then it was that the cries of those present redoubled, and it was impossible to restrain one's tears.

The grave is a kind of vault six feet deep by five, by seven. It was paved and walled entirely in brick. The coffin was placed in the middle on two little brick trestles, about one foot high. Then the walls of the vault were continued to about six or seven feet above the ground, ending in a dome and a cross on the top.

Then some distance from the tomb a slab of white marble was set up . . . on which were written in Chinese and Latin, the name, age and nationality of the dead man, the date of his death and the length of time he had lived in China.[1]

It is these *Lettres édifiantes et curieuses* that reveal more than do any other documents the trials and activities of the Jesuits, the manners, the virtues and the vices of the Chinese, as also those first serious attempts at understanding between two civilizations. Fr. de Chavagnac thus describes the character necessary in a true missionary:

First, we need persons determined for the love of Jesus Christ to accept inconveniences of every kind, and determined to make themselves into new men, not only by a change of climate, of clothing and of food, but, more than all, in manners which are entirely opposed to the customs and character of the French nation. . . . Men who allow themselves to be dominated by their moods are no use here; too quick a temper would do untold harm. The spirit of this country demands that one be master of one's passions, and especially of a certain turbulent activity which wants to do everything and carry all before it by assault. The Chinese are not able in one month to attend to what a Frenchman could tell them in one hour. Without getting angry or impatient one has to bear with this slowness and this indolence of character; one must discourse of religion, and yet not be discouraged, to a nation that fears only the Emperor, and loves only money and is insensible and therefore excessively indifferent to all that concerns eternity.[2]

A none too flattering portrait of the Chinese, but that description shows how serious was the Jesuit approach to the Far East.

The difficulty of the language and of its characters requires further a love of study, although this study has nothing pleasant or attractive about it except the hope of making use of it some day for the glory of God. As there is always something to learn in this matter, there is always reason for study, and one has to accustom oneself to pass repeatedly from activity to study and from study to the daily round of duties. As everybody knows, the Chinese pride themselves

[1] Letter from Fr. de Fontenoy, S.J., to Fr. de la Chaise, 15th February 1703, *Lettres édifiantes*, Tome XVII, p. 248 ff.
[2] Letter from Fr. de Chavagnac, S.J., 1701, *ibid.*, p. 83.

on being the most polished and cultured people in the world, but it is impossible to imagine what it costs us to make ourselves civil and polite according to their tastes. The etiquette of this country is the most aggravating and most irritating imaginable for a Frenchman; it is a labour to learn it and another to carry it out. The sciences of Europe, in proportion to one's excelling in them, particularly dispose the great to overlook their sovereign contempt for what comes from abroad.[1]

The Jesuits were not blind to the shortcomings of Chinese social life. They faced the problem of abandoned children. It is clearly stated by Fr. François Noël:

As for children, many more are baptized, especially those exposed every morning in the streets. The government sends round carts every morning through the streets to gather up those who still breathe and take them to a hospital where doctors and matrons look after them, and where those who survive are educated.

As the population is 'infini' in Peking, and as those who think themselves overburdened with children have no scruple in abandoning them in the streets and public places, where some die miserably and others are eaten by beasts, one of our chief cares is to send catechists every morning to the different districts of the great city to baptize all the infants still alive that they find on their rounds. Of the twenty to thirty thousand exposed every year our catechists baptize about three thousand. If we had thirty catechists . . . few would escape our zeal. In 1694, 3400 infants were baptized, in 1695, 2639; in 1696, 3663, and the same for the following years.[2]

The greatest of the Manchu dynasty, the K'ang-hsi Emperor, was so taken with these charming and learned French Jesuits, particularly Fathers Gerbillon and Bouvet that

the Emperor, seeing his whole empire in perfect peace, decided, either in order to provide amusement for himself, or for something to do, to learn the sciences of Europe. He himself chose Mathematics, the Elements of Euclid, Practical Geometry and Philosophy.

[1] *ibid.*, p. 84.
[2] Memorandum of Fr. François Noël to the General, S.J., 1703, *ibid.*, p. 166 note.

Fr. Antony Thomas, Fr. Gerbillon, and Fr. Bouvet were commanded to write treatises on these subjects. This they did in Tartar. Those who had been their masters in that language revised the work with them. . . . The Fathers put forward these demonstrations and explained them to the Emperor, who understood easily everything taught him, admired more and more the sound basis of our sciences and applied himself with renewed fervour.

So began the education of the Chinese civilization in the physical sciences of the Western World. The writer continues:

They went every day to the palace, spent two hours in the morning and two in the evening with the Emperor. Usually he made them go up to his dais, and made them sit by his side to explain the figures more easily.

His pleasure at the first lessons was so great that even when he went to his palace of Changchung, which is two leagues from Peking, he did not interrupt his work. The Fathers were obliged to go there every day whatever the weather was like. They left Peking at 4 a.m. and only returned as the night set in. Scarcely had they got home when they had to set to work again, and pass a good part of the night composing and preparing the lessons for the morrow. The extreme fatigue of those continual journeyings and vigils sometimes overcame them, but the desire to please the Emperor, and the hope of making him friendly to our holy religion gave them strength. . . . When they had gone the Emperor did not remain idle, he repeated in his private room what had just been explained.[1]

Meanwhile the Portuguese at Macao, afraid of the French influence at the court of Peking, 'seized a young French painter who was bringing our pensions. . . . They put him into prison, and then sent him back to Goa where he died',[2] thus proving that nationalism in Western countries might yet crush this tender plant of Chinese Christianity.

Fr. Gerbillon was the second superior of the French Jesuit mission. It was in his time that the wonderful church was built. The permission to build had been granted by the Emperor in the

[1] *Lettres édifiantes*, Tome XVII, letter of Fr. de Fontenoy, pp. 283 ff.
[2] *ibid.*, p. 299.

days of Fr. Fontenoy. K'ang-hsi had been ill, and nothing which the Chinese doctors could produce would cure him. The Fathers suggested *quinquina* (quinine), and in a few days the fever left him. In 1693 the Emperor gave the French Fathers a house in the enclosure of his palace, a signal favour, and the following year he presented them with a large plot of ground for the building of their church, which was to amaze and intrigue the citizens of the capital and all those innumerable visitors who came there on business. The description of it all is given in a letter dated 20th August 1704 by Fr. Jartoux to Fr. Fontenoy, who had returned to Europe.

In January 1690, the Emperor gave Fr. Gerbillon permission to build a church in the palace enclosure.[1]

He provided the money and part of the material. . . . Four whole years were taken in building and embellishing it. . . . First one enters into a large courtyard thirty feet by fifty feet long. There are two big halls in the Chinese manner; one is used for the sodalities and for instructing the catechumens, the other is used to receive our visitors. In the latter are exposed to view the portraits of the King, Monseigneur, the Princes of France, the King of Spain now reigning, the King of England and portraits of several other Princes, together with mathematical and musical instruments. Besides, all those fine engravings are exhibited, collected into those great books published to let the world know the magnificence of the court of France. The Chinese examine all that with profound curiosity.

The Church is seventy-five feet long, thirty wide and thirty high. The ceiling is entirely painted: it is in three parts; the middle represents a dome (*tout ouvert*) of an ornate design; there are marble columns that carry a row of arcades surmounted by a fine balustrade. The columns themselves are encased in another balustrade of beautiful design with vases of flowers tastefully spaced out: above, the Eternal Father may be seen seated in the clouds surrounded by a group of angels and holding the world in his hand.

We failed to persuade the Chinese that this was painted on a flat surface; they could not believe that these columns were not straight as they appeared to be. . . .

[1] *ibid.*, Tome XVIII, pp. 6 ff.

The reredos is painted just as the ceiling is. . . . It is a pleasure to see the Chinese going forward to examine that part of the Church, which they suppose is behind the altar. When they get up to it, they stop, draw back a little, move forward, put out their hands, to see whether there is really neither elevation nor depth.

Not content with acting the Western schoolmaster or tutor to the Emperor of the East, and so to the whole Far East, Fr. Gerbillon was also instrumental in bringing peace between the Russians and the Chinese. He was to accompany the Emperor eight times on his 'hunting parties' or more accurately, military demonstrations, in Tartary, but on this occasion he skilfully managed a treaty between the plenipotentiaries of both sides; the document was written in Chinese, Tartar, and Latin. Both parties to the treaty signed the Latin version.

Now that we are considering the French mission it is well to move forward a little beyond our chronological scheme. The most typical and most perfect among the company of missionaries in the twilight of the Jesuit period in China, after the fracas over the Rites, was Fr. Dominique Parrenin, a Frenchman born in 1665 at Grand-Russey in the diocese of Besançon. He reached China in 1698 and carried forward the work of Fr. Gerbillon. No missionary was ever so fluent in Chinese and Manchu as he. In European languages he was also proficient. For twenty years he accompanied the Emperor on his annual expeditions to Tartary, and it was he who organized the vast undertaking of mapping the whole of China; he was also first Superior of the College for Diplomats, where young Manchus and Tartars learnt Latin and the ways of diplomacy. By his patience and integrity he saved the Catholic mission in China from complete extinction.

The great names of Fr. Jean Baptiste Régis, cartographer to the Emperor, the historian de Mailla, the artist, Br. Castiglione, and countless others, bear witness to the glory of these years of persecution, when the Emperor had been soured, to the indefatigable labours and selfless perseverance of these wonder-inspiring missionaries.

iii. The Rites Controversy

We have introduced all the actors in the tragedy which is now to be unfolded. The stage is China, though occasional scenes occur in Rome, in Paris, in Macao and in Manila. The chief participants are the Jesuit Fathers, on the one hand, and on the other the Dominicans and Franciscan Friars. In the background the Pope and the Emperor in Peking, and in Europe, far away, men of Spain, France, Portugal, the Jansenists. Various Papal envoys blunder on to the stage. The tragedy itself is the loss of China for the Church; and, in merely political and cultural terms, the failure of the marriage of two minds. It is a tragedy and not a vile crime, because there seems to hang over the whole action a fatality rather than wilful obstruction. All, or almost all, except perhaps the Jansenists of France and their accomplices, acted from good motives. A certain amount of repetition of the story already told is inevitable, but this episode has to be related as a separate whole.

The story begins before any missionary had even entered the Middle Kingdom. In Japan the question had already presented itself, how far to co-operate with, or tolerate, the semi-religious customs of the people. The answer had been an intransigent and complete refusal to countenance anything of the sort.

Ricci, as we have already fully shown, took the opposite view[1] and after a very careful study of the Confucian Classics, had come to the conclusion that the reverence paid to Confucius was no more than a recognition of him as a great man, that the offerings made to him and to ancestors could be benignly interpreted in the same sense, and finally that the names for God which could be used by the Church were those in use among the Chinese themselves, among them T'ien, which signified Heaven or Lord of Heaven. In every way Ricci was eager to avoid offending the

[1] His contributions were 'Ordinances' or instructions to missionaires on how to act on arrival in China, a document known as 'Replies to missionaries of Nanking' (1600), and also 'Instructions for Missionaries' drawn up by him at Peking in collaboration with the Visitor, Fr. Diaz; these were taken by the latter to Fr. Valignano, but they have all mysteriously disappeared.

susceptibilities of the Chinese, in so far as it was allowable to do so.

But to be fair to Ricci and his companions who in those early days shared his views, it must be realized that

> Fr. Ricci and . . . his superiors at Macao . . . did not deny at all that certain Chinese rites had at least the appearance of superstition and that others were really superstitious; but they thought that after carefully eliminating all the Buddhist and Taoist accretions (elements which were certainly superstitious) they would find it possible by stages to laicise completely the rites which were purely Confucian.[1]

The force of the argument of those who objected to the later view lay in this, that whatever the Chinese Rites might mean, or had meant in theory, *in practice* they were idolatrous, especially among the common people, and therefore should be forbidden among Christians.

It is a remarkable fact that even in those early days not all the Jesuit missionaries on the spot were of the same opinion, and most remarkable of all, the very man whom Ricci himself selected to succeed him in his office as head of the Peking mission, Fr. Longobardi, was one of these. As early as 1625 the latter had protested against what he considered laxity in admitting pagan elements into the Christian life.

Longobardi was born in Sicily in 1556: his education as a child was sketchy and at the age of twenty-six he entered the Jesuit novitiate at Messina. He began his Latin studies in 1584 and was ordained priest in 1586. He then taught in Palermo for six years and began his theological studies *leviter* in 1590–2, and mostly unaided. In 1596 he left Lisbon for Goa where he immediately did missionary work. *L'appel irrésistible de la brousse* was strong in him. Japan not China was his assignment, but at the last moment on reaching Macao he was allowed to change to the Chinese mission.

At first he fitted in with the general plan, though a letter dated 1598 shows a restless divergence.

---

[1] Henri Bernard, *Le Père Matthieu Ricci*, Vol. II, p. 143.

A good number of books and pious objects should be sent . . .
because those are the things that give us standing with the Chinese
in accordance with our purpose: a purpose which is not to be
obtained by merely putting on show triangular pieces of glass and
such-like objects. . . .[1]

So far he had no objection to being dressed as a *literatus*. But
his mind underwent a radical change at a meeting which the
missionaries had in 1628 in K'ai-p'ing; he expressed his views,
and he himself forbade the practices.

One of the problems was that would-be *literati*, who had been
converted, were still expected by custom to pay homage to a
tablet of Confucius and pay honour to the ancestors. The Jesuits
set about reading the classical books and then consulted their
three most learned converts Paul Hsü, Leo Li and Michael
Yang, all of whom agreed that to perform the reverence to
Confucius was a 'civil act' merely.

The next move was in 1635 when, a report having been sent
him by the Dominican missionaries of Fukien, the Archbishop
of Manila and the Bishop of Zebut sent objections to Urban VIII
against these very practices. Meanwhile these same Dominicans
had themselves been expelled from the province on account of
their own methods. Their ally was Mgr. Valente, S.J., Bishop
of Japan and administrator of Macao. Both Macao and Japan had
always been rigid on this point. It is only fair to say that, being
better informed, the Archbishop withdrew his objection.

A Dominican, Fr. Morales, therefore went to Rome (1643) as
we have already noted in a previous connection and put the
Dominican case to Propaganda; Pope Innocent X condemned
the Chinese Rites in the form described by Fr. Morales. But that
was not the end, it was unhappily only the beginning of sorrow.
The Jesuits, who not unnaturally felt that their case had not been
heard, sent Fr. Martin Martini to explain what they considered
the true situation. Alexander VII therefore on the 23rd March
1656 approved a Decree of the Holy Office saying that 'from the
report made, the ceremonies were to be tolerated'. However,

[1] *ibid.*, p. 55.

after further remonstrances and counter-remonstrances, on 20th November 1669, Pope Clement IX approved a new decree that both the decisions of his predecessors were to be kept 'according to circumstances'.

By that time the temper of each party had become not a little frayed. A slow-motion argument of such moment across two continents would have been exasperating even to a Job.

Therefore we may say that between 1635 and 1669 things went on indecisively, the Jesuits more or less rigidly keeping to Ricci's plan, the other missionaries, particularly the Franciscans, attempting the method of St. Francis in Europe: the habit, the crucifix, the preaching in the streets. But that was all to be disturbed.

The next phase had already begun in 1665 in the prison at Canton; as a result of rivalry over the reform of the calendar, all missionaries had been ordered out of the country by imperial decree. They were carried off, many of them in cages, to Canton. There, probably for the first time in the history of the Chinese mission, most of the missionaries, to the number of twenty-three, were gathered in one place, and that a prison. Here they could scarcely avoid each other even if they had so desired.

The Fathers took advantage of this unique opportunity to thrash out a common policy in the matter of the Rites. Between them they drew up forty-seven articles which were signed by all the Jesuits, Dominicans and Franciscans, except Fr. Antonio de Santa Maria, a Franciscan and friend of Morales. The 41st article was the decision of Alexander VII, the rest were cases of conscience, and solved in the Jesuit sense.

Then a strange and seemingly unimportant, but in fact momentous, event occurred. The superior of the Dominicans, Fr. Navarrete, fled from Canton, went to Macao and from there to Europe. This happened on the 19th December 1669. In order to avoid trouble with the Chinese authorities a Jesuit from Macao entered secretly into Canton and took his place in his cell; his name was Fr. Grimaldi.

Four years later Navarrete published in Madrid the first of two volumes which attacked the Jesuit tolerance of Chinese

Rites. The second appeared in 1679. 'The question of the Chinese Rites, up to then discussed among competent missionaries, was thus presented to the general public and handed over to impassioned discussions,' wrote Fr. Servière.[1]

Meanwhile, as we have already described, owing to the skilful and patient work of Fr. Verbiest, who had obtained a copy of the futile calendar concocted by Yang Kuang-hsien and showed its utter ineptitude, the Emperor had forced the Board of Rites to reverse its decision against the Christians; and in 1669 the condemnation of Fr. Schall was reversed and he was granted a solemn funeral, although dead since 1666; in the same year the church in Peking was reopened. In 1671 the re-entry of the missionaries into China was granted. In 1692 an imperial edict praised the missionaries and their doctrine, and authorized them to open churches and the Chinese to frequent them. This seems like the prelude to a great victory. But in Europe, as we are in the process of showing, there was being prepared the instrument for the greatest set-back to the missionary efforts ever experienced by the Church.

The publication of Navarrete's book was the signal for a general mêlée.

It is hard for us at this distance to appreciate the subtle influences at work on so abstruse and apparently so remote a subject. But the whole world seemed to be against the Jesuits, except the King of France.

Three men now had more influence on events than all the rest put together. They were Maigrot, Tournon and Mezzabarba, the first a bishop, the second and third Papal envoys.

Charles Maigrot, Vicar Apostolic of Fukien, of the Missions Étrangères, was to start the final act on its way. Though Navarrete's book had created a great stir, more especially as le grand Arnauld, the leading Jansenist, in his venomous hatred of the Jesuits, had used it to belabour them with charges of hypocrisy, etc., yet Rome had no inclination to take action—

[1] J. de la Servière, *Les anciennes missions de la Compagnie de Jésus en Chine (1552–1814)*, p. 45.

rather the reverse. Maigrot had published in 1693 a *mandement* forbidding honours to be paid to Confucius and the ancestors, and forbidding the licence of Alexander VII, on the grounds, he said, that it had been obtained by a false statement of facts. Not content with this, he sent two envoys (Fathers de Quemener and Charmot) to Rome to ask for a reopening of the case. The Holy See therefore reopened the question in 1697.

When the Jesuits knew this they approached the Emperor on the matter. As the question was partly one of the meaning of words, namely the Chinese words for heaven and God, and the meaning of Chinese customs, the Jesuits' aim was to obtain from him an opinion on what the Chinese themselves understood by these words and these actions. They forwarded his answer to Rome. Meanwhile Innocent XII died and Clement XI was elected Pope.

K'ang-hsi's letter arrived in Rome in the autumn of 1701 and it created an excellent impression.[1] A letter from the Augustinian bishop, Alvaro de Benavente (Titular Bishop of Ascalon and Vicar Apostolic of Kiangsi), arrived at about the same time. It too favoured the Jesuit point of view. This was made public in April 1702, and also created favourable comment.

After prolonged examination, by the Sacred Congregation, of all the arguments and counter-arguments adduced by both sides, a decision was finally reached. It was the now famous decree of 1704.

Clement XI and the Congregation of Rites authorized one name and one only for God in Chinese, T'ien-chu, or Lord of Heaven. A typical and unfortunate result of this decree was that an inscription composed by K'ang-hsi himself, for the church of Peking, Ching T'ien, 'honour heaven' would have to be suppressed. Ritual acts in honour of Confucius had also to stop, not even on the occasion of the graduation of the *literati* were they allowed. Veneration of ancestors and even of their tablets

---

[1] Servière remarks that this made some people say in Rome that the Jesuits had submitted a doctrinal point to a pagan prince and that they were duly shocked.

were prohibited by the decree. It was, however, permissible to keep these tablets, provided they had nothing more on them than the monogram of the departed. Offerings on the graves of ancestors were also included in the condemnation.[1]

A Papal Legate had been sent on his way, and the decree was sent post-haste after him. He was Charles Maillard de Tournon, Patriarch of Antioch. So little was the Roman court in touch with the realities of the political implications of the decisions taken in 1704 that Tournon was laden with presents for the Emperor and hopes were high that he would be able to set up an apostolic delegation at Peking. He was fortunate to escape with his life.

He arrived at Canton in April 1705, travelling on a French ship, because the Portuguese authorities would have prevented him reaching his destination at all, had he attempted to sail from Lisbon. The Portuguese were jealous of their authority and resented even Papal interference in China. Tournon was in Peking on 4th December of the same year, but not before the Emperor's spies had discovered his purpose. K'ang-hsi played with him as a cat does a mouse. At first his manner was courteous but in the end enraged, and with little formality (1706) he sent the Legate off to Macao with orders to await a Jesuit, chosen by the Emperor himself, who would escort him to Rome. Tournon accused the Jesuits of this failure. Fr. Appiani, a Lazarist, who had acted as Tournon's interpreter, was imprisoned, bastinadoed and exiled to Canton. The Jesuits had, in fact, behaved with the utmost dis-cretion and charity, even though they saw their whole century-old endeavour being smashed before their eyes.

In the summer of 1706 the blow fell. An imperial decree was issued containing four points of major importance for the Christians. The first was that all missionaries wishing to remain in China must report to the various tribunals in Peking. The second stated that these must swear to keep the rules which Fr. Ricci had laid down concerning the Chinese Rites. The third, that on doing so, they would receive a *p'iao*, or document, which

[1] L. Pastor, *History of the Popes*, Vol. XXXIII, pp. 426-7.

would give them the right to benefit from the edict of 1692. The fourth, that recalcitrants were to be expelled.

Tournon on his arrival at Nanking in January 1707 issued a decree dated 25th January in which he made a selection from the Papal decree that he had brought from Rome, with the ominous addition of excommunication for anyone who refused to comply. On his own authority he forbade the missionaries to accept the imperial *p'iao*.

Tournon had now acted his part and plays but a minor role in the rest of the story, since he was escorted, first to Canton, and then to Macao where he remained, at first virtually and finally openly, a prisoner of the Portuguese secular authority. He died protesting against this lay interference, and asserting the independence of the Holy See. He lived to hear that the cardinal's hat had been conferred on him by Clement XI, but like St. John Fisher, not long enough to receive it.

In view of the fact that his mission was the central act of the tragedy it is right to pause in order to judge whether everything was done which could have been done to save the situation.

We must exonerate the Papacy from precipitancy or lack of caution. The decision of the Holy Office, confirmed by the Pope, Clement XI, on 20th November 1704 was based on the fact that, though the Jesuits might have been right in their understanding of the original meaning of the words and actions in the dispute, for five hundred years the *literati* had used the words for God in a *material* sense of heaven or sky, and the populace certainly were superstitious in regard to the rites. Therefore in order to avoid the slightest danger of misunderstanding or superstition these words and actions were condemned.

The Jesuits throughout had patiently and industriously informed the Holy See of the complexity and delicacy of the problem and had advised moderation. But the Holy See had been turned against their evidence by the combined, though perhaps unconscious, co-operation of Franciscans, Dominicans and Jansenists, the last sworn enemies of the Society of Jesus. The Franciscans and Dominicans had tradition on their side, perhaps some jealousy

of the upstart Order, certainly fear of going too far in toleration
of error. The Jansenists had nothing but hatred for their arch-
enemies who had condemned their teaching.

It was said at the time that 'the eyes of the whole Christian
world are greatly offended by this zeal [of the Jansenists], this
tireless effort, this hope of victory, in an affair which would
bring destruction to that pitiable Christian body'.[1]

But the worst enemy of peace and a wise settlement was
Tournon himself. His behaviour, once he set foot on Chinese
soil, could scarcely have been more calculated to embitter the
quarrel and alienate the Emperor. After having only once asked
the help of the Fathers of the Society, he never again appealed
for their advice. He chose instead as his chief adviser and confidant
Maigrot, who in the presence of the Emperor was proved
incompetent in the Chinese language, and this after Tournon had
assured K'ang-hsi that Maigrot was well acquainted with Chinese
literature. In his behaviour before Christians he showed petulance
by tearing up a petition before their eyes, throwing the pieces
to the ground and stamping on them. Before the special envoys
of the Emperor he would lose his temper and rant even against
the Emperor himself. It was only his bursting into tears that
probably on one occasion saved him and his entourage from
death. Tournon ended his days at Macao, dying of apoplexy in
1710, but neither his withdrawal nor his death ended the dispute.
He set it on a new track.

The immediate result of Tournon's pronouncement from
Nanking was that the Bishop of Macao, the Bishop of Andreville
(a Jesuit), the Franciscan Bishop of Peking, the Bishop of Ascalon
(an Augustinian), nearly all the Jesuit missionaries and a number
of others, all appealed to Rome against Tournon, and took the
p'iao or Government permit to preach. The rest were exiled,
including Fr. de Visdelou, S.J., of the French mission, whom
Tournon consecrated bishop as a Vicar Apostolic in the chapel of
the Franciscan house where he was living under quasi-arrest.

The cardinal's hat which arrived too late to be worn was

[1] Pastor, *op. cit.*, pp. 422–3.

brought by a pushing young Lazarist priest named Theodoric Pedrini, whose chief accomplishment was the ingenious construction of musical instruments. This suited the Emperor, who needed such a man, and they came to live on familiar terms. Their intimacy emboldened Fr. Pedrini to imagine that he could resolve the problem of the Rites where others had so signally failed.

The Emperor, after the Tournon episode, had sent two embassies to Rome; one was shipwrecked, the other reached the holy city in 1711. But Clement XI refused to rescind the decree against the Chinese Rites and on the contrary confirmed them, after the appeals from China had been heard. He confirmed them in Tournon's sense, making failure to comply a matter for excommunication. The chief pronouncement was the Constitution of 1715, 'Ex illa die'. The bishops and missionaries had agreed to prevent the Emperor being informed of these further decrees, not so Pedrini, who, in spite of a promise made to Fr. Della Chiesa not to tell the Emperor, informed him in writing. He wrote to the Pope that K'ang-hsi approved of the decrees against the Rites. This encouraged the Pope to be even more strict, while the disclosure of these decrees put all the bishops in a very delicate position, since the Emperor had told them on no account to keep such a thing from him.

The encouraging but false letter of Pedrini to the Pope also had the effect of stirring Clement XI to one final attempt at resolving the problems by yet another embassy. Consequently he sent Carlo Ambrogio Mezzabarba as bearer of the fateful Constitution 'Ex illa die' of 19th March 1715, the document which confirmed the previous decrees and commanded missionaries under pain of excommunication to swear obedience to the decision of the Holy See on the Chinese Rites. This embassy marks the last act of the tragedy, because K'ang-hsi in his rage had already confirmed, though not put into execution, decrees of the great Tribunals of China dated April 1717; they were: the banishment of the missionaries and the destruction of their churches, the abjuration, by force if necessary, of the Christian Faith.

Mezzabarba, now Archbishop of Alexandria, did all the right things; he went via Lisbon in a Portuguese boat, he sent two envoys ahead, he was received at Macao and entered China by Canton. But all was unavailing. The Emperor was suspicious. Again and again the Legate was cross-questioned by mandarins as to his reason for coming, and was asked why no envoy had been sent from Rome in reply to the repeated messages from the Emperor. He refused to say what the Papal Brief contained but finally consented to say that the Pope had granted some concessions.

A vivid picture of the court at Peking in this year is given by John Bell in *Travels in Asia*. He was an enterprising Englishman who joined a Russian embassy to China in 1719, arriving in Peking fifteen months later. He visited several times all three houses of the Jesuits, who acted as the embassy's interpreters. He was present at the great ceremonies when Mezzabarba was being royally entertained.[1]

On 31st December 1720 the Legate saw the Emperor in solemn audience and at a banquet the latter handed the Legate a golden cup of wine. The embassy seemed to be making headway. Twice more in the next few weeks he had audience. On 14th January, the famous meeting occurred when all except the Jesuit Fathers thought peace had been restored; but when K'ang-hsi said that the matter of the tablets and the dispute over the names of God were trivial things, he spoke, as the Jesuits knew and said, ironically. Mezzabarba wrote a letter to Rome giving the glad news. He had the document translated into Chinese, and it was shown to the Emperor. The latter then asked to see the Constitution. He returned it with the following inscription:

All that can be said about this decree is that one asks oneself how the Europeans, ignorant and contemptible as they are, presume to deliver judgment on the lofty teaching of the Chinese, seeing that they know neither their manners, their customs nor their letters. Today the Legate presents a decree which teaches a doctrine similar to that of the impious sects of the Hoxans and Tassus who tear one another with pitiless cruelty. *It is not advisable to allow the Europeans*

[1] Pinkerton's *Voyages and Travels*, Vol. VII, pp. 381ff.; also cf. ch. IX.

to proclaim their law in China. They must be forbidden to speak of it; and in this way many difficulties and embarrassments will be avoided.[1]

Mezzabarba now told the Emperor of the concessions; but K'ang-hsi refused to annul his decree.

Mezzabarba departed as the others had departed before him. He published eight concessions, benign interpretations of Papal decrees. When Benedict XIV heard of them he countermanded them, thus leaving the missionaries in a state of yet deeper confusion and distress. The Bull, '*Ex quo singulari providentia factum est*', of 11th July 1742 was indeed the end.

This Bull may be summarized as follows: it begins with a survey of the whole matter up to the decree of Clement XI approving the mission of Tournon. Benedict then quotes *in extenso* that decree, then the *Precepto* of 1715. He attacks some 'both disobedient and captious men' who refused to submit to them. He then turns to the permissions of Mgr. Mezzabarba. These he quotes: they sum up all that the missionaries wanted saved from the traditions of Ricci. It must be noted that it is specially these that Benedict XIV condemns. They are as follows:

Firstly, it is permissible for Christians to have in their private houses tablets of the dead, bearing only the name of the dead person, with a suitable explanation on the side, all superstition (thereby) avoided and all scandal put aside.

Secondly, all the ceremonies of the Chinese nation relating to the dead, provided they are not superstitious or suspect, but civil only, are permitted.

Thirdly, the cult of Confucius is allowed, when it is of a civil character; and also his tablets, corrected on the matter of the superstitious letters and inscription, and accompanied by the necessary explanation; it is also allowable to light candles, burn perfumes, present food, before his 'corrected' tablet.

Fourthly, it is permitted to offer candles and perfumes, for use in and for the expenses of funerals, provided a suitable explanation is added in writing.

[1] Pastor, *op. cit.*, p. 478.

Fifthly, genuflexions and prostrations are allowed before the 'corrected' tablet or even before the coffin or the corpse.

Sixthly, it is allowable to arrange tables with cakes, fruit, meat and ordinary food in front of the coffin, where there is a 'corrected' tablet with the required explanation and omitting anything superstitious, the purpose being merely to give some sign of respect and piety towards the dead.

Seventhly, it is allowable to perform the bow called the *Kowtow* before the 'corrected' tablet, both on the occasion of the Chinese new year and at other times of the year.

Eighthly, it is permitted before the 'corrected' tablets to light candles, to burn perfumes, given the required precautions; likewise before the grave, where food may be placed, as said above, with the necessary precautions, as above.

These permissions were condemned in the Bull of 1742 in the following terms:

> We define and declare that these permissions must be considered as though they had never existed, and we condemn and detest their practice as superstitious. And thus, in virtue of our present constitution to be in force for ever, we revoke, annul, abrogate, and wish to be deprived of all force and all effect, all and each of those permissions, and say and announce that they must be considered for ever to be annulled, null, invalid and without any force or power.[1]

There was nothing more to be said.

Already twenty years before (1722), the great K'ang-hsi was dead and his son reigned in his stead. Already, before the promulgation of the Bull of Benedict XIV, persecution had broken out and was to continue intermittently for over one hundred years. Not that K'ang-hsi was really favourable, as can be seen from the seventh maxim of the second Edict, but he saw the use of the Europeans for China's development.

---

[1] cf. A. Vacant and E. Mangenot, 'Rites chinoises', art., in the *Dictionnaire de théologie catholique*, Paris, 1910, Tome XI, the whole article and for this, cols. 2385–9. cf. also Abbé Huc, *op. cit.*, Vol. III, pp. 409 ff., for Clement XI's Constitution on Chinese Rites. cf. also *Catholic Encyclopedia*, Vol. XIII, pp. 37 ff.

As for the doctrine of the Occident which exalts T'ien Chu (Lord of the sky), it is equally contrary to the orthodoxy (of our sacred books), and it is only because its apostles have a thorough knowledge of the mathematical sciences that the State uses them—beware lest perhaps you forget that.[1]

Thus this first full-scale attempt of the West to make contact, to understand and be understood by the East, at this crucial point in the story, failed. Many high hopes had been formed. China was covered by a network of churches, of missionaries, of little Christian communities; Western books were being printed in Chinese, the Christian liturgy had been translated into the native tongue; Chinese priests there were, even a Chinese bishop had been consecrated. The missionaries had reached to the very heart of the Chinese Empire in the person of the Emperor himself. He had been known to sit at their feet as a disciple. He had granted them full permission to propagate their religion; an imperial edict hung before the Christian churches. Within the very enclosure of the palace grounds in Peking was a Catholic church. Intellectually the Jesuits had not only shown themselves to excel their Chinese counterparts, but they had also proved of great service to the Empire. Ricci and others had been so devoted in their efforts at 'sinification' that some of their works have been included in Chinese literary collections.

Never perhaps had one civilization succeeded better in entering into the spirit of another and in being accepted by it, not by force of arms but by force of charity. Yet under the glamour and splendour of that great achievement fatal and tragic problems arose which made for misunderstanding.

The Holy See had thought it prudent to condemn the Chinese Rites. It is not for us to sit in judgement on that decision. There were cogent reasons in favour of that judgement then. Today those reasons no longer hold, and the Holy See has thought fit to reverse that decision in the year 1939.

The Rites controversy was only one of the problems, others were Chinese suspicion of foreigners, jealousy of one foreigner

[1] Cordier, *op. cit.*, Vol. III, pp. 338 ff.

for others, religious rivalry among the foreigners, trade rivalries, the remoteness of the Papal authority, the ambiguities of language. Perhaps the chief reason for the failure was the unpreparedness of many Catholic Westerners for approaching another civilized world, whose history was almost double that of their own in length. It so happened that the West at this period was entering upon its age of smugness, of superiority; it was the least propitious moment to attempt so great a task. Few Europeans of the time were of the calibre of the great Jesuits.

iv. The Century of Persecution

(a) The Beginning of Persecution

Persecution began in a small way in the Dominican mission of Fu-an[1] in the province of Fukien, a year after the death of K'ang-hsi. An apostate Christian denounced the Dominican Fathers to the Magistrate of Fu-an. The Governor of the province proscribed the Fathers and commanded their church to be closed. On the 10th January 1724 this decree was forwarded to Peking for approval by the much-feared Board of Rites, which extended the operation of the decree to all China and to all the missionaries in the Empire. A week later the Emperor confirmed the decree, and everywhere it was put into execution. The spoliation of the Chinese Church was an accomplished fact. The priests and the bishops were all to be deported to Canton. The numbers in Canton, as the result of this decree—apart from nine who had been expelled from Japan—were sixteen priests from the vice-province of China, twelve of the Missions Étrangères, four bishops, those of Shansi, Peking, Nanking and Fukien, three Franciscans, some Dominicans and a few priests of Propaganda. Only those working in Peking were allowed to remain, for instance, Fr. Kogler continued as President of the Bureau of Astronomy.

As was inevitable, there was recrimination, charge and counter-charge. The letter of Fr. de Mailla, attributing the persecution to the imprudences of the Dominicans in Fukien, caused much indignation among them. The following are some extracts from it:

[1] Spelt in French romanization Fu-ngan, and Fu-nan, but wrongly.

Peking 1724. How can one write in the overpowering sadness of the hour, and how give you a picture of the lamentable events which occur before our eyes? The thing we feared all these years, which also we had so often foretold would happen, has at last come upon us. Our holy religion has been entirely banished from this land; all the missionaries, except those in Peking, have been expelled the Empire; the churches have been demolished, or put to profane uses; edicts are published commanding the Christians, under threats of rigorous punishment, to renounce their faith, and forbidding anyone to embrace it. . . .

The first spark which set a light to this all-embracing persecution happened in the month of July last year in the province of Fukien. It was at Foun-Gauhien, a dependent town of Foun-Ning-Tcheou.[1] This mission was administered by two Spanish Dominicans, recently arrived from the Philippines. A Christian scholar, at odds with the missionaries, abandoned his faith; then, having combined with several others of his kind, together they went to the local mandarin and handed him a petition. It contained several accusations, the chief of which were that the Europeans, who kept in hiding, had raised a great temple at the expense of their disciples, that men and women gathered there all mixed together, and that young girls from their earliest age were destined to a life of virginity.

There is no doubt that these practices had been instituted a few years previously, doubtless with good intentions; but with no less doubt with little knowledge of the customs and manners of the Chinese, or with no respect for them.[2]

It will be seen that Fr. de Mailla does not mince matters and in effect accuses the Dominicans of imprudence or ignorance. He points out in the next part of his letter that:

the Jesuits and members of other Orders, who are aware of the delicate sensibility of the Chinese on the matter of the separation of the sexes, have generally taken great pains to avoid giving the slightest offence in this matter, knowing that nothing, in view of the character of this people, could more easily make our religion hateful and contemptible to them.[3]

[1] So wrote Fr. de Mailla, but in our spelling, Fu-an Hsien and Fu-ning Chou.
[2] *Lettres édifiantes et curieuses, nouvelle édition*, 1780, Tome XIX, pp. 327 ff.
[3] *ibid.*

In spite of influential support in Peking and many *démarches* made by the Jesuits there, it proved impossible to prevent the Board of Rites from examining and condemning the Christian religion. The new Emperor, of whom the missionaries had had high hopes, proved unfriendly, and in the second year of his reign, in January 1724, Yung-chêng signed the decree of the Board of Rites which reads as follows: the text of the decree is also given in de Mailla's letter:

> The Europeans who are at the court are useful there for the calendar and they render other services; but those who reside in the provinces are in no way useful. They attract to their religion the ignorant, both men and women; they build churches, where men and women assemble together indiscriminately, under pretext of praying. The Empire gains nothing by this. In conformity with the proposal of the Chung-to of Fukien, those who are useful to the court must be unmolested; as for those spread throughout the Empire, if they can be made useful, let them be conducted to the court; for the rest, let them be sent to Macao.[1]

That the persecution began in Fukien, that the accusations were said to have emanated from there, no one doubts. But the Dominicans then and to this day deny that in fact the spark was in reality struck in Fu-an. Their story will enlighten us on the tense atmosphere between the various Orders, and it will help to give to that scene its sombre colours. A number of the Dominicans wrote home giving their account, none so complete as that of a certain Spanish friar with a most unlikely name for a Spanish member of the Order of Preachers, el padre Oscott. Writing to Fr. Juan Astudillo, O.P., on 9th January 1726, he said:

> . . . I shall state as shortly as possible certain reasons and facts concerning the present persecution which will confirm what you already know. It has been proved that it did not arise through Fukien nor on account of a church being built in Fu-an, but rather from the suspicions of the Emperor roused by the machinations of Fr. Moron. It is certain that before the Chung-to of Fukien laid his accusations against the Church, Fr. Moron had already been

[1] *ibid.*

exiled with the ninth prince, his friend, whom he had attempted to put on the throne. . . . Already the Fathers were prophesying persecution.[1]

The letter goes on:

2. The Emperor, from the moment he was crowned, began to show small concern for the Europeans, for as has been recorded, and it is well known, he would not see them nor did he wish them to be admitted to his presence.

In another letter he suggests that the court was alarmed at the great number of *literati* and of the governing class in the province of Fukien who had become Christian; and that as Fukien was on the seaboard, this strong Christian body there constituted a danger to the Empire.

Whatever the cause, the result was disastrous. It spelt the ruin of great hopes, the destruction of the flourishing Christian Church in China, leaving only scattered and harassed remnants, doubtless capable of survival—for they did survive—but not of growth and cultural development.

(b) *The Situation in the Eighteenth Century*

The situation in 1723 and thereafter is approximately as follows: officially there were no priests in the provinces, all the expelled priests had been brought together in Canton and in 1732 these

[1] The story about Fr. Moron is true. Even before K'ang-hsi had died, he had aired his views on the future Emperor in the presence of a number of high mandarins and some of the Fathers of the Society of Jesus, saying he was inept for governing and suggesting that the ninth prince would be more acceptable. (The same de Mailla records this conversation.) But not content with this Moron set off for the frontier and there attempted to persuade a general to revolt in support of his, Moron's, candidate. At the time of K'ang-hsi's death Moron was at Macao, but in spite of the urgent persuasions of his friends that he should stay at a safe distance, he returned post-haste to Peking, only to be exiled, beyond the Great Wall, with his suggested candidate for the throne. His end was delayed. For years he was in prison and finally was brought back to Peking in chains; he was tortured, returned to Sining, killed and cremated, his ashes were cast to the winds. cf. *Misiones Dominicanas en China (1700–1750)*, por P. José María Gonzalez, O.P. Consejo Superior de Investigaciones Cientificas, Madrid, 1952, pp. 98 ff., and for Fr. Oscott's letter, p. 109, note 30.

were deported to Macao. The churches all over the country were either desecrated, destroyed or taken over by the local Christians who turned them into dwellings. Only the churches of Peking remained open. There were four of these, the oldest, founded by Fr. Ricci, the Nan T'ang which belonged to the Portuguese province, in the south; to the east a dependent church, Tung T'ang, the old house of Fr. Schall; the western church, called Hsi T'ang, belonging to the French Jesuits. This was later called the Pei T'ang, or north church, because the residence of Fr. Pedrini, having become a tolerated church, acquired the appellation Hsi T'ang; these names remain to this day.[1]

During these troubled years the Fathers in Peking endeavoured to make themselves as useful as they could to the Emperor. They had already succeeded in 1688 in bringing to an end the dispute which had arisen between China and Russia concerning the frontier forts on the Amur river.[2] In 1689 at Nertchinsk Fr. Gerbillon of the French mission and Fr. Thomas Pereira a Portuguese Jesuit, acting as interpreters, had helped to settle the dispute. This is in fact the first treaty ever made by China with a foreign Power. Up to then all foreigners had been treated as vassals. The treaty was written in Manchu, Russian and Latin.

Yung-chêng founded a school of interpreters in view of the increasing diplomatic activity of the period. Fathers Parennin and Gaubil taught Latin and the former, in his capacity as head interpreter to the embassies from Europe, introduced in 1727 other Fathers who had come in the train of a Portuguese embassy.

The Church seemed to be concentrated in one place, Peking. All else was done in hiding. It is known that, about 1732, in the Nan T'ang and Tung T'ang, there resided all told eleven priests

[1] Cordier, *op. cit.*, Vol. III, p. 396.

[2] An indirect result of the quarrel over the forts at Albazin on the river Amur was that thirty-one of the Russian or Cossack defenders were taken prisoner, brought to Peking, where they were honourably treated and allowed to build their own chapel, St. Nicholas', and have their own priest. This is the beginning of the Orthodox Church in China. In 1948 there were still only 300 native Chinese Orthodox in China. They mostly withdrew to the Philippines on the advent of the Communists.

and five Brothers; in the Pei T'ang ten or twelve French Jesuit Fathers and one Brother.

On the accession of the new Emperor, Ch'ien-lung (1735–95), there were hopes that, as he was friendly, intelligent and curious, he might mitigate the severity of the laws against the missionaries. But he was weak and did nothing. Still, the great work went on, and in spite of repression, it is recorded that in 1743 Peking Christians numbered 40,000, and each year there were 1,000 baptisms. An encouraging sign was that twelve Chinese priests were helping the foreigners. Two of the Fathers, Fr. d'Incarville and Fr. Benoist, carried on the great survey which had been begun by Fr. Parrenin in the reign of K'ang-hsi in the year 1708.[1] The Brothers Castiglione and Attiret and Fr. Sickelbarth were the imperial painters.[2]

Fathers Florian Bahr and Walter were the imperial musicians. Br. Moggi was a sculptor; Fr. Thebault went round mending the clocks and the mechanical toys, which so delighted the Eastern mind. Glass and enamels were made by Br. de Brossard. The imperial doctors were Brothers Rousset and a Costa.

At the same time, but secretly, the vital work of evangelizing went on. The centres were Hukwang, Honan and King-si. In the first, twelve Jesuits went at the risk of their lives; in Kiang-nan priests circulated from place to place, hiding usually in barges, for in this way they could move secretly.

In 1746 the persecution was intensified. Bishop Sanz, O.P., and four Dominicans were captured, imprisoned and tortured in Fukien.[3] The Bishop was beheaded in the following year and

[1] cf. F. A. Plattner, *Jesuits Go East*, Dublin, 1951, pp. 226 ff.

[2] An example of their industry was displayed in the Exhibition of 'Landscape in French Art' hung at the Burlington Gallery in London in 1949–50. Exhibit No. 626 consisted of sixteen engravings done by Charles and Nicholas Cochin (1715–90) and others, of the conquests of the Emperor of China, Ch'ien-lung. These were taken from drawings made by the Jesuit missionaries in Peking, chief among them the great Castiglione.

In the house of M. Baillard in Paris the writer has seen splendid tapestries made to the designs of these artists of the Emperor, such as that which probably shows K'ang-hsi being taught astronomy by Fr. Verbiest or his successor.

[3] For a full account see José María Gonzalez, O.P., *op. cit.*

four others in 1748. A Portuguese, Fr. Henriquez, and an Italian, Fr. de Athemis, were sentenced by the Prefect of Soochow to be strangled. When the Emperor confirmed the sentence it was carried out and two catechists shared their glorious fate: Joseph Ts'ang and Philip Hoang. In 1750 the Bishop of Nanking, Mgr. de Sancta Rosa died of sheer want.

But these were not the only difficulties the struggling Church in China had to contend with. In 1759 the Portuguese Government under the leadership of Pombal suppressed the Jesuits in all regions under the jurisdiction of the Portuguese crown. Immediately all members of the Society found in Macao, whether Portuguese or not, were crammed into boats for Goa, from where they were shipped to Lisbon, and there thrown into the famous gaol fort of St. Julian. Three, Fathers Boussel, de Neuvialle and a Chinese, Br. Francis da Cunha, died.

A few years later the French Government acted in a similar manner. Four French Jesuits, in order to escape the ban in French territory, left France for China. They were Fathers Bourgeois, de Ventaron, de Grammont and de Poirot.

The last and truly deadly blow against the Society came in 1773, when Clement XIV, brow-beaten by the Governments of Europe, published a Brief suppressing the Society of Jesus altogether, not for any crime or disobedience, but in order to have peace. 'Dominus et Redemptor' was promulgated in Peking. All the Jesuits submitted without a murmur: seven of the vice-province in Peking, three in Kiang-nan, ten of the French mission at Peking, four in Hukwang and one in Canton, as well as eleven Chinese members. The exceptions were de Grammont, de Ventaron and de Poirot, who had left France at the moment of the suppression.

The Pei T'ang was left in charge of the French Fathers. The Nan T'ang was handed over to the new Franciscan Bishop of Peking, de Gouvea, and he took possession of all the property of the vice-province. The French Lazarists were at the request of Louis XVI given the remaining property of the French Jesuits.

The outstanding figure of this doleful period was the already mentioned Bishop of Nanking, the Jesuit Laimbeckhoven. He had been appointed in 1752, but it was four years before he was consecrated in Macao, and yet three years more before he could enter Kiangnan. Most of the time he lived hidden in Honan, which was part of his diocese. In 1760 he began an apostolate which was to last twenty-seven years; he lived in utter poverty, assisted by Fathers Correa and Pires of the vice-province and two Chinese Fathers, Yao and Kuang. He visited Wu-ho in Anhwei province in 1771 and Ch'ung-ming on an island in the Yangtse estuary in 1785. It may well have been his usual place of residence, or hiding, near Shanghai. In 1784 he entered Soochow disguised as a *porteur de chaise* and in the family chapel of the Hsü he ordained four Chinese priests. He died on 22nd May 1787 at T'ang-Ka-Laong, not far from Shanghai, and is buried at Soochow.

Though the death of this noble shepherd of his flock did not mean the extinction of Jesuit influence in the missionary field of China—a number of the Fathers of the Society survived there for many years more, though no longer called Jesuits—yet his death is as it were symbolically the end of one of the most remarkable achievements in the history of missions, the Jesuit approach to the Chinese.

Though this narrative is not concerned to describe the effect upon Europe of the rediscovery of China in modern times, it is to the Jesuit period that we must look for those first and most fundamental influences which China exerted on her discoverers. Here was a world which seemed not to know Christ, but which seemed at the same time to be one filled with nobility, art, wealth, wisdom. Perhaps the missionaries painted the world they discovered in too glowing terms—as it is the way with missionaries the world over—but the result was a Chinese fashion in the eighteenth century, not only in chinoiseries, in lacquer, in ceramics, in landscape painting, but also in philosophy. The naturalist philosophers of the Enlightenment turned to China as the example of mankind, ignorant of revelation, yet noble. But this is a theme which must only be touched on here to show that the traffic was not only one way.

For a time the Jesuits fade from the picture; but this was their finest hour. The new China when it emerges from the ordeal of Communism will once again need the insight and patience shown by these pioneers in understanding.

Their epitaph was sorrowfully inscribed upon a stone. For many years it remained forgotten and unread. But in the year 1835 Dr. Mouly, Bishop of Peking, discovered this epitaph, set up years before by Fr. Amiot, to the memory of the ancient Jesuit mission to China, on the refectory wall of a house belonging to the Fathers of the Society and situated outside Peking. We give the English translation as it appeared in the *Annals of the Association for the Propagation of the Faith*.[1]

IN THE NAME OF JESUS
AMEN
LONG IMMOVEABLE BUT VANQUISHED AT LAST IT HAS
FALLEN
UNDER THE ASSAULTS OF SO MANY STORMS.
TRAVELLER STOP AND READ
AND PONDER OVER THE INCONSTANCY OF HUMAN
THINGS.

Here lie the French missioners, formerly members of that celebrated Society, which in every quarter of the Globe, taught and disseminated in all its purity the worship of the true God, and which, taking Jesus for Model, as likewise it had assumed his Name and imitated Him, as much as such imitation is practicable to human weakness, pursued in the midst of toils and contradictions its exercise of virtue, its Mission of Charity; and making itself all to all, to gain them to God, gave, during more than two centuries of its prosperity, Confessors and Martyrs to the Church.

I, Joseph Mary Amiot and the other French missionaries of this Society, whilst we still retain in Peking, under the auspices and protection of the Tartar-Chinese Monarch, the religion of Christ, sheltered by art and science, whilst our Gallican Church still glitters in the bosom of the Imperial palace, amidst the altars of a thousand false gods, alas! secretly sighing for our last hour, have raised this monument of brotherly affection in funereal gloom. Pass, Traveller:

[1] Vol. XI, pp. 349ff.

congratulate the dead, mourn the living, pray for all; wonder and be silent.

In the year of Christ, 1774, upon the 14th day of October, in the 20th year of Kiang-Louing, the 10th day of the 9th moon.

If love is stronger than death then the Jesuits have yet to play a great part in the Christening of China.

(c) The Lazarists in China

Having completed the story of the justly famous Jesuit mission to China which began with the arrival of St. Francis Xavier at its southern gate and ended with the suppression of the Society by the Pope in the eighteenth century, we must now take up the story of the mission with the coming of the Lazarists who arrived in Peking to salvage what they could of the Church founded by their great predecessors.

As a Congregation this was the first introduction of Lazarists to China, but as individuals some had been sent almost a century before by the Holy See. To round off the Lazarist story, it is fitting to begin at their beginning even though chronology may seem to suffer. But chronology is our servant in history, not our master.

St. Vincent de Paul, contemporary of Henry IV of France and James I of England founded in the year 1625 a congregation of priests. He had a rule that he never undertook any work unless forced into it; this may account for the delay in reaching China. 'We cannot ourselves make a single move to be established in any place whatsoever if we wish to keep ourselves in the ways of God and in the traditions of our company.'[1]

The most astonishing, certainly the most colourful, of the early Lazarists, and perhaps of all the many missionaries who reached China, was Theodoric Pedrini. Italian born (1671), he completed his ecclesiastical studies in Rome, where too he joined the Lazarists. He was no mean scholar, being a Doctor in both ecclesiastical and civil law.

It was the time of the legation of Tournon to the Chinese Emperor. Pedrini was commanded to join his party in the

[1] cf. A. Thomas, *Histoire de la Mission de Pékin*, Vol. II, p. 7.

Canaries, and so set sail from St. Malo in the December of 1703. When off the coast of Peru the ship had to be abandoned. He had already been two years on the voyage. After endless adventures he reached Mexico, and two years after the shipwreck he set sail once again to cross the Pacific. He was now as expert at managing a ship as he was at his legal studies. The boat reached Manila in August. His real troubles had only begun. Tournon, whom he never caught up with, had arrived in China two years before in 1705; his tragi-comedy being played through, he was back in Macao a prisoner. Pedrini made two attempts to reach Macao but twice he was blown back by contrary winds. In Manila he met five Propaganda priests, among them Ripa, an Augustinian, a Dominican and two others. It was they who were bringing the red hat to the much-persecuted Papal Legate.

It was now impossible to get a ship for China, as Philip IV, to placate his Portuguese subjects, had forbidden trade with it. Pedrini therefore took it into his head to disguise himself as a sea-captain, dressing the part and cutting off his beard. He hired a frigate and together with the other priests and the red hat sailed away to Macao. The party reached their destination in January 1710. It had taken Pedrini six years and a month to make the journey from Europe.

Tournon died the following June, so Pedrini's mission was at an end. But the Emperor, hearing that he was a musician, sent for him, and off he went to Peking. His companion, Fr. Ripa, a painter, went there too, in his capacity as artist, while Fr. William Fabri joined the party as a mathematician.

Pedrini was not a man for letting grass grow under his feet. He constructed an organ which, apparently, played by itself—the ancestor of the modern electrical pianola—whilst he, like a child before a gramophone, would conduct it to the delight of his imperial majesty. But this honeymoon period did not last long, for the Rites controversy had reached its peak when these belated travellers arrived at Peking. One day, on account of an indisposition, Pedrini could not attend the new year ceremony. He was put into chains and cast into prison, where he remained until the death of the Emperor. It was a piece of good fortune for him that the new monarch had been his pupil and a friend; he was liberated forthwith. No sooner liberated than he bought in the city a great house of seventy rooms and ten courtyards. It had belonged to the son, now dead, of a viceroy. Pedrini's purpose was to accommodate the priests sent out by Propaganda. He built a chapel for it, and called it the Hsi T'ang. There he remained until his death in 1740.

The other notable Lazarist priest to reach China, as it were out of due time, was Louis Appiani. His life was no less eventful than that of Pedrini had been. Born in 1663, he was sent out to China by Propaganda as Vice-Visitor Apostolic in 1696. His journey took him three years by the now unaccustomed land route. For a time he evangelized Szechwan, but he had the misfortune to be chosen as interpreter for the Tournon mission to the capital. He shared the Legate's disgrace, and during their wretched journey south from Peking, after the collapse of negotiations, Appiani was seized, dragged back to the capital, imprisoned, then escorted to Szechwan where he had preached previously, dragged back to Peking, put in prison or confined with some Jesuits, and finally expelled to Canton. There he languished twelve years. At last by the good offices of Benedict XIII he was set free in 1726. He had lost none of his zeal and started preaching once again, in Canton itself. Expelled in 1732, he died in the house of the Dominicans at Macao.

It is clear that the early entry of the Lazarists was far from peaceful. Nevertheless Pedrini had acquired a house in Peking which proved of inestimable value to them.

When the Papacy, as we have seen, under pressure and most unwillingly, suppressed the Society of Jesus in 1773, it had to find some other missionary body capable of, and willing to undertake their work all over the world, not least in China. Only ten years later the Holy See managed to persuade the Lazarists to undertake this most difficult task. In 1783 Propaganda stated that the *Congrégation de la Mission*, i.e. the Lazarists, had accepted the mission of Peking.

Three pioneers were chosen, not unfitted to carry on the role of scientific missionary. Fr. Raux, born in Cambrai 1754, later to be appointed the head of the mission, had prepared himself by spending a year improving his knowledge of astronomy, botany and natural history. He now went to Picardy to be able to compare its canal system with that of China; he visited the iron 'exploiter' in Champagne. The second member of the party, Gheslain, was born near Chimay in 1751; he had studied experimental physics, especially *pompes à feu*, had made experiments in *électricité simple* and *l'électricité combinée*, with inflammable air, and had dabbled in aerostatic balloons—de Rozier went up in a balloon for the first time the very year that the Holy See had made its choice, in 1783. The third, Br. Joseph Paris, a clock-maker, learned the art of bell-ringing and acquired skill on the *clavecin*.

Macao, living up to its reputation, did not welcome these newcomers; consequently they did not dare land there. On the other hand the Jesuits at Peking sent Raux a letter signed jointly. It reads thus:

> We thank God in all sincerity for having arranged matters so providentially, that you, sir, and your brethren of the congregation of the Mission, should have been, as it were, forced to take over the French Chinese missions, which up to the present have been ruled by your old friends the Jesuits. Nothing assuredly could have given us more pleasure than this choice.[1]

The arrangement among the missionaries in Peking was as follows. The Jesuits did not necessarily leave the capital but carried on as secular priests. These together with the newly arrived Lazarists lived in the Pei T'ang; the Nan T'ang, which had recently been rebuilt by the munificence of the reigning Emperor, having just previously been burned down by some of his subjects, was occupied by the bishop, Mgr. de Gouvea, and some Chinese secular priests; the Tung T'ang was served by secularized Portuguese Jesuits, and Propaganda priests retained the church built so providentially by Pedrini.

[1] It was sent by Fr. Amiot, signed by him, Fathers Bourgeois, de Ventaron, de Grammont, de Poirot and Br. Joseph Panzi.

At this period it was becoming almost impossible to enter China, as the Imperial Government was so suspicious of foreigners. Thus the Lazarists not only had to contend with the avowed hostility of the Portuguese at Macao but also with the suspicions of the port authorities and of every local mandarin throughout the Middle Kingdom. Fathers Richenet and Duzamel, both Lazarists, had to wait four years in Macao for a passport. Even when they got almost all the way to Peking, they were turned back. Finally Fr. Duzamel crept in via Tonkin and reached his mission in Hukwang in 1810, nine years after he had set off. Fr. François Regis Clet, later to be martyred, was sent by the Lazarists to China in 1791, at the height of the French Revolution. In 1793 he was still, with two companions, in Macao. There he was joined by four Chinese priests who had been trained in the College of the Holy Family in Naples, and who had come out with the British embassy under Lord Macartney. Three hopefully followed the English Lord by boat to Tientsin, trusting that they would be allowed to enter the capital by that door and so avoid the Portuguese obstructions. But this time it was the mandarins who obstructed. 'This was not the normal entry' they said, and back the priests went to Macao. Fr. Raux, their superior in Peking, received them only in 1796 after five years of waiting.

The difficulties with the Portuguese never seemed to diminish. Even in the eighteenth century, every missionary going to Peking had first to be presented by the head of the European (i.e. the Portuguese) factory in Canton—the equivalent of a consul—to the chief of the corporation of the main Chinese merchants.[1] It was their duty to draw up a request for the passport and then take it to the mandarin in charge of the police of the outskirts of Canton. Nor was that the end of the affair. This police mandarin

---

[1] This was the so-called Co-Hong. The maximum number of Hong merchants was fixed at thirteen, but the actual number was often less than this. This mercantile organization, which had been set up by the Chinese authorities, enjoyed a monopoly of the foreign trade (itself restricted to Canton) but was not itself a monopoly, as each of the merchants belonging to it traded on his own account and employed his own capital. The Co-Hong had no chief, though some of its members enjoyed more influence than others.

had to pass it on to a higher mandarin and he to present it to the viceroy. At any of these stages in the process the request might be refused. The result was that many of the missionaries went in secretly at their own risk rather than wait about kicking their heels in Macao.

In 1799 the French persuaded the Papal Nuncio in Lisbon to induce the Portuguese to receive French missionaries in Macao. They agreed, but the Senate of Macao refused to present their names to the Chinese authority for permits to enter China proper. Raux endeavoured to set up a business house in Macao for the French mission. Indeed the ex-Jesuit de Grammont was installed, but the Government sent him back to Peking. It is all a story of frustration and pettiness.

Meanwhile England, whose intentions were entirely commercial and whose diplomatic missions had proved lamentable and comic failures, thought of the expedient of using French missionaries as liaisons with the Chinese Government; the English Government therefore approached Raux with the suggestion of a large annual sum of money and free passage for missionaries in English ships, if they would become naturalized English. He refused.

What was happening throughout the Chinese mission during the latter half of the eighteenth century and the beginning of the nineteenth is hard to reconstruct. The most exciting chapters and the most heroic in the history of the Church are chapters of persecution, but the persecuted usually have no opportunity to write their memoirs; they leave few records. China is no exception, for records are scanty. One most remarkable document, however, has survived from that period which goes far to compensate for the dimness of outline in the rest of the story. It is the famous diary[1] written by a Chinese priest who was born in Chingku in 1692 or 1693 and who died in 1774. His name is Andrew Ly.

The diary survives in the archives of the Missions Étrangères in Paris. He was educated by them at their Collège Général at Juthia in Siam and thought of himself as a member of the Congregation,

[1] *Journal d'André Ly, Prêtre chinois, Missionnaire et Notaire Apostolique 1746–1763*, Intro. A. Launay. Hong Kong, 1924.

but he could not in fact be so, seeing that from the Chinese point of view he was not an 'étranger' but rather the opposite and precisely what they were working for, a Chinese priest. An extraordinary fact about this diary is that it is written in fluent Latin and runs in manuscript to 831 pages. That this vast undertaking should be written in correct Latin might seem unbelievable were it not that he was, as just remarked, educated at Juthia. The students there from all over the Far East not only studied Latin but their games were conducted in Latin. Thus it was second nature to Andrew Ly to compose his diary during the years 1746 to 1763 in the common language of the Western Church. From 15th September 1758 to 30th May 1759, there is a gap in the diary.

Andrew Ly was the child of Christian parents in the province of Shensi, whose family had been Christian since the Ming dynasty. When only fifteen years old he followed two priests of the Missions Étrangères into exile, as a result of a persecution raging in the province of Szechwan against priests who had refused to take the *p'iao* or Government permit to preach. Three years later in 1710 he was sent to the Séminaire Général[1] and after only fifteen years' training his superiors considered him fit for ordination. Not without a faint trace of bitterness Fr. Ly refers to scraps of conversation criticizing the Chinese at which he was present. He records for instance, Italians, Portuguese and Spaniards discussing in Macao the problem of Chinese clergy, and someone remarking: 'The Chinese are proud, fickle, ungrateful. That is why they should not be ordained.' On another occasion he heard this remark: 'I refuse to believe anything Andrew Ly may write. Chinese priests are different from European; they have no intention of doing anything unless they are goaded to it.'

[1] The remainder of its story is as follows. When the Burmese destroyed it, in the eighteenth century, in their destruction of Juthia, the seminary migrated to Cambodia, then to India near Pondicherry (1770). The Indian period lasted only until 1782. Then for a time it was in abeyance, as was so much during the revolutionary period. By herculean efforts it was re-established, in 1809, on the Island of Penang in the Malacca Straits. There it remains still, having survived the Second World War and having been overrun by the Japanese armies, which treated the inmates with respect.

This contempt for the native Chinese on the part of the missionaries was a tragic failure of insight and trust in divine Providence; and its effects survived to this century, when there was still in the early decades a reluctance to admit the Chinese to an equality in the hierarchy of the Church.

In 1726 Andrew Ly, recently ordained, arrived in Canton ready to move to wherever his superiors proposed to send him. Fr. Guignes, Procurator of the Society in the Far East, sent him to Fukien with Fr. Thomas Sanchez. Unfortunately he became ill and had to withdraw to his base in Canton. On the journey he was accompanied by another Chinese priest and three Chinese youths who were to be educated for the priesthood. On his recovery he was sent to Szechwan. But the administrator of the area, Fr. Mulliner, refused him entry, because both Ly and his fellow worker, Fr. de Martiliat, were of the Missions Étrangères whereas Mulliner was not. The rivalry between the missionary societies made them jealous to hold on to their preserves even though they had no one ready to do their work. Propaganda, however, confirmed them in their right to enter the province and work for souls.

From this moment the labours of Fr. Ly were unremitting. The passage in St. Paul's epistle where he describes his labours and sufferings could well be applied to this heroic apostle. Arrested in 1744, he and his fellow priest were chained together. On that occasion the gaoler was not above a small bribe and the priests made their escape.

Two years later when the Emperor Ch'ien-lung, one of the most enthusiastic and long-lived persecutors of the Church, issued a decree approving the decapitation of Christians persisting in their errors, Fr. Ly's two companions, European missionaries, withdrew to Macao. At this desperate moment of his life he started his diary at the suggestion of de Martiliat who wanted to be kept informed. He continued it almost without a break for eighteen years.

Now he was alone and without resources except trust in God, for there were years when the meagre annual salary of 400 francs did not reach him. At last in 1750 he received an assistant, Chinese like himself, Fr. Luke Ly, and four years later a French Franciscan, Fr. Urbain Lefebvre, penetrated to the mission. That very year Lefebvre and Andrew Ly were arrested and put in chains. Fr. Lefebvre was escorted to Macao; and if he was disappointed at not being martyred then, Fr. Lefebvre received that crown later, being killed with the Carmelites in Paris in 1792.

Help was at last on the way. Mgr. Pottier, who was to become Fr. Ly's devoted admirer and friend, reached him either in 1756 or 1757. His name for Fr. Ly was always 'le vénérable M. Ly'. But their troubles were not at an end. Pottier was captured in 1760, and on that occasion escaped; the following year Fr. Ly was imprisoned but within the twelve months set free. It was now proposed that the veteran Chinese missionary should be made bishop, Vicar Apostolic of the province; his deafness was an obstacle, so nothing came of it, and some years later Mgr. Pottier was consecrated bishop. Meanwhile the indefatigable Fr. Ly had established a seminary in the remote mountains, near Chengtu; he had also constructed a home for the sick, but this was burnt down and soon after, in 1774, he went to render his account to God; he had saved the Church under his charge by his dogged perseverance.

The great lament of Fr. Ly in his diary is the dearth of indigenous clergy. 'Within a span of nearly fifty years', he wrote, 'scarcely seven of the Chinese seminarists have been considered worthy of Ordination in our Society.'[1] The reasons he gave were, that Chinese youths are flighty and inconstant, that there had been changes of superiors in the seminary and changes of place of the seminary itself. He noted also that in the span of twenty years the Italians at Naples had only ordained nine Chinese. He had no easy optimism, his opinion of his flock was not flattering; 'apart from the name of Christian, in which they glory, they know nothing else of their religion'.[2] He judged that there were eight thousand of these nominal Christians in the province of Szechwan, of whom only one thousand were truly

[1] Launay, *Journal d'André Ly*, p. 179.   [2] *ibid.*, p. 513.

practising. This was the inevitable result of persecution and of lack of priests.

Throughout the eighteenth century and the first half of the nineteenth the problem remained. When the Lazarists arrived, towards the end of the eighteenth century, they converted the Jesuit school of St. Joseph in Macao into a seminary for Chinese priests. The French missionaries in Peking set up a seminary there in the eighteenth century. The Lazarists themselves had one of their own at Peking. In 1788 at the former there were fifteen Chinese students. Fr. Ly himself organized a local seminary in the south of China, but it was destroyed in 1770. His friend and successor, Mgr. Pottier, also established one for a time.[1]

(d) *The Dark Years*

It would be an endless task to record every persecution of the period 1784 to 1840; persecution was endemic. It broke out here or there almost according to the whim or the cupidity of the local mandarin. But some incidents stand out and may be taken as representative, giving as they do a picture of the conditions under which Catholics lived in China during that period.

In the year 1784 four Italian Franciscans, sent by Propaganda into the Chinese mission, were secretly traversing Hupeh on their way to Shensi when they were arrested. This surprise capture of 'foreign devils' travelling incognito through the very heart of China disturbed the equanimity of Chinese officialdom, as well it might. The Emperor forthwith issued an edict commanding the destruction of all Christian churches in the provinces, the apprehending of all European and Chinese priests and the forcible renunciation of their faith by all Christians.

The hunt began, and the bag was a rich one; sixteen European

---

[1] Some idea of the situation in China during this period is provided by the statistics for 1810. In Macao itself there were five Chinese priests. Fr. Brou in an unpublished work, estimates there were 18 in Peking and 6 in Nanking; 8 in Fukien, where the Dominicans were still working; 18 in Shansi, 25 in Szechwan—in all 80 Chinese priests. They had been trained at Manila, Macao, Peking, Penang or on the spot and some at the College of the Holy Family in Naples.

and ten Chinese priests were caught. The former were taken to Peking and put in the Board of Punishments' prison. Besides these sixteen priests, two bishops were caught, the Vicars Apostolic of Shensi and Shansi. The two bishops, the Procurator of the Propagandists, an Italian Franciscan and two priests of the Missions Étrangères died in chains.

In the following year, 1785, at the earnest pleading of the resident missionaries of Peking, the remainder were set free on condition that they either stayed in Peking or left the country for good. Two, Mgr. Saint-Martin and Fr. Dufresse, left and secretly returned to their missions in Szechwan. Fr. Dufresse, later to be Vicar Apostolic in western China, was martyred in 1815.

At the turn of the century, owing to the troubles in Europe, the Chinese mission sank almost to extinction. In 1795, when the Emperor, Ch'ien-lung died, five ex-Jesuits still remained in Peking, two in the Nan T'ang and three in the Pei T'ang. The last of the Nan T'ang to die was Fr. Almeida (1805) and the last Jesuit of all of the Ancient Mission was Fr. de Poirot who expired in 1814. This was truly the close of a chapter. There remained only the churches and chapels as melancholy relics.

The Portuguese Lazarists took over the Tung T'ang in 1801, but it was burnt down in 1807. Four years later the Hsi T'ang was evacuated by the Propagandists and the church demolished. The Pei T'ang became desecrated because the Lazarists were not allowed to replace their Fathers when they died. Fr. Serre the last occupant, President of the Bureau of Astronomy, went to live at the Nan T'ang, and the Pei T'ang was sold. Thus Ricci's old house alone remained. In 1808 Bishop de Gouvea died there, and he had no successor. The Bishop of Nanking, Pires-Pereira, lived on in Peking and administered the Nan T'ang, but he died in 1838 and no European missionary remained to preserve the link. The old residence was destroyed, but, by the kind offices of the Russian Archimandrite, to whom Bishop Pereira had handed the title deeds, the church was saved. It was reopened in 1860.

Chapter Five

MODERN TIMES 1839–1949

Bird's-eye View

The period under review makes a clear unity up to the arrival of the Communist State in 1949; but there is a two-fold division, one chronological, the other ideological. The Boxer Rising in 1900 divides the chapter neatly into two chronologically distinct parts, and the arrival of Protestant missions in the mid-nineteenth century creates a problem of presentation for this last chapter, and forces the writer to cover the same time-span twice. The method adopted is as follows:

We begin with the situation before the Opium Wars; then, taking the nineteenth century, we follow the fortunes first of the Catholic then of the Protestant missionaries. The Boxer Rising is then given its due place between the two centuries as a warning of things to come. The twentieth century it seemed necessary to preface with a short survey of the political scene which so profoundly influenced those years. Here again the space is divided between the Catholic Church and the various Protestant bodies. The book ends with an Epilogue or account of the last years.

PART THE FIRST

THE NINETEENTH CENTURY

A. THE CATHOLIC MISSIONS

i. *Zero Hour*

THE end of the eighteenth century does not mark any significant change in the story being recounted. The significant date was 1839 when the English decided to break through the fragile barrier of Chinese isolation by force of arms.

But, in order to understand the situation from the point of view of the missionaries, it is as well to begin a few years previously. True, as said in the last chapter, it seemed that the Peking mission had come to an end, but in the rest of China good work was being secretly carried on. While the Peking mission, which, as it were, crumbled away in the early years of the nineteenth century, seems to belong to the Jesuit Age, the activity in the provinces during the same period seems rather to belong to the Modern Age. It is therefore to the provinces that we now turn at this most desperate period of their history, the new dawn, though to the workers in the field and to the faithful it must have appeared more like dusk without promise of another day.

All the world, in so far as it was under the direct or indirect dominion of the West, was affected by the upheavals in Europe which began with the French Revolution and ended in the Napoleonic Wars. But in the case of China it was chiefly in the religious sphere that this occurred, as only missionaries dared to penetrate and then only at the peril of their lives. The eighteenth century by its Voltairean attack on religion, the Revolution by its destructions of property and expulsions of religious, the wars which followed, by their hampering of movement, all affected very adversely the missionary activity. Thus the Lazarists and the Missions Étrangères were expelled from France, their home; recruitment ceased. It was therefore increasingly difficult to man the widespread missions and to provide the money. In any case it was impossible to make the journey. The maritime Powers were at war and not interested in the works of peace.

Yet, from the point of view of the Chinese Government, the missionaries, at the turn of the century, were enjoying an unnatural calm. Though the laws of China were set against the religion of Christ, these laws were in temporary abeyance. Perhaps the Chinese felt that there was now no danger from that quarter. They had reasons for being reassured, for, as we have seen, in 1773 the Jesuits had been suppressed by the Pope and the Western Powers were soon at war with one another. In 1787, it is true, the Lazarists had taken over from the Fathers of the Society of Jesus, but the Government, so it must have thought, needed no longer to fear the foreign religion, for it surely could now constitute no threat to the established order; it was a sect like any other, precariously living its life in Peking under imperial protection and supervision, but elsewhere swallowed up in the multitudes that constituted China, and not daring to show its face, for fear of local persecution. Such persecution as there was usually arose, not from religious intolerance or rivalry, but for filthy lucre's sake.

The peace was of course precarious, but it did exist for a time. When, for instance, the old Jesuit church, the Nan T'ang in Peking, was burnt to the ground in 1775, it was the Emperor who gave money for it to be rebuilt. The Lazarists were well received in the capital; and, as the Jesuits had been sheltered in the imperial palace in order to take care of the various scientific instruments they had set up, so the Lazarists, their successors, were expected to perform the same function. During this lull, they received their due reward, for it is recorded that in 1800 there was a public procession of the Blessed Sacrament through the streets of Peking, a sign of tolerance scarcely visible in Europe at that date.

A letter written in 1803 from China by a Fr. Hamel to the superior of the Missions Étrangères in Paris gives some idea of the momentary spell of peace that came over the Chinese missionary field just before a new series of persecutions broke out. He wrote:

> We are extremely quiet on all sides. There is no more talk of persecution, in spite of the fact that the Christians are increasing in numbers, even in the cities, and that they openly practise their religion. This tranquillity is causing a number of conversions. In many parts the inhabitants come of their own accord to ask to be received into the Church, and even in places where there had not been any Christians before.[1]

This lull was deceptive. The following year, 1804, was to begin a chronic condition of suffering and persecution for the Catholic Church in China. The chief years of persecution were 1804, 1811, 1814, 1818–20, 1827 and 1836–45.

[1] cf. *Morceaux choisis des lettres édifiantes et curieuses* ... éd. Antoine Caillot, 4ᵉ édition, Tome 2, Paris, 1823, p. 279.

The historian of any missionary effort is almost sure to be faced with sad episodes of persecution. This is no less, and no more, true of the history of the missions in China than that of anywhere else, for the Chinese have no monopoly of fanaticism; indeed in many respects they have been remarkably tolerant. But it is only fair to the memory of those who risked their lives, to give in some detail an account of the fearful torments they had to face when they stepped ashore in China. Europeans, both Catholic and Protestant, have been no less cruel than the Chinese, and with less excuse; but it is one thing to admire the courage of those who suffered and another to condemn those who caused the suffering. In what follows we write only in admiration of the heroism of those who withstood the onslaught of pain and death for the faith which was in them; no judgement is passed on those who inflicted that pain. 'Judge not that you may not be judged' is a good motto. Indeed the Chinese had some reason for feeling apprehensive of foreigners, even in the nineteenth century, as subsequent history proved.

The incident which intensified the persecution was the discovery in the post for Europe of a geographical map. Fr. Deodat was sending it to Rome as an aid to a decision on the delimiting of the Italian mission in Peking. Now for the first time for over a century the Peking mission itself was menaced. In 1827 the reigning Emperor, Tao-kuang, after expelling the European missioners, declared their establishments confiscated to the State, and razed their beautiful church to its foundations. The Lazarists took refuge in the direction of Tartary. Hsi-wan-tzü grew rich from the losses of Peking. There had been seven hundred Christians in the capital, soon they were reduced by half. Many left the city and set up a parish two or three leagues away.[1] For a time the Peking seminary was established beyond the Great Wall, in

[1] *Annals of the Association for the Propagation of the Faith*, Vol. I, p. 398, London, 1838. A periodical collection of letters from the bishops and missionaries employed in the missions of the Old and New Worlds, and of all the documents relating to those missions and to the Institution for the Propagation of the Faith. This collection serves as a continuation of the *Lettres édifiantes*. In future referred to as *A.P.F.*

Mongolia, where at first a Chinese priest, Fr. Sue, was superior, then Dr. Mouly arrived to take it over.

From beyond the Great Wall, where the Peking Christians had fled, comes an interesting account of their way of life in their self-imposed exile. Dr. Mouly, who had become superior of the Lazarists of the Peking mission, wrote[1] to his superior that his parishioners were all the labouring classes. He and his fellow workers consciously reversed the Jesuit plan of going first to the ruling classes; they now went to the poor. We must not forget of course that, owing to the restrictions imposed by Rome on Christians performing the Chinese Rites, it was difficult to see how any others than the poor could become Christians. The men and women were still kept separate, but at least now they shared the same church. 'Behind the high altar there is reserved for women a space 30 ft. by 20 ft. They can see without being seen.'[2]

Dr. Mouly was very enterprising. 'We have adopted the Gregorian or plain chant of your European churches', he writes, 'which from its great similarity to their own music, the Chinese very soon learn.'[3] They sang the *Kyrie, Gloria, Credo, Sanctus, Agnus Dei*, of Dumont's Mass, 'substituting Chinese words for those used in Europe'.[4] This was sung by a group of children, accompanied by flutes.

A vivid account of at least one corner of the mission field during this period is given by the heroic Fr. Perboyre in letters to the Procurator of the Missions of the Lazarists, who was stationed at Macao. He describes how he travelled in a junk in the year 1836 along the coast from Macao to the eastern extremity of Fukien. He was welcomed with great kindness by the Vicar Apostolic of the area, living there in a remote village, two-thirds of whose population were Catholic. Some whole villages in this area were Christian. Two seminaries were in operation, and many large churches were openly used.

In the evening at the hour of family prayer you would hear the hills and valleys resound with the voices of hundreds singing the

---

[1] *A.P.F.*, Vol. I, pp. 393 ff.   [2] Dr. Mouly, in *A.P.F.*, p. 404.
[3] *ibid.*, p. 403.   [4] *ibid.*

rosary. Two or three thousand fishermen annually assemble and in three divisions go in processional order to make their Easter Communion.[1]

Ministering to this thriving Christian community, he wrote, were sixteen European and eight Chinese Dominicans. It appeared that one of the Chinese Christians had lately been appointed to an official post in Chekiang.

But this almost idyllic existence could not last, and Fr. Perboyre left in March of that year, disguised as a tea merchant, for Kiangsi, which he had to reach on foot, travelling seven to eight leagues a day for two weeks on end. Within a few months persecution broke out again in Fukien. Not long after, Fr. Perboyre was to have the opportunity to accept a martyr's death.

Fr. Huc has left us a fine description of it all.

After the blockade and burning of Kuanintang (the village where Dr. Rameau and Fathers Baldus, Clauzetts and Perboyre were assembled), when the mandarins came the priests were obliged to flee. On the third day . . . Fr. Perboyre's guide, a catechumen, betrayed him to some soldiers for money. Fr. Perboyre was taken to the prisons of Kucheng and finally to Wuchang-fu, capital of the province, where he underwent more than twenty examinations, was beaten with the ratan; when he was struck . . . he covered with kisses and bathed in his tears the image of the Saviour which was presented to him to insult. The judge, on his refusal to venerate idols, commanded some Christians to tear out his hair and beard . . . he exhorted them to obey. . . . 'I should suffer much more if I saw you beaten on my account', said he. He was tortured for four months . . . the Viceroy had four characters marked on his face with a red hot iron—Sie Kiao ho chun, which mean: Propagator of a bad religion. Then he was put in a stinking prison with felons . . . these venerated him. A Chinese priest and some Christians visited him by the help of bribes.

Fr. Huc then quotes a document written by Fr. Perboyre in prison.

. . . four . . . trials awaited me at Siang-yang-fu. During one of them, I remained for half a day kneeling in iron chains. I was kept in this

[1] Dr. Mouly, in *A.P.F.*, pp. 368–71.

position by strong cords, which held me suspended by the thumbs and hair, in such a manner however that the weight of my body should fall on my bare knees. In the city of Wuchang-fu I appeared more than twenty times before the mandarin and I was almost always put to various tortures when I would not reveal what the judges wished to know. If I had made these revelations, the persecution would have instantly spread to all the provinces. . . . At Wuchang-fu I received one hundred and ten strokes of a ratan for not trampling on the cross . . . out of twenty Christians recently arrested two thirds have publicly apostatised.

Fr. Huc continues:

On the 11th of September the imperial decree arrived condemning him to be strangled.

Fr. Perboyre was hanged, his legs tied behind his back, as one kneeling. Five malefactors were hanged first. Fr. Perboyre was three times raised off the ground; twice the rope was lowered. Finally he was kicked in the stomach.[1]

The extreme difficulty priests had in entering China is exemplified in the description given by Fr. Huc.

It was decided that I should depart on Saturday, 20th Feb. towards 7 p.m., in the Chinese junk that plies between Macao and Canton. . . . One of my couriers was promised that the small cabin for four persons should be reserved for our use; that is for my two couriers, a native student whom I leave at Kian-Si with Dr. Rameau and the prohibited European, namely your ever affectionate friend.

Towards 6 p.m. I assumed the Chinese costume; my hair was cut off, with the exception of what I had allowed to grow for nearly two years on the top of my head; other hair was attached to it, the whole was dressed, and I became possessed of a magnificent pigtail that reached to my knees. My complexion, tolerably dark, as you know, was still further deepened by some yellow colouring; my eyebrows were cut after the manner of the country; long and thick moustaches, that I had allowed to grow for a long time, concealed the European turn of my nose, and finally the Chinese clothes completed the disguise. A young Mongol Lama, lately converted

[1] *ibid.*, Vol. v, pp. 10ff.

to the Faith, gave me his long robe; the short tunic put over it, and which almost resembles a rochet, was a relic of Fr. Perboyre, who was martyred last year in the province of Hupeh. This garment was adorned with large spots of blood; it ought to bring me good fortune.[1]

The volume of the Association for the Propagation of the Faith for the year 1840 published a general survey of the Church in China at that date. China had three bishoprics and seven vicariates. The bishoprics were Macao, Nanking and Peking, but all three sees were vacant. Peking was ruled by a titular prelate in Nanking, and he died that year. The most remarkable element in the report is the number of Christians still active. Roughly the figure is 300,000. So we may say that though the numbers had not increased since the beginning of the troubles over a hundred years before, neither had they decreased. In the words of one of the missionaries, 'Up to the present time we have fulfilled in these parts only the ministry of preservation, and not of conquest; thanks be to God we have succeeded.'[2]

ii. The Breach in the Wall

Up to the year 1839, when England broke through the wall of isolation which China had set up round herself, no European country had aimed at more than being able to trade with her. The English action at Canton transformed the whole situation. China was now forced to look the rest of the world in the face. Thus, unlike so many other dates used in history as marking a new departure, a break, but which are not in fact so, the date 1839 is a moment in the centuries when China awoke from an almost ageless sleep.

The Manchu dynasty, ever since the seventeenth century, had done its best to shelter its people from foreigners. But the Modern Westerners were foreigners with a difference, being in the main irreligious, money-grubbing, and technically, both in peace and war, far in advance of the Chinese. Their political ideas of liberal democracy were completely alien to the Confucian

[1] A.P.F., Vol. VI, p. 181.   [2] ibid., Vol. III, No. xvi.

Monsignor Pallu, Bishop of Heliopolis

A Chinese Convert, from the painting by Sir Godfrey Kneller,
1687

graded society. The social theories of the West were surely such as to disrupt the peaceful injustice of the Chinese scene. Consequently, though the Manchu dynasty tottered on up to 1911, and dynastically there is no difference between the eighteenth and nineteenth centuries, the new arrivals, particularly those from the English-speaking world, transformed that antique setting into an arena of contending forces, and ultimately the whole fabric of Chinese society was bound to crumble as though dynamited from within.

The missionary writing home in 1842 from Macao was farsighted when he said:

> The cannons roar round the Celestial Empire . . . cities fall before the conqueror. . . . Might we be on the eve of seeing the Chinese fraternise with the other nations. . . . Everything leads us to this conclusion; policy demands it, and the cannon already exacts it. Indeed the restraints inscribed upon our monuments are already breaking down. In one of my walks I have visited one of those gates on which seemed to be written for ever: 'Thou shall not pass' . . . I, a missionary and a foreigner, have seen it, and passed beyond it and in the presence of an astonished group of Chinese. . . . The time has come for us to raise our voices, hitherto hushed, in the market places of its cities.[1]

The war, in which of course the Chinese found themselves hopelessly outclassed by the 'foreign devils'' superior technique, dragged on till 1842 when a treaty was signed at Nanking in which the Chinese were forced to open their ports and cede territory—particularly Hong Kong. But they refused to legalize the opium trade. This humiliation was imposed upon them by the British after a second war in 1858.

The Protestant English, of course, had no particular reason or wish to protect Catholic missionaries within China. There were no Protestant missionaries. In the first treaty between the two countries no provision was made for their safety. Only in 1844 was a supplementary treaty signed providing immunity for

[1] *A.P.F.*, Vol. v, pp. 420-1. Fr. Blanchin to Fr. Jurine. Macao, 14th February 1842.

missionaries, to the extent 'that they (the Chinese) should no longer put European missionaries to death'.[1]

The French, not to be outdistanced by the English and Americans, sent to Canton an Envoy Extraordinary, M. Theodore de Lagrené, with full powers to negotiate. The party arrived at Macao on 13th August 1844 and by October a treaty was signed at Whampoa on the French corvette, the *Archimède*. The items concerning religion are as follows:

> 'The French shall likewise be entitled to establish churches, hospitals, hospices, schools and cemeteries (in the five ports)' [and further on] 'If Chinese violate or destroy French churches or cemeteries, the offenders shall be punished according to the strictest interpretations of the law of the country.'[2]

The first period after the treaties, at the end of the opium war with Britain, remained one of persecution. Fr. Huc's famous journey from Tartary to Canton gives a very false idea of the situation. By an amazing piece of bravado, he paraded through China without a scratch; but only because he wore the crimson sash which signified to the mandarins that he was kith and kin of the Emperor himself. All around, along the route, he encountered terror-struck little communities of Christians not yet daring to raise their heads. At any moment a fierce burst of bigotry might, and did, break out.

Yet the journey of Fr. Huc and his companion Fr. Gabet is important in many ways. They were both members of the Lazarist Order or Congrégation de la Mission of Paris, founded by St. Vincent de Paul in 1625, and since the suppression of the Jesuits they had borne the burden of the day. Many of their company had been martyred on Chinese soil. Thus, when Fr. Huc published an account of his journeying, it received great publicity in Catholic France. On that score alone this famous journey was important. It stimulated interest. It came as a ray of light over a sombre scene. China was a 'forbidden country',

---

[1] *A.P.F.*, Vol. IX, p. 206. Letter of Fr. Clavelin, S.J., 13th October 1844.
[2] Henri Cordier, *Histoire Générale de la Chine*, Vol. IV, pp. 24–5.

you went there at the peril of your life; but you read of a Catholic missionary parading in his travels from one end of China to the other like a mandarin of the first class.

While this aspect aroused new hope in the Catholic West, the picture it presented was misleading, since it confirmed the idea that, as the result of the Chinese wars with the West, Westerners were no longer molested. In practice the earliest treaties on toleration made next to no difference to the fearful lot of the wandering and hunted priests.

On the other hand it was their fortitude which in the long run gained the admiration of the ordinary people and was the basic cause, under grace, of the conversion of so many. But at that time, of course, all was hidden in the future.

In spite of the optimistic and therefore deceptive atmosphere in the book, it contained the first news of a number of submerged local Catholic communities, particularly those in the far west, those of Szechwan, and also of Fukien.

iii. The 'A.P.F.'

Meanwhile, the missionary activity of the Catholic Church continued, and something had been started in France which was to have world-wide effects, not least in China, especially after the treaties.

A pious woman, Pauline Jaricot, of Lyons, in the year 1822 conceived the idea of creating an Association, called 'The Association for the Propagation of the Faith' and so persuading people to do two things for the foreign missions, first to pray, second to contribute a small sum regularly week by week, or month by month to help those missions. This, in spite of its small, unnoticed beginnings, grew into a world-wide movement.

Article XII of its original constitution is as follows: 'The chief means by which the Association hopes to arrive at the proposed end are prayer and gifts.'

Article XV read: 'Each Associate contributes for Missions five centimes ($\frac{1}{2}d$.) per week.'

The first year it collected a little over 22,000 francs; in 1913 about £325,000; in 1955 £4,900,000. The A.P.F. provided the sinews of war, war against ignorance of the Catholic Faith in non-Christian countries. It performed another service by publishing letters and reports from the mission fields, a worthy continuation of the famous *Lettres édifiantes et curieuses* of the preceding century. Herein can be found the first-hand information, the stuff out of which history is made. But more important, such accounts of heroism, trials, often martyrdoms, stirred the Catholic world into a response. Missionary work, which had sadly languished at the beginning of the century, now revived. Indeed the nineteenth century must surely be considered one of the great missionary periods in the history of the Church.

iv. The T'aip'ing Rebellion

In the middle of the nineteenth century two types of war overcame China and the missionaries, the first was civil war, known to history as the T'aip'ing Rebellion, the second, war with the Western Powers.

Hung Hsiu-ch'üan, the originator and leader in the T'aip'ing Rebellion, is an important figure in Chinese history not only in the political but also in the religious sphere. The rising was primarily a religious affair. He was born in 1813 thirty miles north of Canton, and in his youth was a diligent student, but never passed a public examination in the whole of his scholastic career. He was disillusioned, soured, a typical member of the intelligentsia. During one of his visits to Canton, where he failed in an examination, he came in touch with Christian doctrine but rejected it. However, when in 1837 he had failed once again and was in very bad health, he had what in modern parlance would be termed a breakdown. It was then that he began to experience visions of his future greatness. Ten years later he failed in an examination yet again, and once again he came in touch with Christians, but on this occasion he gave their teaching more serious thought. He was instructed by an American missionary, the Rev. Issachar Roberts, whom Latourette dubs eccentric but earnest.[1] He had gone out to China at his own expense, and he belonged to the American Baptist Board of Missionaries.

To return to Hung. His ecstatic visions, which were intensified perhaps by overwork, undernourishment, and similar causes, took on a Christian tinge, not fully Christian but nevertheless making use of certain Christian teachings and interpreting them, doubtless in good faith, in his own sense. He taught the existence of God, the Father, and of Jesus, Son of the Father. He taught a doctrine of Heaven and Hell, good men going to the former and bad to the latter. He and his followers believed in the Ten Commandments—with modifications. The ordinary fellow, the rank and file, had to keep to monogamy, but the leaders were allowed several wives. He himself had eighty-eight consecrated wives and innumerable concubines. It was, however, in the doctrines concerning his own person that Hung most disturbed the basic teaching of Christ. Christ was the heavenly Elder Brother and he, Hung, was the heavenly Younger Brother. There is a sense in which that could have an orthodox meaning. We are all brethren in Christ through grace. But Hung went much further; it would appear that he was not satisfied with a brotherhood of grace, he would claim a brotherhood of nature with Christ. He is said to have claimed to have had the same mother. The Bible was the book of the sect, used at their services. They kept the Sabbath day holy, sang hymns, read passages of the Old and New Testaments. About the Lord's Supper they were vague. On the other hand the enthusiasm with which they destroyed idols must have had plenty of scope. The disciples offered up animals as sacrifice and drank ritual tea. Sacrifices or offerings to ancestors were forbidden. Adults were baptized and some practised their founder's gift of ecstasy. It will be seen therefore that a very great deal of the trappings of the Christian belief were used by

[1] Kenneth Scott Latourette, *A History of Christian Missions in China*, London, 1929, published by the S.P.C.K. About 600 pages are devoted to the nineteenth and twentieth centuries, evenly distributed between Protestant and Catholic; it contains an immense bibliography, is balanced and impartial to a degree unusual in writers on such a thorny subject. My indebtedness to this great scholar is very profound.

Hung and his friends in the creating of their new sect, 'The Society of the Worshippers of Shang Ti'—Shang Ti being in Chinese a term for 'Lord of Heaven'. Hung assumed the imperial title in 1851, and by 1853 the rebels had won their more spectacular victories, capturing and burning Hankow. In the same year they took Nanking, which they made their capital. Now was the moment for a march on Peking, but this proved a failure, and the rebellion may be said to have been defeated in principle from that date. Meanwhile the European Powers looked on perplexed. By 1865 the imperial armies and a European force under Major Gordon had completely overcome the T'aip'ing armies. In so doing they granted the effete Manchu dynasty another fifty years of life, and it is even thought by some that the convulsions in China during the twentieth century might have been spared the Chinese had the T'aip'ing been acceptable and accepted by the British Government of the day.[1]

Thus, while it is true as C. P. Fitzgerald[2] stresses, that the T'aip'ing was primarily a religious revival, it was of a very peculiar kind and not an attempt to initiate China into the Western culture in its Christian entirety.[3] For quite apart from its un-Christian dogma and moral teaching, the T'aip'ing destroyed Christian churches and killed many of the faithful; hundreds were massacred in Nanking, Yangchow and Chinkiang and in other places. Yet the Manchu government saw in the T'aip'ing a Christian rebellion; consequently the Catholics were also maltreated by their armed forces and a new wave of persecution began.

To the Government the rebellion was another sign of the danger of Christianity, to the Catholics it was a proof of the danger of disseminating religious tracts, as Protestants had been doing, without explanation. To the Protestants, at first, it seemed like a break in the clouds. In fact had Hung been amenable to

---

[1] cf. A. W. Hummel, *Eminent Chinese of the Ch'ing Dynasty*, under Hung Hsiu-ch'üan.

[2] C. P. Fitzgerald, *China, A Short Cultural History*, London, 1935, p. 566.

[3] A. J. Toynbee, *A Study of History*, Vol. VIII, London, 1954, p. 327, note 3.

reason, it might have been an opportunity for social reform and being rid of the Manchu. But Hung was a fanatic who thought he was God.

v. The Wars

The war that broke out in 1857 between the Great Powers on the one hand and Imperial China on the other was even more humiliating for China than the earlier war over opium, for it reduced China finally to that state of permanent inferiority from which it emerged only after the Second World War. It began with the judicial murder of Fr. Auguste Chapdelaine and it ended with the burning to the ground of the summer palace of the emperors some miles outside the old city of Peking.

Auguste Chapdelaine was born in the Huguenot stronghold of La Rochelle, the ninth child of a farmer. He was destined for the Church from the tenderest age, but not initially for the foreign missions. After passing six years in a *petit séminaire* and then more at the *grand séminaire* of Coutances, he became a curate at Boucey. But in 1851 he withdrew to the Seminary for the Missions Étrangères in Paris and the following year he was already on his way to the Far East, and China. Within three years he had been betrayed by one of his own neophytes in Kwangsi. By good fortune the local magistrate was favourable and let him go free on parole to the town of Hsi-lin (Western Grove), a county town in the extreme west of Kwangsi. Unfortunately, when a new governor arrived, he was once again imprisoned, this time never to be liberated. It was now that he went through a slow martyrdom by torture before he was actually given the *coup de grâce*: he received three hundred strokes on the cheek; he was suspended in a cage. Finally they beheaded him outside the city; his Chinese catechist, Agnes, was martyred at the same time.

Mgr. Guillemin, Prefect Apostolic of Kwangsi sent a report of the deed to M. de Courcy, France's *chargé d'affaires* in China, asking him to intervene with the Viceroy of Kwangsi, according to article 23 of the Treaty of 1844, whereby any Frenchman taken into custody in the interior of China by

Chinese authorities, should be conducted to the nearest French consulate.

The French *chargé d'affaires* protested to the Chinese Government, which replied that Chapdelaine had broken Chinese law, and it refused to do anything about it. De Courcy informed Sir John Bowring, Minister of Great Britain to China. He informed his government at home, and the case of this Catholic missionary was given much publicity in the British Government's Blue Book on the Chinese situation.

In October two years later, 1856, some Chinese sailors, belonging to a British ship, the *Arrow*, owned by a Chinese settler in Hong Kong, and lying off Canton, were arrested by Chinese officers who boarded her and carried off twelve of the crew. The British bombarded and breached the wall of the city of Canton.[1] Meanwhile the French claimed reparations for the murder of Fr. Chapdelaine, being stung into action by the interest Protestant England had taken in their countryman. The war dragged on.

When, in 1856, Yeh Ming-ch'e, the Viceroy of Canton, was approached by the Powers with the suggestion of a peace treaty, they received the curt reply, 'No. No concessions to the barbarians.' In 1858 Canton was captured by the British, and six months later treaties were drawn up by the British and the French. But when their representatives approached the mouth of the Pei-ho for their ratification, the plenipotentiaries were fired upon by command of the Emperor. The following year the second campaign was therefore undertaken; this time the objective was the occupation of Peking itself.

When the allies were within twenty miles of the capital, the Emperor seemingly abandoned the struggle. Again plenipotentiaries were sent. This time they were ambushed and seized, and some died in chains in the Old Palace in Peking. Lord Elgin, who was in charge of the expedition, marched on the capital and took it on 13th October 1860. The British, to their shame, for

[1] *The Second China War*, edited by Bonner-Smith and Lumby, Navy Records Society, 1954.

reprisals burnt the old summer palace to the ground. The French did their share in this act of vandalism, as vividly described in *l'Illustration*.

However, that was the end of the war. By the Convention of Peking the Chinese were made to say that the Christian religion was excellent and to grant full liberty to practise it. It was now that permanent legations were established—until then the Empire had always clung to the illusion that all other nations were tributary and not sovereign—these were set up in the capital, Peking. Any Christian was allowed henceforth to appeal to the legation against Chinese law. The French legation was to have a practical monopoly in these transactions when ecclesiastics were concerned.

There was some ambiguity over the French and Chinese texts of the Convention, which differed materially in details. These differences were probably introduced partly to save the face of the Chinese. For instance, in the Chinese text, all anti-Christian legislation is 'pardoned', while in the French text it is 'abrogated'. Another reason may have been to allay the anti-clerical feeling in political circles in France; for instance the French text did not mention the right to buy land and to build; the Chinese did. It was seen that this ambiguity would lead to trouble and shortly afterwards the two texts were made to conform.

These wars were of profound importance in the history of international relations and of course in the history of the relationship between the Christians as such and the Chinese people. The liberty won for Christians had been won at the point of the sword, and it was to be maintained by the threat of force. This would not easily be forgotten; it could easily be recalled in times of anti-foreign agitation. The attacks on Chinese sovereignty, however justified they might appear to the harassed European—because of the injustice of the Chinese behaviour towards foreigners—could only appear to the Chinese as violent aggression, and for them to submit would be a stain on the honour of the race. All foreigners now seemed to them barbarians, tyrants, robbers.

vi. The French Protectorate

In this atmosphere of international unrest and war, of suspicion and even hatred of the foreigner, in this period of civil strife, the missionaries nevertheless began to make great headway, partly because they were now protected by the power of France and partly because at home the nineteenth century was one of very great prosperity.

In order to explain the legal basis upon which the French founded their right to support the missionary in China, the texts of some of the treaties and conventions must be presented here.

After the first Chinese war, M. Lagrené, the French representative, had inserted into the Whampoa Treaty of 1842 between France and China the following 22nd article:

> Every Frenchman who, in conformity with the stipulations of art. 2, arrives in one of the five ports, shall be able, whatever the length of his stay, to rent houses and warehouses for the storing of merchandise, or to acquire land and there build himself houses and warehouses. The French may also in the same manner set up churches, hospitals, hospices, schools and cemeteries. For this purpose, the local authority, after having agreed with the consul, shall designate the districts which are most suitable for the French residence and the places where the aforesaid building operations may be constructed. . . .
>
> If any Chinese violate or destroy churches or French cemeteries, those responsible should be punished according to the severest laws of the country.[1]

After the second war which ended with the Treaty of Tientsin in 1858, the 13th article of that treaty runs as follows:

> The Christian religion having as its essential purpose the leading of men to virtue, the members of all the Christian communions shall enjoy entire security in regard to their persons, their property and the free exercise of their religious practices, and an effective protection shall be granted the missionaries who go peacefully through the interior of the country, provided with regular passports, of which there has been made mention in art. 8.

[1] For this and following passages from treaties, cf. Cordier, *op. cit.*, Vol. IV, pp. III-14.

It will be noticed that the French undertake to protect not only Catholics but missionaries of any denomination.

No hindrance shall be put in the way, by the authorities of the Chinese Empire, of the acknowledged right of any person in China to embrace Christianity if he wishes and to practise its tenets, without being liable to any penalty imposed for so doing.

Everything which has been previously written, proclaimed or published in China by order of the government against the Christian religion is completely abrogated and is a dead letter in all the provinces of China.

After the capture of Peking, a Convention was there signed in 1860. The 6th article of this Convention ran as follows:

In conformity with the imperial decree issued by the august Emperor, Tao-kuang, on 20th March, 1846, religious and charitable institutions which have been confiscated from the Christians during the persecutions of which they have been the victims, shall be restored to their owners through the mediation of his Excellency the Minister of France in China, to whom the Imperial Government will hand them over, together with the cemeteries and other buildings which depend upon them.

The last article quoted seemed to imply that all property ever confiscated from the Catholics had to be restored. This, of course, was not the intention of the framers of the article, nor was this property restored. However, such buildings as the famous church, the Nan T'ang, in Peking were given back to the Catholics and also the sites where the others had stood, the Pei T'ang, the Hsi T'ang and the Tung T'ang.

Another representative of France, in order to clarify the wording, had a further Convention signed in 1865 called the Berthemy Convention. This again was definitively drawn up after some minor alterations in 1895. It is in the latter form that it is given here: 'In future, if French missionaries buy land or houses in the interior of the country, the seller . . . must specify in drawing up the act of sale, that his property has been sold in order to become part of the collective goods of the Catholic missions of the locality. . . .'

The purpose of this was, apparently, to emphasize to the Chinese that the land had not been alienated from Chinese ownership, nor passed into the hands of a foreigner, but that it still remained Chinese property, though Christian Chinese property. Alone of all foreigners, the missionaries thus were able in practice to own land outside the Treaty Ports and in the interior.

It would be an error to suppose that the earliest of these treaties was the prelude to actual peace. It is true that the Catholic missionaries now went about the country openly, that property was bought, that churches and schools were built. Indeed this was an unimaginable release from living in hiding and being hunted from village to village. But persecution burst out fiercely from time to time during almost all the second half of the nineteenth century and in most of the provinces. Sometimes it was, as it were, by accident that the Christians were killed; this occurred when the Mohammedan minority in the western provinces would rise against their masters. More often an attack would be positively anti-Christian or at least anti-foreign. Thus in 1867–9 in Kwangtung Catholic priests and their converts and their mission houses were attacked. In 1868 in the province of Chihli at Hienhien a priest was killed and the following year an orphanage was pillaged. In that year the missionaries of Hankow were stoned in the streets of the town. In the same period hundreds of Christians were killed in Kweichow. The French, in order to protect their nationals and the Christians sent two warships to Nanking.

Christ, so it seemed to the Chinese onlooker, was coming not with a Cross but with the sword, and the fateful prophecy must have been present to the minds of the more thoughtful, that those who take up the sword, perish by it. This question of the forcible defence of the rights of Christians to live as Christians is an age-old one, and will not be opened here. It is the fact that a historian must record, and the effects of its use. The Chinese responded in their inscrutable way, much as any subject people has always done. Resentment filled their hearts. In the long run the Portuguese protectorate had proved harmful, the same could be said of the French protectorate. Are these lessons we can learn today?

As an example of the Chinese reaction we may take an extremely significant and ominous Chinese attack on Christianity, which comes from Hunan in 1869; it was a placard circulated through the length and breadth of the Empire. Hosea Ballou Morse summarizes it as follows:

> The adherents of Christianity do not honour their ancestors nor the spiritual powers; converts are required, in proof of sincerity, to destroy the sacrificial tablets of their ancestors.

This was an old complaint and in substance true.

> Baptism is essential, and for it an unguent is made from the corpses of priests; this is administered with a stupefying drug, to the chanting of a magic charm. The convert is thereby so fortified that, even under persecution, he must cling to his folly.

This and most of the rest is sheer fabrication, but none the less good propaganda.

> 3. After this ceremonial the converts are afflicted with madness, so that they take their ancestral tablets and break them into a thousand pieces, destroy all idols, and even raze to the ground every sacred temple they may come across. 4, 5 and 6 (too obscene to be printed). 7. When an adherent of this religion is on his death-bed, his co-religionists require his relatives to leave the room, while they read prayers for his soul. In reality, however, while the body is still breathing, they take out the eyes and tear out the heart, to be used in making counterfeit money, for, as they allege, the prayers assure his eternal salvation, but the body is then no more than a broken tabernacle. 8. To make converts, they count much on the power of money. The poor silly fools, to sell their souls for a little money. 9. The propagandists of this religion employ reciters and physiognomists, both men and women, to entice people by their smooth words. Then they take them off, men and women, and sell them to depraved foreigners; sometimes their bodies are even used as ground bait for the fisheries of the south seas. (An allusion to the evils of emigration.) 10. Foreign merchants claim, under the treaties, entire exemption from foreign control over their trading

operations, and the missionaries are the spies of these trading bandits. It is said, too, that the religious bandits have destroyed the temple of Confucius in Shantung; but the people rose, killing some and driving out the rest. Alas! If the doctrines of Jesus drive out the teaching of Confucius, what sort of a world will it become? Let each of us draw the sword for vengeance. If any refuse to join in the common cause, they are even as these outrageous creatures.[1]

These words have the same ring that the attacks made against the Christians had in the early centuries, when they were being persecuted and killed by the officials of the Roman Empire. The Communists produced much the same accusations when they came to power in 1949.

In endless succession periods of persecution followed periods of peace during the second half of last century. Thus the Tientsin Massacre may be taken as a symbol of this uneasy arrangement. In 1858 the French had made use of an old temple-cum-palace as their headquarters. This was insulting enough. But when in 1869 the French missionaries added the further insult of building their cathedral in the town on the very site of the temple, the Chinese could contain themselves no longer. The actual incident to start the massacre was an epidemic in the home of the Sisters of Mercy. They made a habit of paying people to bring in the abandoned children. Some of these employees are supposed to have, and indeed may have, kidnapped some children in order to get their pay. Dying children were also accepted. But during an epidemic as many as thirty-four of these children died. Rumours were not slow in spreading that the nuns had killed the children. Crowds mobbed the convent and disinterred the bodies. The French consul, who should have kept his head, threatened a Chinese official with a pistol; he even went to the length of firing it, and hit one of the official's servants. The mob killed the consul and fired the cathedral, destroyed the convent and also the Protestant stations and chapels. For three hours the massacre continued.

[1] Morse and McNair, *Far Eastern International Relations*, U.S.A., 1931, pp. 278–9.

vii. The Geographical Distribution in the Mid-nineteenth Century

In mid-nineteenth century the missionary societies were located in China as follows. The Dominicans were still in Fukien, with their base in Manila and ultimate base at Santo Tomás in the valley at the feet of the walled city of Avila in Old Castile. They had been in Fukien through good times and bad since the early seventeenth century. Now life was to be bearable once again. They were thus able to consolidate their position. The Jesuits, dissolved a century before, had now returned to China, but not to Peking, which was the province of the Lazarists who had taken on their tasks. In 1842 the Society of Jesus was given Kiangsu, Anhwei and south-east Chihli. Five years later they settled at Zi-ka-wei near Shanghai, which later became their Observatory. The Paris Missions Étrangères were spread out over Kweichow, Yunnan, Kwangsi, Kwangtung and even Manchuria and Tibet. The Franciscans had immense areas: Shansi, Shensi, Hupei, Hunan and Shantung. Most of their missionaries came from Italy, but it was not usual for Frenchmen and Germans to join them. The Lazarists were in the old Jesuit areas: Hopei, Kiangsi, Honan and Chekiang. But these for all their zeal were not numerous enough to cope with the new situation provided by the French protectorate; thus the second half of the nineteenth century saw the arrival of newcomers to the Chinese missionary fields. The Milan Foreign Missionary Society went to Hong Kong in 1858, the Scheut Fathers to Mongolia in 1865, the Augustinians returned in 1879 to Hunan. The first two were new institutions and form part of the immense revival of missionary fervour in the Church. The Steyl Society of the Divine Word, of the German province, went to China in 1879. It was to be from the ranks of this new Society that would come China's first Cardinal. The Roman Seminary of SS. Peter and Paul came six years later. An unusual experiment, and one destined to provide China with some of its finest confessors during the Communist persecutions, was begun in 1883, when the Trappists started a foundation.

Another innovation was the sending out of nuns. Very

fittingly the first to venture, since the Lazarists had already laboured in China so long, were the Sisters of St. Vincent de Paul, who went in 1847; in the following year the Sisters of St. Paul de Chartres. There were others, the Canossian Sisters, the Helpers of the Holy Souls, the Franciscan Missionaries of Mary, Dominican Sisters and finally Carmelites, who made a foundation in Shanghai. Such a list as the above can give no idea of the heroic work done, it can only demonstrate that the Chinese mission was far from stagnant in the second half of the nineteenth century.

Statistics in the early years of the century are inevitably unreliable, and to some minds dull, but they give some indication; and it is roughly estimated that at a minimum there were close on a quarter of a million Catholics in China in 1800, and that half a century later the figure had risen by another hundred thousand. In 1900 the figure given is three-quarters of a million, which shows a remarkable increase during the second half of the century. This was clearly manifested to the world by the increase during the same period in the hierarchical divisions. In 1844 there were only ten such divisions, in 1865 this was more than doubled, being twenty-two vicariates and prefectures. In 1900 we find this figure itself was nearly doubled. There were forty-one.

The problems nevertheless remained fundamentally the same as they were before the great onslaught on the missions at the beginning of the eighteenth century. The Catholic Christians were not permitted to pay the ritual respect to Confucius or to their ancestors which was customary among the Chinese. They could not aim at office in the State nor compete in the public examinations, as these required such ritual acts of respect to be performed. Thus the Christians came from the uneducated portion of the community, and consequently could have no standing in the political or intellectual life of the country.

The problem of native priests still remained acute, and this concentration of the faithful in the uneducated classes increased the problem. The long training, the cost, the Latin language, all remained obstacles that only the more heroic and patient and persistent would surmount. China in consequence still remained

Dom Celestine Lou

Father Vincent Lebbe

from the Catholic Church's point of view a markedly missionary country.

One of the old problems appeared to be in the course of solution. The great persecution of 1724 had had as one of its professed reasons the fact that in the Dominican churches in Fukien there was a mingling of men and women. Up to that time and also for many years after also, women did not go to the men's churches. This disability was a considerable inconvenience not only to the women but also to the church officials; yet, to have broken with the custom at the time would have offended the susceptibilities of the Chinese. The change came first in Peking in the early part of the nineteenth century when Mgr. Mouly was Vicar Apostolic. He successfully broke with the tradition of separation at the request of the faithful themselves. At first the arrangement was that the women should be on one side of the nave with a barrier cutting them off from the other. Then the barrier was taken down. Then women went in by one door and the men by another. This advance took place about the year 1860. When the Hsi T'ang church was rebuilt, it was built without a women's chapel.[1]

Owing to the enhanced standing of Christians, as a result of the recent treaties, another problem arose, which was to distinguish between genuine conversion and the conversion of a man with an eye to the main chance. This was all the more difficult as, by the new legal arrangement, any Christian could claim to be judged by the French law. All he had to do was to put himself under the protection of the missionary on the spot. In the province of Kweichow, evangelized by the Missions Étrangères of Paris, when Mgr. Faurie was bishop, a group of Chinese estimated at one hundred thousand asked for conversion. It is true that Faurie had mediated between the rebels and the Government, but neither he nor his fellow missionary, Lions, had any illusions; they suspected that the motive of these would-be

---

[1] On Mgr. Mouly's first arrival in Peking, the local Christians asked him, 'Are you an astronomer, a painter, a clock-maker?' He answered, 'God wants the Christian religion to be spread now by humility, suffering and the cross.' cf. B. de Vaulx, *Histoire des Missions Catholiques françaises*, Paris, 1951, p. 311.

converts was 'to put themselves outside the power of Chinese injustice'.[1]

Neither Faurie in Kweichow nor Mouly in Peking had any hesitation in accepting the indemnities after the T'aip'ing Rebellion. The latter used the considerable sum he received in order to rebuild the ancient churches of Peking. The former claimed 50,000 francs, even demanding compensation for the loss of clothing of one of his priests, Fr. Lions, and 90 taels for wounds received. They were paid.[2]

The Holy See, specially through Propaganda, kept the problems of China continually in mind. As early as 1845 Propaganda urged the Chinese Church to have regular synods and even proposed that one should meet in the winter of 1849 or 1850 at Hong Kong; it put forward very definite proposals regarding the hierarchy: three archiepiscopal sees, one in Peking, another at Chengtu, a third at Kaichow, and with the astonishing suggestion that Peking should have thirteen suffragan sees, Chengtu nine and Kaichow eight. Not unnaturally the Vicars Apostolic were opposed to these vast ideas.

Nevertheless, Rome took advantage of the meeting together of the Vicars Apostolic in the Holy City for the Vatican Council in 1870 to discuss their common problems, including the burning one of Chinese clergy. It was decided 'neither too much to depreciate them nor too much to raise their self-esteem'. The secretaries of the Sacred Congregations were asked not to give to the Chinese clergy too high-sounding titles. Such things went to their heads. When the first all-China Synod met in Hong Kong in 1880 the views of the leaders of the Catholic Church in those parts had not changed. It was agreed that for the time being until circumstances changed, the missionaries should be in charge of the Chinese clergy. It was to take the Western missionaries nearly a century before they were ready to admit Chinese to equality as workers in the Lord's vineyard.

[1] cf. A. Launay, *Histoire des Missions de la Chine, Mission du Kouy Tcheou*, Tome II, p. 350.
[2] *ibid.*, pp. 11–12.

viii. The Use of the Printed Word

The printing press in the second half of the nineteenth century became one of the chief agents of propaganda the world over. At the same time the printed word became a major influence in the spread of the message of Christ. Just as there were difficulties in this matter peculiar to China, such as the Government's suspicion of any printing press, the difficulties of making a fount, of training technicians, so China presented certain advantages. If they could read at all, those countless millions could read, in their own almost different languages, the same printed page, since the signs on them were not letters but ideographs. Not only the Chinese but the Koreans, the Japanese and the Vietnamese peoples also can read the Chinese ideographs.

While it is true that the use of the printed word in China developed widely only in the nineteenth century, the early missionaries had not been idle. The present writer can remember browsing in Mr. Dawson's shop in Wigmore Street, London, and finding there a beautifully printed book on astronomy, the very first printed by the French Jesuits in China, c. 1700, with the signatures of that distinguished group printed at the end.

Fr. Ricci was printing works on Christian doctrine in Chinese at his press in Peking in the seventeenth century. In 1622 Mgr. Pallu, before leaving Paris, had the liturgy printed there, with spaces between the lines left blank for inserting the native languages. In 1672 M. Langlois of the same Society proposed having a printing press at Juthia in Siam. The press set up by the Jesuits in Peking was not abandoned when the Society was suppressed; the Lazarists took it over, carrying on the good work. But the end of the eighteenth and the beginning of the following century were troubled times and not ideally suited to such works of peace.

On the other hand, by the end of the nineteenth century the Catholics in China had three great printing centres, that of the Lazarists in Peking, already mentioned, a Jesuit installation in Shanghai, and in Hong Kong the printing works of the Missions

Étrangères. In the present century one might add that of the Salesians at Macao and another at Peking, set up by the Society of the Divine Word in connection with the one-time university in Peking. All these were completely up to date with their machines and methods of printing and binding.

In order to give some idea of how seriously this work of printing had taken hold of the minds of the missionaries, a few statistics tell their own tale. Besides these major institutions already mentioned, many others existed before the Communists confiscated them all. There were two each in Manchuria and Shansi, Kiangsu and Szechwan, three each in Hopei, Hupei and Kwangtung, and one each in Hunan, Chekiang and Fukien.

To return to the chief centres; the Lazarists at the Pei T'ang printing works in Peking between 1864 and 1930 produced more than five hundred publications in Chinese, Mongolian, Tibetan, French, Latin, English, German, Flemish, Italian, Spanish; all this was achieved in spite of the fact that part of the machinery had been melted down for ammunition during the Boxer Rising. The matter published included grammars, prayer-books, theology and the works of Huc. Incidentally, they were also the printers to the Chinese railways and of the Chinese Law books.

The Jesuit venture began with an act of mercy. In 1848–50 a severe famine occurred in the neighbourhood of the Jesuit mission at Zi-ka-wei. The Fathers founded an orphanage in order to deal with the abandoned children, the orphanage of Tu-ssŭ-wei. As occupation a printing press was annexed to it, and by 1870 it was well in its stride. When therefore the Aurora University was first launched at that mission, ready to hand was the printing, which increased enormously in importance and quality. The school of the *Hautes Études industrielles et commerciales* started in 1923 at Tientsin provided more grist for the mill; then there was the Jesuit observatory at Zi-ka-wei which provided yet more work. The chief fame of this press is, however, its publication of the learned sinological studies of such scholars as Fr. Havret, for example the *Variétés Sinologiques*, which by 1936 had reached sixty volumes. In this way the latter-day Jesuits hoped to emulate their forefathers. But times were different and the age was that of the common man.

The press of the Missions Étrangères had an eventful career. In 1884 it began on the deserted but sacred Island of Sancian, where St. Francis had breathed his last. The threat of pirates forced it to move to Macao, but the unfriendliness of the Portuguese sent it scurrying over to the neighbouring British Island of Hong Kong. The scheme thought out by its initiators was that there should be a rest and retreat house for the Fathers on the mission stations where they, in their leisure hours, would lend a hand, albeit an amateur hand, to the permanent staff, in the lesser skilled departments of the work. Before the *débâcle* of the present time this press had three rotary printing machines in full production.

B. THE PROTESTANT MISSIONS

i. *Introduction, the Early Days*

It is not unfair to say that the Protestant bodies in Europe during the seventeenth and eighteenth centuries had very little interest indeed in spreading the Faith beyond the bounds of their own countries, and none at all in doing so in China. This is not the place to discover the reason, but the fact is important. Though the Dutch and the English were in Far Eastern waters in the first half of the seventeenth century, their activities in those parts consisted often enough, from the religious point of view, only in spreading untrue and dangerous rumours about the Catholic missionaries, or in behaving in such an unruly way as to jeopardize the whole missionary work of the Catholic Europeans. In this they were not worse than most of their Portuguese opposite numbers, the merchants for whom St. Francis Xavier had few good words.

Caron,[1] who worked for the Dutch, remains one of the greatest and most trustworthy sources of information, for the Dutch, who made this infiltration, of which he had charge, had no illusions on this point. We might be tempted to suspect a

[1] François Caron, *A True Description of the Mighty Kingdoms of Japan and Siam*, London, 1935.

Catholic who wrote in this strain; but Caron is speaking from the Dutch side.

He wrote a long and detailed account of Dutch activities in the Far East, particularly the founding of Dutch trading centres in Japan. He lived there many years, and witnessed more than one persecution of the Catholics; his evidence is therefore first hand.

The Dutch in the Far East were interested in trade and did not hesitate to stoop to the lowest means in order to discredit their rivals, the Portuguese. An example, though concerning Japan and not China, may be allowed. When the news of the martyrdom of the heroic Fr. Sebastico Vieyka in Japan (1633) reached Macao, the populace and notables were proud of him; he had, in their eyes, done the noblest act a man could perform: offered his life for the Faith. They celebrated his martyrdom by horse-races, pageants and fireworks as well as by *Te Deums*. An account of these festivities got into the hands of the Dutch. Immediately they sent a copy to the Japanese Government in order to discredit the Portuguese the more.

It is precisely this kind of international back-biting, designed to undermine the confidence of Japanese and Chinese Governments in the Portuguese, which did such immense harm to the Catholic missions. The example of the Philippines was repeatedly quoted: the Spaniards had come to convert and remained to conquer. That was the fate awaiting any nation which allowed Catholic priests within its borders. The cruellest persecution ever undergone by the Church, that experienced by the Japanese converts, was in great measure the result of this dishonourable and underhand propaganda. In China, the exquisite tact of Fathers Ricci, Schall, Verbiest and others staved off the blow for some time.

The first appearance of the English at the mouth of the Pearl river at Canton was not calculated to reassure the Chinese as to the pacific intentions of the new arrivals. It was in 1637. Instead of abiding by the subtle rules of procedure laboriously distilled as it were by the Portuguese and Chinese authorities, they left Macao, advanced up the estuary, disembarked at Canton and, having roused the extreme anger of the Chinese, who attacked them, they seized a fort. In the end, by the good offices of the Portuguese—who must have been very relieved to see them go—they left Macao in December of the same year.

The attitude of hostility was mutual between the newcomers and the Portuguese, who lost no opportunity of preventing the English from getting a foothold. But the Dutch and English were interested only in trade, the Portuguese also in missionary work.

Another incident, which showed both the unruly spirit of the Dutch of that time and the delicate position in which the Portuguese missionaries were placed, is that of the Dutch attack on Macao in 1622.

This attack was unprovoked; it was undertaken in a spirit of commercial and political rivalry. Its effect was a serious threat of persecution. The Portuguese, who got wind of the impending attack, set about fortifying the city, putting up earthworks. It was to the omniscient Jesuits that they appealed—and not in vain. But these military preparations were looked upon, not unnaturally, with very considerable suspicion by the Chinese. It took much patient explaining to persuade the Chinese officials that the fortifications were not being erected against them.

In one place, Formosa, which the Dutch used as a base for commercial operations with China, they did a little evangelizing. The English, who abandoned the Far East for the time being, did none.

It was in the nineteenth century that Protestants awoke to the necessity of spreading their faith. This is not the place to account for their sudden emergence as missionary churches. Perhaps the spirit of Wesley, himself an apostle of untiring energy and faith, is at the root of this growth in missionary endeavour.

Exhaustive research into the history of missions in China during the last hundred years has been done by Professor Latourette and need not be done again here; the results of that monumental labour are clearly set forth in his book. This chapter is largely indebted to his excellent account.[1]

[1] Latourette, *op. cit.*, p. 219.

The earliest period, which extends to the treaty after the second Chinese war in 1856, is one of remote preparation. There was practically no penetration of the country: the Bible was translated by Dr. Morrison; a college was set up at Malacca—the Anglo-Chinese College—with William Milne in charge (1818), and, strangest of all efforts at evangelization in the whole history of missionary technique, boxes of Bibles were floated off in Chinese waters with the hope that they would drift ashore, be opened and read.

ii. The Nineteenth Century

(a) The First Arrivals

Dr. Morrison, being the pioneer among Protestant missionaries to China, deserves special notice. He was born in Northumberland in 1782; in his youth he learnt Latin, Greek and Hebrew, and in spite of almost insuperable difficulties, which included the Napoleonic Wars, he set off for China via New York in 1807, as a missionary attached to the London Missionary Society. Arrived at Canton he was not well received by the Catholic clergy, but he persisted. Already he had transcribed a copy of the New Testament in Chinese which he had found in the British Museum, now he set to work to translate and print the whole Bible. This task he completed in 1824.

As it was impossible, or rather exceedingly dangerous, to penetrate into the mainland, he divided his time between Canton and Macao, taking on work as employee and translator to the East India Company. At the time of his death in 1834 he had received ten converts. His remains were buried in Macao.

The Catholic priests from Europe who were spread throughout the Empire attended to the needs of Catholics, but they could not preach openly. The Protestants had no 'faithful' yet and therefore their presence in China was almost useless until such time as the permission to preach openly the word of God was granted.

In 1800 not a single Protestant Christian lived in China, no 'Anglican' Chinese, no Wesleyans, no Quakers, no Calvinists, no Congregationalists. The only Christians in China. were

Catholics, scattered in isolated pockets everywhere, a down-trodden minority; and a few Orthodox lived round about Peking. In 1853, after fifty years of growing effort, the number of Protestants amounted to 350 communicants; but in 1889[1] the number was 37,289. This phenomenal increase demands an explanation. Catholics too, had increased with rapidity, but the Protestant figure is the more astonishing. Catholics in 1800 are estimated, as we have said, at about a quarter of a million; in 1850 they were about 330,000 and in 1890 near the half million.

The most important reason for the success of the Protestant missions was undoubtedly their zeal. They were indefatigable, giving both of their time and of their wealth. The directness of their approach, the very simplicity of it, must have appealed to the simple Chinese. It was, too, a democratic approach, befitting the Age of Democracy, where the poor were as good as the rich, and indeed even more important.

The great increase at this time of Protestant and Catholic was, of course, the result also of the increased liberty of movement for the missionary. But the Protestant now had certain material advantages over the Catholic. It was the English-speaking world which was sending Protestant missionaries; they were wealthier and better equipped with the material benefits of scientific discovery. It was, too, the English devil who had beaten the Chinese in war and the Chinese were ready to learn from their conquerors even if they heartily detested them.

Lastly, and this is not said in disparagement but merely as a contributory factor in the situation, most of the Protestant missionaries for whom 'Conversion' was the fundamental tenet, believed in the less dogmatic form of Protestantism. Thus reception into the communion of these bodies was simpler than to become a Catholic.

In the period between the two nineteenth-century wars against China the Protestant bodies, mostly from England and America, confined their activities to the Treaty Ports and to making

[1] Latourette, *op. cit.*, p. 479.

excursions of twenty to thirty miles inland. It was a period of reconnoitring and exploration. Some men, later to be very well known, were learning the work: Medhurst, Griffiths, John, Legge. The chief organizations concerned were the London Missionary Society, which moved its college from Malacca to Hong Kong—Medhurst, for example, went to Shanghai. The American Board of Commissioners for Foreign Missions got moving as early as 1843; the American Presbyterians sent D. B. McCartee to Ningpo in 1844, others followed later. The Protestant Episcopal Church in the United States had Boone made bishop and he too went to Shanghai. The American Baptists had missionaries in four Treaty Ports by 1856. The Church Missionary Society had two members in Ningpo in 1848. Gutzlaff wrote from Hong Kong and roused Germans to missionary ardour. Besides all these, American Methodists, English Wesleyans, English Presbyterians and others sent earnest missionaries. This was a bewildering array of Christian messages.

Yet, as Latourette remarks: 'In spite of the community of interest and purpose among Protestants, little attempt was made to approach China unitedly.'[1] In the matter of translating the Bible, however, some measure of co-operation was attained.

The methods used in these early days were the dissemination of the Bible, the setting up of educational establishments and medical centres.

As the Protestants rarely ventured outside the Treaty Ports they shared little in the persecutions suffered by the Catholics.

It is of interest that during the first twenty-six years of Protestant missionary activity in China (1834–60) the Americans outnumbered the English by two to one. The United States opposed the trade in opium. They had therefore from the Chinese point of view a more legitimate right to come and teach the Chinese the moral law than the English, whose compatriots seemed by their actions not to care a jot for that code. While the British Government neither opposed opium smuggling nor defended it, the United States officials opposed it.

[1] *op. cit.*, p. 261.

The first true American missionary for China was Dr. Elijah Coleman Bridgman; he deserves fame not only for being the first from the New World to the Old but because he founded the *Chinese Repository*, a periodical rightly famous since it did immense work in spreading information about China, not only among the Europeans who lived on its borders or within it, but all over the world wherever it was sent. He had come to China in 1829, sent out by the American Board of Commissioners for Foreign Missions, together with a David Abeel, whose business was to be the spiritual care of American sailors in Chinese waters. The latter soon left, but only to carry on a great crusade for the missionary field. Bridgman received the inestimable help of a press in 1831; it was through this that he was able to begin the *Chinese Repository*.

In 1845 twenty American male Protestant missionaries were in China, but only ten English and one German. In three years time the position was even more in America's favour, which had forty-four to the nineteen English, two German and two Swiss. To take another sample, in 1855 there were twenty-four English and forty-six American.

The dissemination of Christian literature by Protestants, enthusiasts for the written Word, helped unwittingly to produce a most surprising result. The T'aip'ing Rebels were, as has been said, certainly in sentiment a quasi-Christian sect, created by enthusiasts who had read these tracts.

The indiscriminate spread of Protestant literature indirectly provided the pseudo-spiritual background for the T'aip'ing Rebellion (1850–65) which was, doubtless, at root the uprising of land-hungry peasants. In lives the Rebellion cost China 20,000,000, while eleven provinces were laid waste.[1]

The Tientsin and Peking Treaties of 1858 and 1860, which followed, opened the door into China in a manner that had not occurred since the imperial edict of 1692. Both Catholics and Protestants took full advantage of the new freedom. The first phase lasted until the Boxer Rising in 1900; the second phase,

[1] *Encyclopedia Sinica*, p. 589.

which began in 1900, was for the missionaries a matter of accommodating themselves to the changing political conditions following on the slow collapse of the Manchu dynasty and the rise of the Chinese democracy.

Mgr. Michael Navarro, Vicar Apostolic of Hunan, gives an interesting sidelight on the effect of the first appearance of Protestant missionaries in their midst.

> At the beginning of April, 1865, we suffered painful trials. Three American Protestant ministers arrived in Hangchow towards the end of March. It was the time of the general examinations, and the number of students had risen to at least ten thousand. The arrival of the strangers excited general emotion, produced by the unheard of sight of Europeans who were not clothed in Chinese fashion. The latter, becoming frightened, took refuge in the tribunal of the prefect. But the excitement among the students was so great, that it was feared this asylum would not be sufficiently safe, and the strangers returned to their ship on the advice even of the prefect. The students threw themselves into boats, crossed the river, and entered the ship. ... On the following morning, the public papers contained the most horrible accusations, and appealed to the popular passions, exciting the people to kill all the Europeans, and to destroy, as they did before,[1] our church and our dwelling.[2]

The only security was to appeal to the French legation, and peace was restored.

It would be tedious to catalogue all the multitudinous Protestant Societies that spread their wings over China in those first thirty to forty years. But three points may be observed. Those Societies which were already there did not each spread right through China, but, as it were, staked out a claim only to a part. It was like a spiritual partition process. The second point is that almost all the organizations were evangelical, not what today the members themselves would call 'Catholic or Anglo-Catholic'. The word and the idea of 'Catholic' were abhorrent. The Catholic Church was not the mother of churches but the 'scarlet woman' and so forth.

[1] In 1862 the bishop's house, two churches, etc., had been burnt.
[2] *A.P.F.*, Vol. xxviii, pp. 84 ff.

In the words of Professor Latourette:

In all these pioneering efforts Roman Catholic missionaries were practically ignored. To the Protestant it was as if the Catholics had never come to China. Protestants nearly always thought of themselves as the sole representatives of the Gospel and spoke of 'opening' cities and provinces to the Christian message even when Catholics had been there before them. This was natural. By the average Protestant of the time Rome was thought of as anti-Christ. At best, Roman Catholicism was regarded as a corrupt form of Christianity from which the Reformers had, at great cost and suffering, escaped to restore the Gospel in its purity.

Then note that the Professor goes on to say, and doubtless justly: 'The Roman Catholic, on the other hand, had nothing kind to say of the Protestants. They were as he believed, dangerous heretics who were hindering the work of Christ.'[1] This state of affairs could not but have a bad effect upon the would-be convert, who was taught the doctrine of universal love as the essential of the Christian faith, and yet beheld unseemly and sometimes bitter disputes between the apostles of this message.

One organization, and one only did in fact aim at covering the whole area, the famous China Inland Mission inspired and organized by Hudson Taylor.

(b) *James Hudson Taylor and the Pioneers*

James Hudson Taylor was born in 1832 in Barnsley in the West Riding of Yorkshire. He was a Yorkshireman by birth, and he seems to have had the dogged temperament which we associate with that part of England. His pious parents always hoped he would become a missionary. This he did. He went to China first in 1853 as a preacher for the Chinese Evangelization Society. Ill-health, however, forced him to return home; but instead of giving up the struggle he worked with almost superhuman energy at medicine and then returned to the land of his choice.

The most outstanding qualities of the man were his utter reliance

[1] *op. cit.*, p. 361.

on God and his consequent optimism. Within his lifetime he had covered China with missionaries after his own heart. He had begun with little money and less backing. Another characteristic was the almost extreme view that no man could be saved unless he had heard and accepted the true Gospel. Now, most of the Chinese had never heard of the Gospel at all, and, as he thought, those who had, knew only a false gospel, that preached by the Catholic Church, an institution which was for him anathema. The idea that so many souls were going to hell oppressed his soul.

At his death in 1905 there were nearly a thousand missionaries of the organization which he had founded, the China Inland Mission. His first appeal in 1865 was for two dozen helpers. By 1866 they were on their way. In 1876 he made an appeal for eighteen and they were forthcoming; five years later for seventy and within two years they were on their way; in 1886 there was an appeal for a hundred and they came. Hudson Taylor had an appeal made for a thousand, to fill the ranks of the various Protestant missions, and they were provided.[1]

The China Inland Mission was peculiar in many ways. In the first place it was undenominational. It did not link itself with any special Church: any man could join its ranks provided he accepted the doctrines of Heaven and Hell, the Trinity, the Fall, the Redemption through Christ the Son of God; the Bible was the only rule of faith. In time the members grouped themselves into their respective Churches and were concentrated in certain parts of China; thus the Anglicans were in Szechwan.

The second peculiarity of the Mission was its unconcern about setting up a church or worshipping community in those parts where its agents went. This activity it left to the groups concerned, believing that for itself the allotted task was the spreading by word of mouth and by literature of the *Gospel*. As soon as 'the Churches' created communities in various towns, the Mission withdrew and sought out remote and untouched areas. The third peculiarity was this: its members imitated the Society of Jesus in that they wore Chinese costume.

[1] Latourette, *op. cit.*, pp. 389–91.

Anyone wishing to have a modern and no doubt typical account of the work of members belonging to the China Inland Mission could scarcely do better than read *Through Jade Gate and Central Asia* by Mildred Cable and Francesca French. Perhaps in the earlier days the hardships were greater and the risks more perilous, but the spirit is the same. It is not for the present writer to criticize the method or the ideals; the sincerity is undoubted.

In contrast to the purely evangelical approach to China, which had more in common with that of the early Franciscans, is the work undertaken by Timothy Richard, in its way so akin to the technique of the Jesuits. But just as the China Inland Mission lacked the central idea of a church or institution, which of course the Franciscans possessed in its fullness, so did the activity of Timothy Richard lack anything approaching the theological, or dogmatic formation characteristic of the Jesuits. While the Franciscans tramped through the countryside preaching Christ Crucified, as Hudson Taylor did, yet they created mission centres, churches, a stable Christian life; and while the Jesuits became the greatest intellectual force at the court of the Chinese Emperor, they also preached the full Catholic doctrine.

Timothy Richard was a sincere believer of the Baptist persuasion. Born in 1845 in Wales, he had been converted as a youth during one of those Revivalist meetings so typical both of the nineteenth century and of Wales. He joined the English Baptist Missionary Society and reached China in 1870. Perhaps it was the experience of the great famine in Shansi, where he helped in the relief work, that turned his mind to the purely secular side of Chinese life. It was clear to him that the Chinese, besides needing the Gospel, needed Western knowledge. What Ricci, Verbiest and Schall had done in the past he would do in his own times.

The chief methods used by Richard were the press and education. He became Secretary of the Society for the Diffusion of Christian and General Knowledge in 1891. He saw to the foundation of the first public school for Chinese in Shanghai and of the University in Shensi. Lastly, he made a point of getting in touch with the official class. In this he was closely following the Jesuits. But in the nineteenth century it came again as an innovation, because the mandarin class had lost touch with the Christian message as a result of the Rites controversy.

Regardless of public opinion among his fellow workers, he left the poor and associated with the ruling class, in order, as he would have said, the better to help the poor. He was the friend of the leading liberals, he associated with officials of all kinds. It seemed that the time had arrived for the 'great awakening' of China. But it was to be a hope not so soon fulfilled.

The nineteenth-century Chinese were in a more unhappy position than their forebears. It might have been possible for them to catch up with the West in the physical sciences in the days of Matteo Ricci. But, they missed that opportunity, and by the time the great Western Powers were once again beating at their gates, this time more peremptorily, they were too late to compete, they were outclassed. But having been so sadly distressed by what must have seemed to the Chinese an almost unbelievable military defeat and humiliation in 1858 and 1860, with foreign troops in the capital and its palace burnt, the time had come to discover why it was that the 'foreign devils' had been so successful. That was Timothy Richard's opportunity and he took it.

The Chinese Government proved, however, to be so incapable of admitting this cultural defeat that, instead of putting their house in order, they allowed themselves to be led by the fatuous and criminal Dowager Empress, and she did nothing; or rather she actively impeded reform and ruthlessly persecuted reformers. An obscurantist attitude was encouraged, and these enlightened missionaries were associated with hatred of the foreigners. There were good reasons, too, for this animosity. Opium was the curse of China and the English were making a fortune out of the tragedy.

When the Boxer disturbances began in 1900 they were cleverly twisted by the Government into an anti-foreign demonstration.

The ensuing massacres were grievously detrimental both to the Catholic and Protestant missions. The former were almost inured to such things; for the latter this horror was in many cases their first experience, and their demeanour was worthy of the name they professed.

During the riots much Protestant property was destroyed and many missionaries lost their lives. At first sight it seemed to be a major calamity; but it proved in the long run a great incentive. Here was a present-day story of Christian heroism, the age of the early Church revived.

c. THE BOXER RISINGS

The political life of China and its international relations are for the religious historian not alien matters, but closely linked with the fate of the missionary efforts. This fact has been abundantly proved throughout the history of Christianity in China, from the first suppression of the Nestorians to this latest incident of the Boxer Rising. It has been even more abundantly shown in the last development of all, the ruthless Communist crushing of Christians.

The Boxer Rising was no sudden and unexpected occurrence. It was the fatal and almost inevitable result of the pressure put upon China by the foreign Powers, standing round her like vultures to devour her at the first signs of collapse. That moment came when China was soundly defeated by her neighbour Japan in 1894-5. This Chinese calamity opened the way for the 'Break-up of China'. Each of the Great Powers was to take a hand in annexing part of the dying Empire, or at least in controlling some part of it. Inevitably the missionaries and their work were linked with the unscrupulous proceedings of their compatriots, the Germans, the French, the British. Alone the Americans, with noble self-restraint, refrained.

In 1897 two Catholic German missionaries, Franz Nies and Richard Henle, were murdered in Kiachwang in south-west Shantung. The deed was done, not by the Chinese local government, nor even by incensed citizens; but by robbers. This, however, was an excuse for the Germans to annex Kiaochow Bay. They then forced the Chinese to give them sole railway rights and mining and trading rights in Shantung. This was a

terrible blow to Chinese pride and it was effected in the name of
retaliation or compensation for the murder of two Christian
missionaries of German nationality. Little wonder that the Chinese
associated in their minds Christianity, and international banditry.

This incident encouraged the Russians to snatch their part of
the spoils. In the same year, 1898, they acquired the lease of
Port Arthur; France in April, a month after Russia, settled in at
the Bay of Kwangchow. England, to offset the acquisition of
Port Arthur by Russia, acquired Weihaiwei and was given
possession of the Kowloon peninsula opposite Hong Kong, a total
of 376 square miles, 286 of which were on the mainland and the
remainder on islands.

Even before the Sino-Japanese War the anger against foreigners
had been growing. In 1893 there had been considerable riots in
several provinces and it was the missionaries who received the
brunt of the attack. They were there to receive it. Thus in May
riots occurred against French, English and American missionaries
in Chengtu in the province of Szechwan, in August against the
English and American missionaries in a town of Fukien. For the
latter riot twenty people had their heads cut off, an act not
likely to encourage enthusiasm for the foreigner or for the foreign
missionary.

During the parcelling out of China among the Powers in 1898
there was considerable disturbance in the Isle of Hainan, at Shasi,
at Sungpu, at Yanchow and in Hupei. A French priest was
killed in Kwangsi. Conditions were dangerous in Shantung for
two whole months. These spasmodic upheavals, now here now
there, were the prelude to the general slaughter which was to
come in the first year of the new century.

Meanwhile the patriot Chinese had not been idle, but were
powerless to do more than remonstrate and draw up protests to
the Government. One such patriot was Sun Yat-sen; he drew up
a memorandum and had it signed by a number of the gentry of
Kwangtung and sent it to the throne, and this even before the
Sino-Japanese War broke out. Societies for reform sprang up
everywhere; Kwangtung students, who had been studying in

Japan or the United States, and a few in Australia, returned full of democratic—and therefore revolutionary—ardour.

The Emperor was sympathetic and in touch with several of the leaders in the reform movement. In 1898 he even issued a number of reforming decrees. But the 'Old Buddha', as the Empress Dowager was familiarly called, took fright. She had the Emperor Kwang-hsü, and a leader of the movement, arrested. The latter was killed, and so ended the last chance of reform by constitutional means. The *status quo ante* was restored. The Emperor remained on the throne but was confined to his palace in semi-imprisonment.

In December of 1899 Mr. Brooks, an Anglican missionary, was murdered in Shantung, the centre of nationalist feeling. The Governor had refused to check the rioters; and, although he was withdrawn after a protest by the Powers, he was soon after made Governor of Shansi. The Germans in retaliation burnt down two villages. In January of the fatal year, 1900, the Americans, British, French, German and Italian Governments sent a stern joint note to Peking calling for the suppression of the I Ho Ch'uan (i.e. Fists of Righteous Harmony, that is the Boxers) and the Ta-tao-hwei (i.e. the Great Sword Society), which had begun by being anti-Manchu, but which had now been deftly turned by that Government into anti-foreign societies. The Government's reply to the note was that the Governor of Shantung and the Viceroy of Chihli had suppressed the said societies. Nevertheless, Peking refused to make the decree public.

In February 8000 troops joined the Boxers. The situation had now seriously deteriorated. Mgr. Favier, Bishop of Peking, gave a very serious warning to the French legation in the capital, and as a result some reassuring decrees were published, but the state of affairs was beyond curing by decree. On the 25th May the houses of converts of the American mission at Pachow, sixty miles south of Peking, were destroyed and nine Christians killed. June began with the killing of two English missionaries at Yungtsing. These atrocities were a warning to the foreigners in Peking to gather in self-defence in part of the 'legation area', i.e. the American and British legation, some in the American Methodist compound and especially at the Pei T'ang, in the imperial city, where they were guarded by forty-three French and Italian marines. The priests and nuns who were at the Nan T'ang were brought in to join them.

A number of cases of incendiarism occurred—one railway after another was destroyed, beginning with that of Pao-ting. Detachments of troops were sent to Peking (31st May), by the English, Americans, Italians, Japanese, French and Russians. They had to turn back towards Tientsin without being able to make their way to the capital. In order to feel safe, the foreign contingent demanded the surrender of the forts which controlled Taku and the harbour. But the Chinese Government refused to hand them over, and indeed opened fire on the international force. The court, and at its head the Dowager Empress, were openly on the side of the rioters. The siege of the Peking legations where the Europeans and the Christian missionaries had taken refuge now began. On the 13th June the massacre of the Chinese Christians of Peking took place. On the 24th the Empress issued a decree commanding the killing of all foreigners. A relief force finally arrived at Peking to save the British legation and the Pei T'ang, the Catholic cathedral stronghold.

Because the viceroys of the rest of China promised the Powers to keep order in their areas and defend the lives and properties of the foreigners, and because the representatives of the Powers, on their side, promised not to intervene except in the north, the massacres did not spread.

The 'incident' was over by October 1901.

The harm done to the Church was immense; firstly, three Catholic bishops lost their lives, as did thirty-one missionary priests and about thirty thousand Catholics, the vast majority of whom were Chinese.[1] The Protestants lost nearly two thousand. The harm done to property was on a vast scale. The famous Nan T'ang was burnt, the Tung T'ang and Hsi T'ang were destroyed. The slaughter was worst in Shansi, Mongolia and Manchuria.

[1] On 24th March 1946 a number of Boxer victims were beatified.

The twentieth century was ushered in sombrely dressed for the Church in China. The next few years, however, were years of strong growth. These very recent heroic deeds and deaths had again roused the imagination of the Christians in Europe and America.

As with the Catholics, so with the Protestants, the Boxer Rising caused much loss of life and great damage to missionary property. It was only because the number of Protestants in China was less than the number of Catholics that their deaths were fewer. The worst suffering was in the north, especially Chihli, Mongolia, Shansi, Manchuria. Not only missionaries faced death but numberless Chinese, often with much constancy.

Hudson Taylor, in the name of his great society, the China Inland Mission, refused any indemnity after it was all over. Heirs of martyred missionaries of American Societies received each a sum of 5000 dollars.[1]

Timothy Richard, in a spirit of conciliation, suggested that some of the indemnity should be utilized in China and for the benefit of the Chinese. In Shansi he was asked by the provincial government to help. At his suggestion, with some of the money collected, a university was founded at T'ai-yüan for teaching Western culture.

The space given to all this political ferment may seem to some excessive. But it was precisely politics which permeated the spirit of the missionaries, especially the French Catholic ones, as a result of these riots for the next thirty years. The French protectorate of the missions now became almost a doctrine of belief among the foreign priests in China.

PART THE SECOND

THE TWENTIETH CENTURY

D. THE POLITICAL BACKGROUND

THE first fifty years of the twentieth century in China have the shape of a tragedy with a clear beginning and an equally clear end. It begins with the aftermath of the Boxer Rising and ends with the conquest of the whole of China in 1949-50 by the

[1] Latourette, *op. cit.*, p. 524.

Communist armies of the north. Before examining the fortunes
of the Catholic Church and of the Protestant bodies during this
period, we must pass in review the chief happenings in the life
of the Chinese peoples, in so far as those happenings influenced
the fortunes of the missions and the faithful.

The history of China from 1900 to 1950 may be roughly divided
into the period of anticipation leading up to the disappearance of
the Manchu dynasty in 1911. This is followed by the second
period, that of a nominal Republic but mostly 'war-lordism' and
civil war. It lasts until 1926 when Chiang Kai-shek marched
North. The third period is that of Chiang Kai-shek and lasts
until the beginning of the Japanese War in 1937. The fourth
period is one of endless war and the infiltration of Communism
into power. The final scenes of that period come towards the
end of the Second World War with the uneasy alliance between
the Chinese Communists and the Nationalists, and the former
setting about the conquest of the whole country for themselves. This they achieved by the end of 1949. The curtain fell
that year.

It will be seen at a glance that all this period except for the
first eleven years was far from ideally suited to the propagation
of the Gospel message. Even the first, the aftermath of the Boxer
Rising, was in some ways scarcely the atmosphere in which to
speak of Christ, especially for missionaries who came from those
countries which had reduced the Chinese State to one of complete
subjection.

An immediate result of the suppression of the Boxer Rising
was the successful attempt on the part of the Great Powers to
re-establish in the country their nationals and their trade. Large
indemnities were demanded and paid. As most of these missionaries were nationals of one country or another much money
passed into their hands. The collecting of money, the payment
of it to the foreigners there in China, as can be imagined, was
extremely mortifying and not conducive to a receptive frame of
mind.

Psychologically the effect of their national humiliation was to make the Chinese realize at long last that they could not afford to ignore the great superiority in scientific skill possessed by their Western conquerors. The passion for education grasped them, as it has so many other backward peoples before and since. The one thing they wanted was schools of the Western learning. They not only flocked to Christian schools, but the Government itself set up a Ministry of Education in 1905. In the same year the old examination system based entirely on the Confucian classics, which had been going on for two thousand years, was abolished. It was England which at the time stood out as the most flourishing nation. It was the British missionaries, none of whom were Catholic, who were prepared to provide the schools and the teachers. So English became the lingua franca, and the popular enthusiasm was for English political ideas. The man who more than any other at this time furthered the creation of an educated class in China was the veteran missionary Timothy Richard.

The inevitable by-product of this sudden increase in the educated class was the creation of an intelligentsia. An intelligentsia has been described as a group of educated people in a country which cannot find them any other occupation than that of undermining the traditional institutions which keep that country from being in the front line of 'progress'. China certainly found herself with this irritant in the early years of the twentieth century. Inevitably it was not long before revolutionary societies were organizing the downfall of the completely inept Manchu régime.

The 'Old Buddha', the Dowager Empress, died in 1908, lamented by none. The same year her nephew, the Kwang-hsü Emperor, died also. That left the throne to a boy of three. Three years later the revolutionaries proclaimed the Republic, though the child Emperor did not abdicate until 1912.

Meanwhile in the international field a great European Power had been seriously defeated by an eastern neighbour of China. In the Russo-Japanese War of 1904 the Japanese had defeated the Russians, thus showing for the first time since East and West had met in the sixteenth century that the West was not invincible. It was a considerable reassurance and invitation to the Chinese to imitate their neighbour and, by learning the foreign devil's own tricks, to beat him at his own fierce game of war.

Sun Yat-sen, the founder of the Chinese Republic, had not waited for this startling *dénouement* of the aggressions by the Western Powers, but as a boy in his teens had followed his elder brother to Honolulu in the eighteen-eighties. There he went to Iolani School, of which the headmaster was an Anglican, the Rt. Rev. Alfred Willis, and there he was baptized and became a Christian for the rest of his life. His brother, displeased at this desertion from Chinese ways, sent him back to his native village—this was in the summer of 1885. There, good Christian that he was, he smashed the idol in the local temple, an aggressive act which caused him to flee to Hong Kong for sanctuary. Sun Yat-sen studied in Hong Kong and Honolulu, but at the same time was continually fomenting a revolutionary spirit wherever he went. Every new attack by one of the Western Powers on the integrity of China urged him to greater efforts. At first his headquarters were Japan, but when the latter began to persecute the Chinese student body in its midst, he moved to Annam. He travelled extensively over America and England in order to rouse the interest and support of the Chinese *diaspora*. From 1902 onwards there was scarcely a year without some uprising in China organized by his revolutionary group.

In March 1911 an abortive rising in Canton was to cause the death of seventy-two of the party, but in October of the same year a second attempt, this time at Wu-ch'ang, succeeded in seriously embarrassing the Government, which had to send a powerful army under a well-known general, but who was in disgrace, Yüan Shih-k'ai, to quell the rebels in Wu-ch'ang. The revolution spread to Canton, Shanghai and Nanking. In January 1912 Sun was sworn in as provisional President of the Republic. In February he stood down and Yüan Shih-k'ai was elected President—Sun's reason for this gesture was the avoidance of war between north and south. Unfortunately Yüan chose in 1915 to aspire to be an Emperor and to start a new dynasty. But he died the following year, leaving the country of his betrayal in the throes of civil strife, from which it never recovered. From the moment of the setting up of the revolutionary government in 1911 to the unified rule of China in 1927, the country was racked by civil war. First of all there was the rivalry between the old régime and the revolutionaries, then the rivalry between the general turned Emperor, Yüan, and his fellow war-lords, then in 1921 onwards between the newly constituted revolutionary government in Canton under Sun Yat-sen and the government in the north. China knew no peace during all those years.

The war in Europe between 1914 and 1918 left Japan more or less a free hand in the East. China however had hoped to wrest from Germany her rights over the province of Shantung. She therefore joined the Allies and sent representatives to the Versailles Conference, trusting to receive at least that concession for her participation in the war. To her dismay the politicians of the Great Powers, who also had promised to reward Japan for her services, decided according to their promise to transfer the German rights in Shantung to Japan. The Chinese delegates left the conference table in disgust. It was this disgust which provided Sun Yat-sen in 1919 with his opportunity to build up once again his revolutionary government in Canton, and indeed all over the country.

The disgust was so universal throughout China on the return of the delegation from the Peace Conference that the students of colleges and universities all over the country staged protests. This movement among the students is called in history 'the May the Fourth Movement', and it had considerable importance for the missionaries because it was essentially an anti-foreign intellectual movement directed to a renaissance of Chinese culture. In so far as Christianity was foreign, to that extent did it lose caste in the eyes of Young China at this date. The movement began in Peking under the inspiration of intellectuals of Peking University. But it soon became a demonstration of widely-felt national feeling among the urban working class, and most of its leaders, two years later, helped to found the Chinese Communist Party.

Up to 1923 Sun Yat-sen had turned to the democratic Powers

to provide him and his party with the money for the prosecution of revolution. They saw in him and his party a beginning of a Far Eastern democratic rule. But in 1923 a new giant, Soviet Russia, was on the horizon, in some ways more akin to the revolutionary character of the Chinese leader than the cautious Western democrats. This new Power had overthrown the Tsarist régime, as Sun Yat-sen and the Kuomintang had overthrown the effete Manchu dynasty. In that year messages of friendship were exchanged and two important members of the Communist Party were sent from Russia to Canton. They were Borodin, the experienced propagandist, and Galen, a military expert, also known as Bluecher, later Soviet commander in eastern Siberia. Meanwhile the Communist Party in China was officially affiliated to the Third International (1924).[1] This was a fateful alliance. Nor was it a good augury for the Christian missions. They were to suffer grievously from this *mariage de convenance*.

On the Island of Whampoa in the river estuary off Canton a young man, Chiang Kai-shek, was put in charge of the military academy there. In Whampoa he forged the instrument, which would have made it possible to conquer all China, had it not been for the splintering activities of the Communists in the ranks of the combined party.

So long as Sun Yat-sen lived the divided disciples could be kept fairly well together. He was the acknowledged leader. But when he died in 1925, rifts occurred, and it was clear that the Communists were determined at any cost to command for themselves alone. The left wing of the Kuomintang set up a government in Wuhan. All this time the attacks on Church property and on missionaries were becoming more numerous and ferocious, although Chiang Kai-shek was in control of Shanghai. In 1927 the opposition of these two centres of power was publicly known. In April of that year Chiang set up a rival capital at Nanking and made a great purge of Communists from the Kuomintang. By the end of the year the Central Government forces had advanced

[1] The Chinese Communist Party had resolved to join the Comintern at its Second Congress held at Hangchow in May 1922.

on Wuhan (the name given to the constellation of great cities: Hankow, Wu-ch'ang and Hanyang) where the opposition had been in command. The Communists were defeated and withdrew to a restricted area between Hunan and Kiangsi; and there they gradually consolidated their hold, while Chiang was bringing one northern province after another into line with the Government at Nanking.

The years 1928 to 1937 were comparatively quiet in South and Central China. Already, however, the Japanese were probing vulnerable points in the north and east. The Communists still held out in their stronghold, and Chiang became fully aware of the danger from this core of opposition in the centre of his empire. In 1930 he decided to crush them. It is said that he used as many as 600,000 troops in the operations, which lasted until 1934. In that year the Communists, realizing that their position was untenable, withdrew. Nearly starving they trekked across country to Yenan on the north-western frontier of Shensi. That march is one of the most amazing in all the annals of military history; it was a distance of over 6000 miles.

The last period, before the Communist advance to power, really begins in the year 1935. The Japanese by that date were leaving no one in doubt of their intentions to create in China a sphere of influence which ultimately would bring China under her suzerainty and oust the Western Powers altogether. It is not the purpose of these pages to describe the long agony of China during these years. Suffice it to say that by 1937 the position was sufficiently serious for the Kuomintang and the Communists to agree to make common cause against the enemy. An alliance was struck[1] between them which lasted until the end of the Second World War.

The years from 1945 to the present day shall be left for the final chapter which is told in the form of an Epilogue. It cannot yet be called history.

[1] This was after the Communists had persuaded (in December 1936) Chiang's kidnappers at Sian to release their captive. Chiang had been arrested in that city by the Manchurian troops of Marshal Chang Hsüeh-liang.

e. The Catholic Church in China

i. The Old Ways

The Catholics, during the first ten years after the Boxer Rising, consolidated their position. Apparently no new methods were tried, no heart-searchings made. The Chinese clergy were still kept down to the lower ranks of the hierarchy: the main concentration of energy was still directed to evangelization. Unlike the Protestants in China, who saw the value of schools, the vast possibilities of education were not greatly exploited by the Catholics, partly from lack of funds, partly from the conviction that the essential purpose was to preach Christ. It is true, the Catholics had numbers of schools, but they were of a religious rather than a secular type, schools for teaching the Catechism to small children, schools for the formation of catechists, and as many as sixty seminaries preparing young men for the priesthood.

In 1900 the Catholic Church in China was divided into forty-one dioceses and vicariates. During the next eleven years these remained static except for the creation of the Hangchow, the Ningyuanfu and the Paotingfu vicariates in 1910, and the Changchow vicariate in 1911. It was a period of political ferment and doubtless Church authorities were being cautious.

Equally static, or almost as static, was the development of religious Orders and Congregations. At the beginning of the period there were already in position the Augustinians, Dominicans, Franciscans, Jesuits, Lazarists, the Society of the Divine Word, several groups of priests of Foreign Missionary Societies, that of Paris, those of Milan and Rome, the Scheut Fathers, some Benedictines and one house of Trappists. During the first phase of the twentieth century the only newcomers were the Salesians and the Parma Foreign Missionary Society. Again it would seem that the missionary field was dormant.

In a population[1] of four hundred and fifty million a few hundred thousand are insignificant; nevertheless, the growth of the Church

[1] It was estimated in 1900 that the population of China was between 450,000,000 and 500,000,000.

in numbers tells a tale of considerable if not spectacular expansion. It is estimated that in 1900 there were three-quarters of a million Catholics in China; ten years later, in 1910, the million mark had been passed with the approximate figure of 1,292,000. On the other hand the proportion of Chinese to foreign priests was depressingly low. At the beginning of the century the Chinese priests numbered not quite five hundred and by the year 1912 the number had risen to 729. Compare this with the number of foreign missionaries in the country at the time. They numbered almost exactly double the Chinese clergy. This strikes one as astonishing after three hundred years of missionary activity. The comparison or contrast of Saxon England haunts the mind. How is it that in the first hundred years of Saxon Catholicism there were native priests, bishops and saints, and in China after three hundred years so few? There was still no Chinese bishop.

While one must lament the partial failure of the missionaries to take full advantage of all the opportunities offered for advancing the cause of Christ and the Church, certain other elements of the situation must be recalled, which undoubtedly hampered growth. The chief Catholic country occupied with missionary work at this time was France, which had fallen into the hands of anti-Catholic Radicals and Freemasons, who made no secret of their antagonism to the Church. The French Government was expelling the religious Orders, and in 1905 the Law of Separation was passed in the French Chamber. The following year the French minister in Peking relinquished the protectorate, exercised by his country since the middle of the previous century, over nationals other than French. Each country was expected from that date to look after its own. In practice the French still helped Catholic missionaries.

The first years of the Republic, which were so soon to be followed by the First World War, were scarcely propitious for missionary work from France or Europe, and undoubtedly the Catholic missions in China suffered from that great world calamity. In spite of war it is heartening to mention one major missionary venture made in China during those years. The

Maryknoll Foreign Missions Society began its fine career in the Far East in 1917.

The Maryknoll Missionary enterprises, being the first in time of the Catholic Church in the United States, deserve special mention. The Society itself was started in 1911 by Fr. James Anthony Walsh, the Director of the Association for the Propagation of the Faith in the United States, also founder of the missionary bulletin *The Field Afar* (1907), and by Fr. Price, the apostle of North Carolina. During a visit to Rome in 1911 they received encouragement both from the Cardinal in charge of Propaganda and from the holy Pope, St. Pius X. In the same year the seminary for missions abroad was started.

It was not until 1917, towards the end of the First World War, that they felt able to undertake their first assignment. Fr. Walsh set sail in that year for Japan, Korea and China, in order to offer the services of his institution for work in that missionary field. It was only when he reached Canton and met once again Fr. Robert and the Vicar Apostolic of Canton, Mgr. de Guebriant, that he and his fellow enthusiasts were accepted. The first missions in China given to the Maryknoll Fathers were the two centres of Yeung-kong and of Loting in the southern province of Kwangtung.[1]

The early Republic of China was more friendly to the Church and to Christians generally than almost any Chinese Government before or since. Many of the leaders had been educated in Christian schools; many of them were Christians. Here it is apposite to mention the most famous Catholic among them, Lou Tseng-Tsiang, who for a short time became Foreign Minister and who was one of the representatives of China at the Peace

---

[1] From reports handed to the Internuncio, Archbishop Riberi, in 1952, they had, at that date, mission centres in the dioceses of Meiesien (Kaying), and of Kongmoon, and in the prefecture of Kweilin. A notable feature of their missions was the presence of Maryknoll Sisters, and another was the high proportion of Chinese priests—at the time of writing most of them are in prison for their faith, or killed.

For a lively account of the beginnings of the Maryknoll foundation see: *The Early Days of Maryknoll*, by Raymond A. Lane, M.M., D.D., New York, 1951; for a similar and extremely vivid account of their missionary efforts see *The Maryknoll Story*, by Robert Considine, U.S.A., 1950.

Conference at Versailles in 1919. He ended his days as a Benedictine monk in the Abbey of St. André in Belgium, having, as he
described it, sought out the most ancient thing in the culture of
the West and the most ancient institution in that most ancient
thing. He found the Catholic Church and the Rule of St.
Benedict. His life was a symbolic act of homage paid by the
noblest element in the Far East to what was best in the West. His
life will not have been wasted. His death occurred in Belgium in
1949. Lou Tseng-Tsiang was born in 1871 in Shanghai, between
two worlds. His father was a Chinese Protestant catechist,
spreading the seeds of Western culture broadcast, distributing
tracts to all, whether willing or unwilling to listen. The family
belonged to the London Missionary Society. He wrote in later
years: 'I have the deepest gratitude for all the charity and kindness
shown towards me by these missionaries.'

In 1892 he began his diplomatic career. He was fortunate in
having as his guide a notable man, M. Shu King-Shen: Lou
Tsing-Tsiang records this parting advice given by his old friend
before he set out for Europe.

The strength of Europe is not to be found in her armaments: it is
not to be found in her science; it is to be found in her religion. In
the course of your diplomatic career you will have occasion to study
the Christian religion. It comprehends various branches and societies.
Take the most ancient branch of that religion, that which goes back
most nearly to its origins. Enter into it, study its doctrine, practise
its commandments, observe its government, and closely follow all
its works. And later on, when you have ended your career, perhaps
you will have the opportunity to go still further. In this most ancient
branch, choose the most ancient society. If you can do so, enter
into it also. Make yourself its follower, and study the interior life
which must be the secret of it. When you have understood and won
the secret of that life, when you have grasped the heart and strength
of the religion of Christ, bring them and give them to China.[1]

That response to the problems which gripped and still hold
China was a noble and profound one. Abbot Celestine Lou had

[1] Pierre Celestine Lou, *Ways of Confucius and of Christ*, London, 1948, pp. 11–12.

discovered a solution on the spiritual plane. Unfortunately this was not the solution of the mass of the intellectuals. They had received their 'three R's' in Church schools, but at times the specifically Christian element was somewhat vague, and the main stress was placed not on religion but on material prosperity. The youth of China tended to put aside the deepest elements in the things they learnt from the Western missionaries, namely doctrine and ethical teaching, in order to concentrate rather upon a political solution. Great Britain and the United States were the leaders in the West, they were democratic: the Chinese not unnaturally were won over by the democratic creed. In this they were probably wise; and if they had had time to make it work, time to learn the advantages and the pitfalls, doubtless China would have found economic salvation. But democracy is not enough, it needs behind it, underlying it, permeating it, the spirit of the Gospels. This Dom Celestine Lou and his wise master had known and acted upon.

ii. New Ideas

(a) Fr. Lebbe and the Holy See

Though the old ways persisted up to the end of the First World War, already some minds were at work questioning, searching, finding a way out of the impasse which the Catholics had reached in China. They were losing ground to the Protestants and they were not making that impact upon the Chinese people that the Church should, and indeed could have made.

The three chief agents of the forward movement were Pope Benedict XV, his successor Pius XI and Fr. Vincent Lebbe. These three worked as one. It is common knowledge that Pius XI wished to be called the Pope of the Missions, but less commonly appreciated that his predecessor was equally alive to the realities of the situation. This zeal for the missions is all the more remarkable as his pontificate was so soon after the War of 1914–18.

The man, however, who towers above the rest at this time and who is to be compared to Fr. Ricci, a symbolic figure, is a Lazarist, Fr. Lebbe. He was of mixed Flemish and English descent. Born in 1877 he joined the Lazarists at eighteen years of age. On account of his ill-health he was sent in 1900 by his superiors to Rome, as they supposed that the climate might be more congenial to him. There he met Mgr. Favier, the Bishop of Peking, back in Europe after having escaped from the massacre of the Boxer Rising. The Bishop made the prophetic remark '*tu seras missionnaire en Chine*'. It came true, for not long afterwards he arrived in Peking. For a time he was curate in a village, then parish priest at Chu-Chow. Already he was aware of something fundamentally wrong. He could not bear to see the Christian missionaries protected *from* the Chinese, from those very souls his duty and his desires told him to win for Christ. You cannot win someone whom you are holding down by force. He refused to accept the protection of the French consuls.

On one occasion the French Consul of Tientsin seized more land for the French Concession than was legally right. Fr. Lebbe gave this act its true name. He was living by his principle of being on the side of his adopted country. As an immediate result he was ecclesiastically banished to an area whose language even he did not understand, near Ningpo, south of Shanghai. It was during this period of exile that he wrote a long letter to his Bishop on missions in China (1917). This letter his Bishop sent to Rome. It was the beginning of the close collaboration between this holy and zealous apostle and the Apostolic See.

Fr. Lebbe now summarized the missionary methods under four heads; the legal method, the Spanish method, the method of good works, and the alms method. In each case he considered them inadequate and proposed a fifth method, that of *love*.

One of Fr. Lebbe's root ideas was 'that to convert a soul to the truth it is not enough to know that that soul is not Christian, it is essential *first and foremost* to discover its aspirations and desires, to disentangle all there is which is legitimate and true, and to make use of that to conquer that soul entirely'. The second principle upon which he based his apostolate was the complete de-Europeanization of the Church. The Church in China was foreign, and it had to become indigenous, Chinese.

Thus wherever, as we have seen, there was a conflict between the French authorities and the Chinese law he took, on principle, the Chinese side. In and out of season he preached his doctrine, in China and in Rome: the Church in China had to be Chinese or perish. Whether his theories were right or wrong, Rome shared them.[1]

The first great victory for the ideas spread by Lebbe was the encyclical letter of Benedict XV 'Maximum Illud', undoubtedly an echo of many of his ideas, which was published in 1919. It is of such fundamental importance for the study of missionary activity in the twentieth century that an extract is justified.

The Pope urges the heads of missions to find vocations from among the people of the place:

> Finally, the point on which all those who rule over Missions must fix their principal attention, is to educate and instruct members of the sacred ministry from among the people with whom they live, for in this is contained the principal hope of the new Churches. For the native priest, in as much as he is one with his countrymen in birth, in character, in feelings, in interests, has a peculiar power of introducing the faith into their minds: for he knows far better than any other the right way to persuade them of any point.

Benedict XV does not believe that the Chinese clergy should be kept only for menial tasks, as it were, of the ministry: 'The native clergy is not to be trained in order to assist the foreign missionaries in humbler offices, but in order that it may be equal to the accomplishment of its divine task, and in course of time duly to assume the government of its own people.'

The aim of a missionary enterprise is to make itself superfluous. 'Where there exists a sufficient number of indigenous clergy, well instructed and worthy of their vocation, it may justly be said

[1] For recent discussion cf. *Etudes*, Dec. 1955; *La Revue Nouvelle*, Jan. 1956 March, 1956; *Etudes*, April 1956.

that the missionaries have successfully completed their work, and that the Church has been thoroughly well founded.'

The Holy Father lamented the failure of those in charge not in one but in several missionary countries, to create an indigenous hierarchy.

> It is to be deplored that there are regions in which the Catholic faith has been introduced for centuries, without any indigenous clergy as yet to be found there except of a lower order: and that there are certain nations, which have long been illuminated by the light of the faith, and have emerged from a savage state to such a degree of civilization that they possess men who excel in all the varieties of the civil arts, yet, after many centuries of the influence of the gospel and of the Church, can show no bishops to govern nor priests to teach their own countrymen.

The new Pope, Pius XI, wasted no time in showing his mind. One of the first acts of his pontificate was to establish in 1922 an Apostolic Delegation in China, thus abolishing the French protectorate over Catholic missions which had survived since 1860. In the following years two Chinese priests were made Vicars Apostolic, one in 1923 and the other in 1924, by the recently appointed Papal Delegate, Mgr. Celso Constantini. This was followed by the first plenary Council of the Church in China, held in May 1924. The consideration shown by the Holy See for the standing of the Chinese nation and State was reciprocated by the Chinese when in 1925 at the funeral of Sun Yat-sen they showed their appreciation by granting the same honours to the representative of the Holy See as they did to all other diplomatic representatives.

Pius XI in his encyclical '*Rerum Ecclesiae*', in which he reiterated all the principles of the letter of Benedict XV, especially in his insistence upon indigenous clergy, put his own principles into action by creating in China two prefectures which were to be governed entirely by Chinese clergy, that of P'uch'i in Hupeh and that of Lyhsien in Chihli. Meanwhile Pius XI called Lebbe to Rome. He selected a friend of his, Mgr. Philip Tchao, for a bishopric and in 1926 six Chinese priests were raised to the

episcopate. Lebbe himself in order to give proof of his devoted-
ness to China had himself naturalized as a Chinese citizen.[1] He
returned to China in 1927.

(b) *New Arrivals*

Whatever the cause, it is certain that after the First World
War the missionary zeal of the Church grew, and mighty efforts
were made in the rich field of missionary activity.

A number of Orders and Societies took up the ancient challenge
and made foundations during the twenties of this century: the
St. Columban Foreign Missions in 1920, the Passionists in the
following year, the Picpus Fathers in 1922, and in the same year
the Betharramites. Three groups of Benedictines ventured out
in 1925, 1926 and 1928; the Salvatorians in 1923 and during the
next few years the Stigmatins, the Quebec Foreign Missionary
Society, the Scarborough Bluff Foreign Missionary Society,
the Conventuals, the Bethlehem Foreign Missionary Society, the
Recollect Fathers of St. Augustine, the Redemptorists; in the
thirties, the Canons Regular of St. Augustine, the Missionary
Society of the Immaculate Heart of Mary, the Sulpicians.

(c) *The Sinification of the Chinese Mission*

The encouraging act of Pius XI in consecrating six Chinese
bishops was, as anticipated, only the beginning of the sinification
of the Chinese mission. The time was very appropriate, just
when Chinese national consciousness had reached its climax in
the nineteen-twenties.

Gradually the Chinese were put in command of the vicariates
and prefectures, and their staffs of priests were in some cases

---

[1] During the Japanese War he organized a band of stretcher-bearers. Promising
two hundred, he in fact brought two hundred and sixty. During the Second
World War he was captured by the Communists (though theoretically on their
side). Some of his Little Brothers had already been buried alive by these
soldiers, but on account of the great veneration felt for him he was freed.
However, some time later he was severely wounded and died on his way to
Chungking. He was being brought back by air expressly at the command of
Chiang Kai-shek. His death occurred on the 24th June 1940.

entirely Chinese. In the north eight ecclesiastical divisions were, at the end of the Second World War, ruled by Chinese, in Hopeh, Mongolia and Manchuria. In the east there were five, in Kiangsu and Chekiang; in the west four, in Szechwan and Yunnan: in the centre six, in Shansi, Shensi and Hupeh; in the south four. These dioceses now ruled by native Chinese had almost all been initiated by great missionary congregations. The Lazarists had provided five in the north, one of them the archdiocese of Peking; the Missions Étrangères of Paris had provided six, including the archdioceses of Mukden and Canton; the Franciscans all in the central provinces; the Jesuits mostly in the north; the Scheut Fathers two.

It may seem that to allow only twenty-seven of the one hundred and forty-four dioceses which existed in 1951 to be under Chinese control was meagre fare for national aspirations. But if one considers that these twenty-seven include the chief centres of Chinese and Catholic life, the figure will be seen in due proportion. These dioceses include Peking, Mukden, Canton, Shanghai —all commercial and intellectual centres in China. Besides these one must add four other units under Chinese Lazarist and Chinese Franciscan control. Of the twenty-seven dioceses, nine had no foreign missionaries in them at all, and another nine had only five or less. These were changes indeed.

The proportion of Chinese to foreign priests during the period 1925-48 is significant of the change. In 1925 the number of foreign priests was 1806, and it rose to 3015 in 1948. The Chinese clergy in the same period rose from 1220 to 2676. It will be seen that the foreigners increased by just over half their original number, whereas the Chinese clergy were more than doubled. The advance was even more marked if the figures are taken from 1939. In the nine years between that date and 1948 the increase in foreign clergy was just over one hundred, while the increase in Chinese priests was 646.

For the training of native clergy the Church had established fourteen central seminaries at Peiping, Sienhsien, Tatung, T'aiyüan, Tsinan, Yenchow, Chengtu, Siccawei, Kaifeng, Suanhwa, Hankow, Kiukiang, Ningpo, and Hong Kong. This list of names reads like a triumph. It is a deep sorrow that the triumph was so short-lived. The great hope of the complete sinification of the Church was cut short by the coming of Communism.

(d) Education

The progress of the Church bore some relation to the political situation in China. During the years 1927-37, that is, the period when Chiang had more or less control over most of the country, the Church strode ahead, particularly on the new lines laid down by Benedict XV and Pius XI, under the guidance of the Holy Spirit and certainly through the insight and zeal of men like Vincent Lebbe, little as some other missionaries agreed with him.

Apart from the question of indigenous clergy which we have already examined, there was also the urgent question of education. The Protestants had long been in the lead, having begun in the nineteenth century, but now Catholics all over China were setting up schools and colleges and even universities to cater not only for the Faithful but also for any other Chinese who were prepared to come and be taught.

Of all modern Catholic education institutes in China the most famous, and rightly, was the magnificent Aurora University on the outskirts of the city of Shanghai. Its history is both typical and exemplary.

The beginnings came even before the Boxer Rising in 1898, when by the initiative of Chinese students themselves a start was made at Zi-ka-wei, one of the oldest Jesuit mission stations. After some misunderstanding it was reopened in 1905 under the direct control of the Fathers of the Society of Jesus. Gradually the numbers increased, the courses extended; buildings, playing-fields, libraries and all the paraphernalia of higher studies were set up. In 1932 the Chinese Government recognized it as one of those national universities whose degrees would now have equal standing with any other university in the country.

In this experiment the Jesuit Fathers were the first in the field among Catholics, but they were following in the wake of Protestants, notably of Timothy Richard. The work was not encouraged as a direct but as an indirect apostolate. The students would by no means all be Catholic. The teaching and atmosphere of Aurora University aimed at creating an *élite* worthy of its position as the ruling class, so imbued with sound moral and social principles, so free from all prejudices against the Faith, as to be a profound and beneficial support to the State and at the same time, indirectly, of great assistance to the missionaries in the field.

For years the notables in the various districts had shown antagonism to the missionaries and the simple folk had been afraid, out of human respect, to approach them or to be baptized. Now, as a result of this centre of higher studies under Catholic direction, young men were growing up throughout China whose attitude to the Church was one of gratitude and admiration for their teachers. 'Human respect is the great obstacle to conversion in China and Catholic Universities are the only remedy for this state of affairs', so said Fr. J. Rutten, the General of the Scheut Fathers. The wheel had come full circle, and we are back at the missionary technique of Ricci, Schall and the rest.

Besides the Aurora University there was also the Fu-jen Catholic University of Peking, founded by the American Benedictines, but later taken over by the Society of the Divine Word. In 1922 the French Jesuits set up the Higher Studies Institute in Tientsin. These institutions also, unlike in the early days of the nineteenth century, were attended by a great number of non-Catholics. Of the 2140 youths attending 'faculty courses' only a tenth were Catholics. The same is true of the secondary schools belonging to the Church. In the fifty or so in existence, out of the ten thousand boys all told only a third were Catholics; in the case of the girls, the proportion was higher, about half the children were of the Faith out of a total of nearly 7000.[1]

[1] The Church directed 252 high schools for boys in 1937, the proportion of Catholics to non-Catholics was 7378 to 9697, and in the 180 high schools for girls, 4229 girls were Catholic and 5291 were not. At a lower level, in the catechetical schools, of which there were over eleven thousand, all, of course, would be Catholic and the numbers for boys and girls in each case was approximately 10,000 and over. These statistics are taken from *The China Year Book*, 1939.

But what was the use of all this higher education if it still remained impossible for a Catholic to take part in public life? And what use all this energy expended if the Chinese took all the technical knowledge the West could offer, but not the religion which gave it substance and stability? The first question was answered by the Holy See in 1939. The second question remained unanswered. The Chinese took all the scientific and democratic ideas of the West, transmuting them; but in the main they did not become Christians, though remaining grateful to their Christian mentors.

(e) *The Rites Again*

This particular difficulty of Catholics taking part in public life dated back to the period of the Rites controversy. No *literatus* could hold civil office and become Catholic, because, if he were received into the Church, he would still have to pay reverence to the tablets of Confucius and to his ancestors. This, as we have seen, had been strictly forbidden by Benedict XIV on the ground that such an act was a religious service. But now, after the Revolution of 1911, were not the circumstances different? When the educational system, which had survived nearly two thousand years, and by which the children learned the Confucian Books by heart, was entirely done away with, it was expressly stated by the Government that the ceremonies performed before the tablets of Confucius had no religious significance. Might it not be possible to rescind the ancient Catholic legislation prohibiting Catholics from performing these bows and reverences?

In 1939 the Congregation of Propaganda issued a Decree (8th December) which reads as follows:

1. Inasmuch as the Chinese Government has repeatedly and explicitly proclaimed that all are free to profess the religion they prefer, and that it is foreign to its intentions to legislate or issue decrees concerning religious matters, and that consequently ceremonies performed or ordered by the public authorities in honour of Confucius do not take place with intent to offer religious worship, but solely for the purpose of promoting and expressing honour due to a great man, and proper regard for tradition, it is licit for Catholics

to be present at commemorative functions held before a likeness or tablet of Confucius at Confucian monuments or schools.

2. Hence, it is not to be considered illicit, particularly if the authorities should order it, to place in Catholic schools a likeness of Confucius, or even a tablet inscribed with his name, or to bow before such. Where scandal may be feared, the right intention of Catholics should be made clear, etc.[1]

It would be difficult to over-estimate the importance of this document. Up to 1939, and ever since the crisis over the Rites controversy and its pitiful conclusion in 1740, no man of any standing could become a Catholic. He could not pass the test of reverence to Confucius. Now at long last that impediment had been removed. But also now in 1940 deeper shadows are falling, greater trials are in store for the Faithful of China. The permission came too late to be of much value.

(f) *War*

The date 1937 is really the beginning of the end for this fourth chapter of the Church's story in China, since it was in 1937 that the war with Japan began in grim earnest; the war did not end until the collapse of Japan under the frightful experience of the atomic attack in 1945.

As the war swirled north and south, east and west, the property of the Church, the schools, hospitals, churches, were devastated, the Christian population, with the rest, killed or hounded down everywhere. It was not a period of material construction; and yet on the other hand it was a period of spiritual fruit. The marvellous work done by Catholics, priests, laymen, nuns and nurses, to alleviate the sufferings of others brought out in singular relief the true nature of the Church, a body of people whose life's motive was love, not self-interest. It would be impossible to give all the examples. The Generalissimo on more than one occasion praised this great work of mercy performed by the Catholics, and also the Protestants. It brought the Church into prominence as never before.

[1] cf. *The Tablet*, 20th January 1940.

Outstanding in the works of mercy were the Little Brothers of St. John the Baptist, a body of stretcher-bearers, organized and led by Fr. Vincent Lebbe. For the latter's uncompromising patriotism he was first given the honourable title of captain, then lieutenant-general in the Chinese army and finally that of national hero. In February 1940 twelve of these Little Brothers were buried alive by the Communists, even though they were all supposed to be fighting and working on the same side. But the important point, which this merely exemplifies, is that the Chinese Catholics were at this date, as never before, identified with the just cause of their country. Catholicism seemed no longer an alien thing, it was part, and a noble part, of the national life.

But while the Faithful were endeavouring to the utmost to defend and support their country, the allies of Chiang Kai-shek, the Communists, were playing a double game, which everyone in China knew, but which few outside China realized. Instead of fighting the Japanese they did all in their power to hinder the national cause, all in their power to create chaos and in the ensuing interregnum to seize power.

The only comparable situation was that of Yugoslavia, in which there were two organizations supposed to be fighting the Germans, each accused by the other of working for its own hand. This tripartite war is well described in *In the Land of Mao Tse-tung* by Fr. Carlo Suigo, who experienced it. He wrote:

> In every village the shadow of the Japanese terror became a nightmare . . . but when towards evenings, the Japanese returned to the city, the village once again fell into the hands of the Communists. Those guilty of collaboration with the enemy . . . were liquidated. . . . When these (the Nationalists) felt themselves sufficiently strong they initiated a counter-offensive to stem the tide of active Communist propaganda. The Reds, for their part, did not intend to allow themselves to be overwhelmed by an 'army of traitors who had retreated before the enemy'. So by night (not by day for fear of the Japanese) there were fierce encounters, and those who suffered were the unfortunate villagers.[1]

[1] p. 16.

(g) *The Interlude*

When the Second World War was over the position of the Church in China had never been so flourishing. The year 1946 may be taken as an interlude between one great catastrophe and the last which is upon it now; and the picture of the Church in that short breathing-space gives one some idea of the progress made and of the state of the Church before the last and most terrible blow of all, that delivered by the Communists.

Almost all the main centres of population in which the Catholics found themselves in any numbers were under the spiritual direction not only of a Chinese bishop but of an entirely Chinese clergy. There were twenty-eight of these in all.[1] It is difficult to imagine how strong and almost ubiquitous the Church was at that date, in spite of the utmost material devastation. England for instance with its three to four million Catholics has a handful of dioceses, China had one hundred and thirty-eight.

Although foreign priests still outnumbered Chinese by about a thousand[2] the immense increase in Chinese vocations to the priesthood over the last half century was little short of the miraculous. It would be hard to find a parallel anywhere. Less than five hundred Chinese priests ministered to the Faithful in 1900, now in 1946 the figure was four times as great.

Naturally in order to keep pace with this remarkable increase in vocations the Church had established a network of seminaries and minor seminaries. In spite of wars and all the dislocation such calamities bring in their train over a thousand young men were busily studying for the priesthood in the sixteen major seminaries of the country. Numbers in minor seminaries are always deceptive, as usually the overwhelming majority of the students do not persevere to the end. They are of course perfectly free to depart at any time. However, bearing that in mind, it is significant that in the hundred and more *petits séminaires* or junior seminaries over five thousand Chinese boys were being educated with the ultimate, remote aim of being priests.

[1] Although twenty-one of these had a Chinese bishop.
[2] 3064 foreign, 2073 Chinese priests.

To crown all, as it were, it was in the year 1946, the first—and last—year of peace for the Chinese, that the Holy See decided to give the Church of China full status. Up to that date, although there were bishops in every diocese, these were called Vicars Apostolic, which in simple language means they were acting, not so much in their own name as supreme authorities in their own areas, as in the name of the Pope, as his vicars or lieutenants. Once, however, a Church in a missionary country has become well established, this temporary arrangement comes to an end. It came to an end in China in 1946.

This Catholic population then of between three and a half and four million found itself in 1946 possessed of twenty archiepiscopal metropolitan sees—England has three—and seventy-nine suffragan episcopal sees. Some of the old divisions, in the less settled areas, remained under the old system, thirty-eight in all. As the final jewel in the crown, Pope Pius XII appointed the first Chinese ever to receive the honour, a Chinese prelate, to the purple: Cardinal Tien, a member of the Society of the Divine Word. Truly the Chinese Church had come of age.

Perhaps the most heartening sign was the increase not only in the number of Chinese priests but also the existence of a great number of Chinese sisterhoods, in charge of hospitals and schools. Besides the missionary institutes of nuns which numbered fifty-eight, there were as many purely Chinese similar organizations, attracting the best of Chinese womanhood to their ranks.[1]

Meanwhile the Catholic schools and universities opened their doors once again, if they had ever been completely closed. But now more than ever before students flocked to the classes and lecture rooms. More than 3600 students attended the Catholic universities alone and close on half a million went to school in Catholic institutions of one kind or another.[2]

But in that year already, for those who had eyes to see, the doom of China was sealed. It was only a matter of time before the abandoned Chiang would be driven from the country and

[1] For the last attempt at statistics (1941) cf. Appendix III, p. 292.
[2] cf. *The Tablet*, 1st June 1946.

the whole stretch of Eastern Asia with its stupendous number of souls, four hundred or even six hundred million strong, would be controlled by the tyrannical, materialistic and atheistic Communist armies.

Once again the prize of the Chinese soul was wrested from the hands of the Church. It now remains only to tell something of the story of the persecutions, more cruel than those of Ancient Rome, more thorough, more annihilating, more devilish. But before doing so we must conclude the parallel story of the Protestant missions during the first fifty years of this century. In the end the blood of the martyrs of all Christ's followers mingled, and we shall treat the final scene as a single whole, which it is.

F. THE PROTESTANTS IN CHINA

i. *The First Years*

The Protestants, like the Catholics, had a number of serious problems to solve as they faced the new century in China after the baptism of blood, which we call the Boxer Rising. Like the Catholics they had to re-establish their stations; they enlarged their printing campaigns; as with the Catholics, so with the Protestants education was to play a very important part; the Protestant bodies too were in the process of becoming more Chinese and less missionary; they too would suffer the Japanese War, the Second World War, and Communist pressure.

In a number of matters the Protestant problems differed from those of the Catholics. The Protestant bodies on the whole had plenty of money. They could be lavish with their schools, hospitals and universities. On the other hand they were scarcely a united body, but rather many independent units with very varied theologies. Unity of action was difficult if not at times impossible. But valiant efforts were made, as we shall see, to overcome this permanent obstacle to progress. The great number of sects, as the missionaries crowded in, made for a certain amount of overlapping in the missionary work, and not a little disagreement.

Quarrels increased rather than diminished in the early years of the century, as the theological temperature rose in religious circles in Europe. The fever spread to the Far East as Modernism began to be a live issue.

The story of the Protestant missions in China in the twentieth century is one of almost unbroken progress until about 1920, when a set-back occurred. After the Boxer massacres the long-established bodies like the London Missionary Society and the China Inland Mission made good their losses and enlarged their stations. But on the whole little new ground was covered. Most of the chief centres of China had already been evangelized, and there seems to have been a tacit agreement that the various bodies would not 'poach' on each other's territory.

A new phenomenon, however, now appeared: a locust swarm of out-of-the-way and, in some cases, eccentric bodies flooded the Chinese missionary field. A mere list of the names is sufficient to give an idea of the confusion that this invasion must have caused in simple minds. For these Christian folk were not ready to leave alone the Christians already settled in China, they must needs Christianize the Christians, each sect believing that it was the only true brand of Protestantism. Their advent was a major disaster to the Protestant bodies and no small embarrassment to the Catholics.

The following is a list of some of these bodies:

The Seventh Day Adventist General Conference (who consider Saturday to be the Lord's Day).

The Assemblies of God in the U.S.A. and Foreign Lands.

The Broadcast Tract Press and Faith Orphanages.

The Metropolitan Presbyterian Mission.

The Church of God Mission.

The Canadian Holiness Mission.

The General Mission Board for the Church of the Nazarene.

The Ebenezer Mission.

The Evangel Mission.

The Hebron Mission.

A Faith Mission.

Mission Alliance.

The Mennonite Brethren Church.

The Pentecostal Holiness Mission.

The Pentecostal Missionary Union for Great Britain and Ireland.

And finally, a more important body, The Board of Foreign Missions of the Conference of the Mennonites of North America, and various other samples of the Mennonite persuasion. And this list is incomplete. Only by such a tabulation is it possible to realize the utter confusion such a variety of faiths would inevitably create in the minds of the Chinese. 'One Lord, one faith, one baptism' must have sounded little more than a pious wish in the ears of the neophyte, except in Catholic mission centres where the teacher could say that the Catholic Church always spoke with the same voice.

It was inevitable that many Protestant bodies should realize the need for some unity. Consequently, in the early years of the twentieth century, numerous efforts were made to create some link between, or union among, the Churches, or to achieve at least their federation. These efforts had only a very partial success, since those who were most sincerely convinced that they themselves were right were the least ready to give way. Only after the end of the First World War was it possible to get anything positive done, though much preparatory work went on from 1913 onwards.

ii. The Position of Protestant Missions in China after the First World War

When the First World War shattered peace everywhere, it did not disorganize the Protestant missions in China to such an extent as it did the Catholic. The Protestant bases were chiefly England and America, and these Powers had command of the seas. The Catholic missions on the other hand had their centres in Germany or Belgium or Austria and in devastated France. Psychologically also the Protestants stood to gain, because the Chinese would hear of the efficiency of the Anglo-Saxons, their strength, their political wisdom, the glories of democracy, and also of the principle of nationalism and self-determination. Their missionaries could add to their zeal and wealth, the aura of victory.

But the war once over, the Chinese experienced a revulsion of feeling against even the victors. The Treaty of Versailles, as we have already noted, did not give them redress: the foreign concessions still remained; China still appeared in the family of nations as a subject. In 1925 this anti-foreign feeling reached a crisis. The incident which brought it to a head occurred in Shanghai on 30th May of that year. Eight employees of a Japanese spinning firm in that city made representations to their employer, on behalf of the mass of workers, for better wages and shorter hours. The employer, in a fit of rage at this lack of submissiveness, drew his revolver and shot the leader of the party dead. It should be remembered that Japan had gained the 'concession' which Germany lost in Shantung. Considering the temper of the Chinese people, at that juncture in their history, this Japanese shooting act was not only a crime, it was also a supreme political blunder. China as a nation was roused, not only against foreigners but against their religion; and there were not found wanting men prepared to exploit such a deed. It became a symbol of China's past subservience to foreign devils and bullies, to those imperialist nations and in particular to Britain.

The situation was not improved when seven students, part of a demonstrating crowd, were shot dead by order of the British Chief of Police; nor were peace and amity restored by British, Japanese, French and Portuguese ships firing on demonstrators in the streets of Canton.

The incident two years later, when in 1927 at Nanking British and American warships shelled the city, gave ample justification for the anti-foreign demonstrations and acts of violence which followed. Of the eight thousand Protestant missionaries still in China at that date a bare five hundred remained; this outburst of violence caused a great exodus. Meanwhile large numbers of Chinese Christians apostatized, chiefly on the grounds that to be

Christian was to side with the foreigners and so to be disloyal to China.[1]

Once the crisis was over, many missionaries returned to their old posts, but things were never quite the same. A significant change had come about. Protestant leadership in China had definitely gone over to the Chinese. The National Christian Council—a recently formed body representing a large number of Protestant communions—was now ruled by a majority of Chinese on its staff.

Mention of the National Christian Council leads naturally to a consideration of the efforts during this period towards union among Protestant bodies in China.

iii. The Ecumenical Movement and China

It was only after the First World War that the ecumenical fervour swept over the rest of the world and over China also. The need for co-operation had of course been felt in the previous century. As the Bible was the chief instrument in the Protestant apostolate, they had in the nineteenth century co-operated in producing a standard agreed Chinese version, no mean feat. No union or federal arrangement was, however, created in those days. The time was not yet ripe; but it is remarkable that as early as 1877 a National Conference of Protestant missionaries was held in China. In the educational field, the Christian Literature Society, of which Timothy Richard became a secretary and prime mover, was inter-denominational. It even happened that a number of groups of different communions combined to set up universities and colleges, for instance, the University of Nanking, and the Shantung Christian University. It will be remembered too that the China Inland Mission, though Methodist in theology, was prepared to accept in the ranks of its evangelists members of almost any group.

But it was the justly famous 1910 meeting in Edinburgh of representatives from all over the Protestant world which gave a real impetus to the ecumenical movement in China. 'In many

[1] cf. The China Missions Year Book, 1929, p. 49.

ways that church', Professor Latourette is speaking of the Protestant bodies in China, 'was still divided, for it had been planted by more than a hundred different societies representing scores of denominations from many different lands.'[1] The problem was to bring them to unity. One of the difficulties was that the Chinese Protestant had little sense of what was even meant by 'church'. He was not always a churchgoer, even though a Christian. The problem remained acute, as new sects were appearing yearly with regrettable fertility. Even as late as 1938, '123 separate non-Roman missionary organizations were at work in China'.[2]

As we have seen, the beginning of the twentieth century saw the arrival in China of many new sects. A start in the move to union was made before 1914. In order to bring some kind of order out of this babel of voices, and as a direct result of the Edinburgh Conference of 1910, a committee called the Continuation Committee met in Shanghai in 1913. It represented the Protestant forces in China and a third of its number were Chinese. The work of this committee, which met regularly, was only brought to fruition by the calling in 1922 of a National Christian Conference: this consisted of over one thousand delegates, at least a third Chinese and representing almost all of the Protestant bodies then working in China. Out of the twenty-two bodies which originally belonged, by 1939 sixteen still maintained their membership. It included the Anglicans, the Methodists, Baptists, Congregationalists, Evangelicals, etc. The strength of this federation was about 300,000, that is, half the total Protestant strength in China.

Besides this fairly cautious *rapprochement* between the various Protestant religious bodies in 1922, a far more enterprising and far-reaching movement was on foot at the same time which culminated in the amalgamation of a number of churches into a single unit which called itself the Church of Christ in China.

[1] Rouse and Neill, editors, *A History of the Ecumenical Movement, 1517–1948*, London, 1954, p. 380.
[2] *ibid.*, p. 458.

This title was doubtless chosen to offset the title chosen by the Anglicans in the country, the Holy Catholic Church in China, and the ancient title of the Church whose centre is in Rome. In fact this new Church was made up of a section only of the Protestant bodies and kept very much to one particular theological colour, namely the presbyterian or non-episcopal kind. The Anglicans and the Methodists—an offshoot of Anglicanism—kept aloof from this body. It will be seen from the appendix[1] that while some Baptists joined, the majority did not. On the other hand the Congregationalists on the whole did, two-thirds of the Presbyterians did, so too the whole of the United Church of Canada. But despite the fact that the China Inland Mission and the Anglicans and the Lutherans did not, this new body became overnight the second largest group of Protestant Christians in China. Their first national assembly took place in Shanghai in 1927 and the great majority of the delegates were Chinese.

The theology of this group was extremely simple: faith in Jesus Christ as Redeemer and Lord—no mention of the Godhead of Christ—the Bible was the supreme authority 'in matters of faith and duty', since it was inspired by God. The Apostles' Creed was accepted as the expression of the faith. It was with this Church that the Communists tried to come to terms and with which they would have wished to associate all other Christian bodies. In this they failed. The reason that they chose the Church of Christ in China may have been the most markedly national spirit of that body, and also its extremely undogmatic content.[2]

iv. The Sinification of the Missionary Bodies

The sinification of the Protestant bodies in China was not in itself a bad thing, rather the reverse. It would have been well if the Catholics had advanced along that road much faster also. But in the case of the Protestants there were peculiar dangers. The Protestant Chinese neophytes were undoubtedly zealous,

[1] Pages 294-5.
[2] cf. Rouse and Neill, *op. cit.*, chapter by Stephen Charles Neill, p. 459.

but they were not so well grounded in their religion, so well
instructed as the Catholics. Were the Chinese Protestants sufficiently well grounded in Christian truth to be left to themselves? Their dogmatic formation was weak, more especially
as the form of Christianity that these bodies represented was on
the whole evangelical and moral rather than dogmatic. Thus,
once the European or American direction was relaxed, the
dogmatic allegiances relaxed also; and the tendencies were
towards Modernism on the one hand, or to social work on the
other. This latter tendency was to make it fatally easy for many
Christians brought up in a philanthropic Christianity to shift in
the direction of Communism, not realizing the theological
implications of this new creed and its incompatibility with the
true teachings of Christ.

It is interesting to see the great increase in Chinese among
the directors of the various religious bodies by 1937. Over two
thousand Chinese men were working as ordained pastors and an
equal number of unordained men formed part of the staffs.
About the same number of women also were helpers in the cause.
The foreign staffs still numbered nearly six thousand. It is significant that the majority of these, in the year 1937, were women,
and this demonstrates what a large part was being played by
women in the Protestant communions.[1]

The Chinese had control not only of the National Christian
Council, they also now had control of Church schools and of the
medical branch of the missionaries' work. Both the Y.M.C.A.
and the Y.W.C.A. were also under Chinese administration. The
foreign missionaries meanwhile withdrew to the remoter parts.
It was noteworthy also that most of these missionaries were over
fifty years of age.

The sinification of the missionary bodies in China was further
accelerated by the difficulty of filling the gaps left by the death
or departure of missionaries. This created a problem: to find and
educate suitable candidates for the ministry.

---

[1] Of these non-Chinese, 1084 were ordained ministers, 1002 not ordained,
1617 were wives and about 2000 single women.

v. The Problem of the Ministry

By far the most important and also the most disturbing problem among the Protestant Chinese bodies during this pre-Communist period was that of the ministry. As has already been pointed out the number of missionaries fell sharply in 1937 from eight to four thousand; of these about a thousand were ordained pastors, a thousand were children, one thousand six hundred were wives. Meanwhile the process of creating a Chinese clergy, as with the Catholics, was slow. As far back as 1823 the first Protestant Chinese evangelist had taken the road; his name was Leang A-fa. But very little headway was made until 1877, by which time twenty theological seminaries of an elementary kind had been erected. Just after the turn of the century, in 1905, over seven hundred men and over five hundred women were being trained as evangelists and pastors in a large number of seminaries up and down the country. This was a great achievement. It looked promising indeed. But once again troubles arose in the nineteen-twenties and thirties, stunting the growth. It is all best described by the Rev. Stanley Smith in his work on the subject.[1]

As he points out, the disturbing problem was that by no means all those who had begun went on to the ministry after completing the course; and it is to be noted how few in the higher grade there were in 1941. It is known that in 1935 only sixty-seven left for the ministry from these colleges. There was thus a great dearth of vocations and a considerable lowering of educational standard among the ministers, compared with the older type of pastor arriving from Europe; and these were coming in much smaller numbers.

'During the 1937–45 war it was estimated that 20 to 23 per cent of the Protestant ministers in China gave up their posts for other occupations.'[2]

[1] *The Development of Protestant Theological Education in China*, Shanghai, 1941. There were in 1941 in China:

    20 students of college graduation standard: 17 men and 3 women
    241 students of senior middle graduation standard: 210 men and 31 women
    268 students of junior middle graduation standard: 264 men and 4 women.

[2] So said Dr. T. C. Chao at the International Missionary Conference of Ontario (1947).

As the training became more sketchy so did the theology become more nebulous. True, some kind of unity had been achieved among many of the Protestant bodies working in China after the First World War, but it was unity at the expense of orthodoxy. For example The Church of Christ in China according to the *Christian Year Book* of 1931 said it had not yet formulated any creed, because it believed that when one was adopted 'it should be the product of the Chinese Church, expressive of her doctrinal convictions'.[1] This fatal loosening of theological ties had, in 1931, led Dr. Leighton Stuart to make the following serious pronouncement:

> There is little in the present situation to encourage the hope that China will ever be Christianized by continuing indefinitely the evangelistic and ecclesiastical processes hitherto conducted. Nor can a nebulous appreciation of the principles and spirit of Christ among individual Chinese get very far in spiritual regeneration. There is the danger that Christian faith and practice crystalizes in forms fashioned for it by promoters abroad. There is equally the disastrous possibility that Chinese awakenings, instinct with life, but formless and lacking definite aims or trained leaders, may fade into nothingness.[2]

All the Protestant institutions of education were thriving at this time except the theological and Bible schools, about which a report, *Education for Service in the Christian Church of China*, was published in November 1935. It is interesting to compare the conditions then with those of an earlier account given in the Burton Report of 1922. In 1922 there were nearly fifty Bible schools for men: by 1934 five of these had changed to higher grade schools, only nineteen remained as Bible schools, the rest seem to have ceased independent existence altogether. The theological colleges still remained at fourteen after twenty-two years, but two of them were now for women only. Further, women were now admitted to most of the others on an equal footing with men. In spite of this energetic effort to maintain theological education, the number of students with college education went down by over fifty per cent. Consequently the

[1] *op. cit.*, p. 151.   [2] cf. *Chinese Missionary*, 1948, p. 299.

teaching imparted was less and less doctrinal. This is yet another indication of the growing undogmatic texture of the Protestant approach to China.

Another serious difficulty has also arisen in the nineteen-thirties. At one time it was profitable for a Chinese who had been through one of these Protestant seminaries to take a job as catechist or preacher. Now that they could go to other schools and acquire a smattering of learning and get a moderately paid job elsewhere, there was little monetary incentive for them to enter one of the Protestant theological schools, and as a result the Protestant churches were tending more and more to rely, not on paid staff, but on voluntary workers. In many ways this would lead to better service. On the other hand their theological knowledge might be of the scantiest.

vi. The Protestant Missionary Methods in Recent Years

Though the latest chapter of the Protestant missions in China is over, the lessons to be drawn from the last hundred years and more have an important interest and should be stated.

On the surface the successes had seemed immense. Merely from the political point of view the Protestant faith had penetrated far. Sun Yat-sen, the founder of the Republic, had been a staunch Christian, Chiang Kai-shek was a professed follower of Jesus. The Soong family was Protestant, as were such well-known figures as C. T. Wang, Wang Chung-hui and Feng Yü-hsiang. Thirty per cent of the delegation that went to Europe for the Treaty of Versailles were Protestant.

The Evangelical methods used have been conveniently listed under three main heads: Revivalism, a teaching of social responsibility, and long-term religious education.

The first of these methods is supposed to have been discarded, but in practice it was much in use.[1]

A fair example of the technique called 'social responsibility' is to be found in the work of Stanley James. This work was sound enough in itself; but it is legitimate to wonder whether the

[1] *The Chinese Recorder*, 1933, p. 486.

Christian dogmatic content of it was really any more than a cry for more food and better wages. Might it not degenerate into mere Humanitarianism?

Undoubtedly one of the most practical methods of evangelizing used by Protestant bodies was in the realm of education. They outshone in this matter their Catholic rivals, certainly in the number of boys attending classes and also in efficiency. The peak year for Protestant primary schools was 1920, when there were over six thousand schools with 174,481 pupils. This was nearly four times as many children as in 1905.[1] It was in that very year, 1920, that the Chinese Government began to show jealousy of the foreigners and that they attempted to put a number of legal restraints upon them. After the Second World War, the situation had deteriorated so seriously that in 1947 it was estimated that of the six thousand only about five hundred of these schools had survived. Since the Communists won control, these institutions have ceased to exist except in name.

The Protestants made great strides with secondary education during the same period. The Protestant Boards were responsible for 339 middle schools in 1924. During the 'troubles', round about 1927, more than two-thirds of these failed to survive. Just before the Second World War the figures for secondary education had improved considerably. Then came that catastrophe of war, but the position was almost restored in the number of schools and even in an overall number of pupils, namely 74,320. They did not, however, reach the 1920 figure. 'They have trained millions of Chinese children and youths', so wrote *The Chinese Recorder* in 1940, 'who otherwise would have been deprived of the benefits of education. . . . If Our Lord and His message are known to thousands of Chinese educated people, the merit must go to Protestant schools and colleges more than to any other evangelical agency.'[2]

In 1940, Dr. Leighton Stuart, a Protestant minister and later American Ambassador to China,[3] made the following perhaps too

---

[1] 2196 primary schools with 42,546 pupils.　　　　　　[2] Page 292.

[3] He was confirmed as American Ambassador to China, 11th July 1946.

damning remarks on the subject of the effect that Protestant schooling had had on the Chinese mind. 'Something is very wrong with a situation in which such a small percentage of students, leaving College as professed Christians, continue to identify themselves with the local church in their future place of residence.'[1]

At university level, Protestant bodies have certainly led the field. In 1936 they had under their charge thirteen such universities, and immediately after the Second World War, in spite of almost complete disorganization during it, the enrolment of students was almost doubled.

Critics of Protestant missionary technique in China during the twentieth century concentrate on the failure of the Protestant schools and universities to turn out strong Protestant graduates. But these critics forget two things: the first is that the educational activity of these institutions was not primarily or immediately aiming at conversion, but rather preparing the ground for it. The second point is that many students, called Christian during their student days, were only very superficially so. No long course of instruction was necessary there before calling oneself a Christian, as was necessary for a Chinese wishing to be a Catholic. The call for 'results' may also have led to unduly optimistic and hasty 'results' being presented. We should therefore accept the criticisms with caution. However, here follows a criticism from a Protestant pen.

> . . . church-consciousness, at best weak among Chinese Christians, [the writer is referring to Protestant Christians] was almost entirely absent in a large proportion of Christian students. . . ; a large proportion of the students, out of whom should have come the leadership of the church, were lost to it. This was strikingly true of former students and graduates of the union universities. They found adjustment to the local congregations, usually small, without much vision, and with poorly trained pastors, so difficult that either they formed no connection with them or, if they did so, tended to be inactive or to drift away.[2]

[1] *The Chinese Recorder*, 1940, p. 292. [2] Rouse and Neill, *op. cit.*, p. 385.

Lack of deep doctrinal instruction may have had something to do with this falling away. This seems to be a recurring note in the story of the rather markedly untheological brand of Protestantism propagated in China.

The educational side of missionary work, as we have seen, played an enormous part in the Protestant method. But it must be remembered that their pupils were not necessarily Christians and the subjects taught were mostly secular: science, agriculture, the arts, engineering, medicine, commerce, law, public affairs. Indeed, it was these matters that interested the Chinese most. They were eager to catch up with the foreigners who seemed to be taking over their country. If missionaries were prepared to provide them with this secular information almost free of charge, they were quite ready to accept the terms of the bargain, namely the gift of a Bible and classes to understand it. In the year 1936–7 the total student population of Protestant theological colleges and universities was seven thousand; of these only a thousand were from Christian homes.

These many bodies between them carried on a very remarkable work of medical attention and training. Before the Japanese looted and the Communists confiscated their establishments the Protestants had as many as three hundred hospitals in China with nearly five hundred male doctors and a hundred and fifty women doctors working in them. Apart from the medical faculties in their universities, they had set up six medical colleges with over five hundred students. For those many derelict children, the remains of war, they had twenty-six orphanages; they also had two homes for the aged. Five of their hospitals were exclusively for cases of leprosy. One cannot but admire their zeal, their charity, their efficiency.

All this and the educational work, besides the direct missionary work undertaken, required a vast sum of money. It was only when all this money went into the coffers of the Communists as fines for supposed crimes committed that the flow ceased.

The printed word has always been a major instrument in the Protestant technique of evangelization. The first founts of

Chinese type made by Europeans were cut in 1815 for use by Dr. Robert Morrison and William Milne. With the opening of the Treaty Ports and the safe-conducts of the middle of the century, the distribution of Bibles or portions thereof became one of the chief means the Protestants had for getting the Christian message to the Chinese. It seems, however, to be a fact that in the main the printing was done in England and other Western countries. Latourette[1] records that by 1895 ten missionary presses had been established by Protestants in or near China. They were run on a denominational basis. It is of interest to record which were the enterprising groups; the following list is given by Latourette: the American Presbyterian Mission, the American Board of the Church Missionary Society, the English Presbyterians, the National Bible Society of Scotland, the Society for the Diffusion of Christian and General Knowledge, the Methodist Episcopalian Mission at Foochow, the Central China Press, the China Inland Mission Press. By 1914 the number had increased to nineteen. The vast majority of the publications were Bibles or portions of them. There seems to have been an almost frantic effort to outdo the distribution of each previous year. The peak was reached in 1924 when more than nine million copies of Bibles or parts of them were distributed. After this date the number receded. In 1937 68,127 whole Bibles and 67,818 New Testaments were distributed.

Besides the distribution of Bibles the Protestant missionaries, in their more modern approach, made much use of the newspaper, even from the beginning. There were four newspapers by 1838, one of which, *News from All Lands*, was the first to be produced on the Chinese mainland, in the city of Canton. The others were produced at Batavia, Malacca, Singapore. One of the most important ventures of that century was the *Chinese Repository*, a monthly, begun by the American, Dr. Elijah C. Bridgman, in 1832. In 1868 *The Missionary Recorder* carried on its work, as the former had ceased in 1852. *The Missionary Recorder* in its turn failed and *The Chinese Recorder* carried on its task until

[1] *op. cit.*, p. 437.

suppressed by the Communists. It was the most important Christian periodical in English in China. The Seventh Day Adventists produced *Signs of the Times* which in 1937 had a monthly circulation of 70,000 copies. The printing of periodicals was a chosen method for many of the Protestant organizations. Over two hundred were being sold in 1933, and eight of them had circulations of more than ten thousand copies.

All this printing and distributing of literature, quite apart from the daily running of thousands of mission centres, cost huge sums of money. The relevant details may be found in *The China Year Book*. To give some idea of the sums of money which went into the effort it is of interest to record that the American Missionary Boards alone in the year 1936 sent 4,058,132 dollars; the largest contributors were the U.S.A. Presbyterians with 662,560 dollars, and the Seventh Day Adventists with 369,377 dollars.

We have not often had occasion to mention the Buddhists in China, except in the earlier part of this narrative, but even to this day they remain a force, though a lesser force, in the life of the people of China. The Catholics seem almost to have passed them by, though we hear of Ricci visiting one of their monasteries, but a group of Protestants in the twentieth century made a direct effort to present Christ to them.

At Sha-tin, a place on the mainland of China, yet part of the British Crown Colony of Hong Kong, was a mission of Buddhist priests, organized by some Scandinavian missionaries. These Buddhist priests spent their whole lives wandering across China, staying at monasteries or convents, seeking 'Tao', or 'the Way'. This mission was built exactly like a Buddhist monastery, and the wandering priests or bonzes who stayed there were given an introduction to Christianity through Buddhist ideas and symbols.

The symbol of the Cross on a lotus blossom was everywhere to be seen—the lotus being the Buddhist symbol of the spiritual life—and great use was made of Buddhist scriptures which, they pointed out, contain remarkable similarities to Holy Scripture.

The theological approach of these Scandinavian missionaries was what is commonly known as 'undenominational', but the experiment was interesting. It may seem that too much space has been allotted to this venture. But physical size is not the measure of a spiritual activity. This approach, which links hands with that of Ricci to the Confucian *literati*, was a noble and inspiring experiment and deserves to be remembered.[1]

vii. *For Those who Like Statistics*

In order to have some idea of the relative importance of the various denominations in China, at the end of the book in an appendix will be found a tabulated list of Protestant bodies with their approximate numbers during the years 1932–5, according as they are given in *The China Year Book* for 1939. Here a few conclusions are drawn from that table. Only one body, the China Inland Mission, had more than a thousand missionaries, and it was one of three groups that had over a thousand Chinese evangelists. The China Inland Mission shared this distinction with the Methodists, the Presbyterians and Reformed Church of Christ in China and an amorphous collection called 'Other Baptists'. These all had about a thousand, whereas the China Inland Mission had well over three thousand; it had also 80,000 communicants. The next largest group, the Methodists, had 78,000; the Presbyterians 58,000. The Anglicans with their 500 foreign missionaries, their 900 Chinese evangelists and pastors and their 34,000 faithful, present quite a notable body, but the others had at the most 15,000 faithful, many a few thousands only.

We take leave of the brave Protestant endeavours with the overall picture of the situation as it appeared to the compilers of *The China Year Book* in 1939. After about a century of intensive work the total figure of communicants for the year 1936–7 was just over the half million, 536,089, out of a total of baptized Protestant Christians, 618,000.

---

[1] This information was given me by Mr. Philip Smiley while he was serving in Far Eastern waters in 1946.

EPILOGUE

THE present and the very recent past are no subject for history. We cannot truly guess the workings of Providence, we cannot foretell the future, gauge the significance of present events in the light of the not yet unfolded years ahead. The following pages therefore must not be read as history but merely as fragmentary glimpses and impressions of one who views this present in the light of the past, without any thought that the events he chooses to record can in any real sense be considered, in ultimate analysis, the most relevant.

The political and military background to the present sombre scene is as follows. During the war against Japan, from 1937 onwards, the Communists in the north-west and the Nationalists agreed to work in unison for the defeat of the common enemy. As soon as the Japanese accepted the conditions laid down at Potsdam, the Communists, without agreement with the Nationalists, threatened to march into the Japanese-occupied territory in the north and north-east. After much consultation and pressure the Communist leader Mao Tse-tung was persuaded to go to Chungking for consultation with Chiang Kai-shek. Meanwhile the two allies were waging a civil war against each other. In January 1946 a cease-fire was agreed to; the following month a fusion of the two armies was settled and a national constituent assembly was promised. In spite of these paper agreements the Communists continued their advance and were descending on Tientsin and Weihaiwei. The Americans, however, forestalled them by transferring Chinese troops there by plane from Nanking to Peking. The Communists then refused to assist at the national assembly. In July 1947 Chiang Kai-shek called upon the whole nation to support him in an effort to quell the Communist rebellion. It was war to the death.

In 1948 the civil war seemed to have reached the stage of stalemate, but in the following year the whole atmosphere changed. The Communists took the offensive and captured Peking in January. They had been given the Japanese arms by the Russians. The Yangtse was crossed by them in April with only a token resistance; in October the far south was overrun and Canton taken; by December every province of China was in Communist hands and China virtually Communist-ruled. It remained for the Party to digest the biggest catch it had ever made —a quarter of the population of the globe.

Fr. Rétif in a careful article in a recent number of the French review, *Etudes*,[1] has shown that the attitude of the Communists to the Catholic Church has followed a clearly defined policy; throughout China the same attitude has been followed, and throughout China it changed as though by command from a central authority. Thus from 15th August 1945, the day that Japan capitulated, to the summer of 1948, that is, just before the great advance on the south heralded by the capture of Mukden (September 1948), there was a most violent persecution wherever the Communists held sway. The area of their power was the northern provinces.

It is known that at least fifty-eight priests, mostly native, were killed or died of the cruelty they received at the hands of their captors. Sixteen Brothers and thirteen religious also lost their lives. It is reported that the Protestants had twenty-five martyrs for Christ in the province of Shantung alone. The worst period of this time was the bloody winter of 1947-8. Mob trials took place in every village. The church of Shunghi-Siwantze (in Chahár) was burnt and the Christians massacred. In the province of Jehol, priests, religious, laity were dragged over the frozen roads and then died either from blows or from exposure.

Of all the incidents for this period the best known is that of the martyrdom of the Trappist monks from the great monastery of Yangkiaping among the mountains north of Peking. First of all

[1] March 1950.

two priests and th... lay brothers were dragged off to a neighbouring town and went through the ordeal of a mob trial, a
'People's Trial'; these were then killed by having their heads
crushed between two heavy stones. The two priests were
Chinese and so were the three lay brothers. There were other
similar trials, and among the dead were French, French Canadian
and Dutch priests. In all thirty-one out of the seventy-five
monks were killed. Father Peter Chang, the parish priest of
Ling Yuen (Jehol) was whipped, then hung by his arms. They
were trying to make him apostatize. He was beaten so hard that
his legs broke. As he was dying he was heard by the fifteen
priests in the cubicle next to his to whisper: 'Conscience remains
up to the very last sigh.'[1]

In spite of all these fearful attacks, the order from Rome and
reiterated by the Papal Internuncio, Mgr. Riberi, was that no
one was to leave his station except if made to by force, or through
old age or infirmity. He himself remained at Nanking until the
Communists arrived, and only left because he was forcibly
ejected.

The Protestants also remained until 1951, when however,
perhaps wisely, the six hundred missionaries of the China Inland
Mission were withdrawn.

The Times, 19th February 1951, had this piece of news:

The Rev. W. J. Mitchell, Secretary of the China Inland Mission,
states that more than 600 missionaries are to be withdrawn from
China. This will be the first mass withdrawal ordered since the
mission was established in 1865. Missionaries are not being ill-
treated, but they are made to feel that they are unnecessary.

The Church in China was very strong, he said, and at present
enjoyed independence, but the ruling régime has made it clear that
it will remain so only while it is free from outside influence. That
meant that the missions were not getting the help they should from
the churches. About 100 of the missionaries being withdrawn were
from Australia and New Zealand, and the others came from the
United Kingdom, the United States, Canada, Europe, and South
Africa. Nearly all represented Protestant denominations.

[1] cf. *Outlook*, April 1948.

A number of Catholic missionaries also withdrew at about the same time, but, as we recalled, the Holy See called a halt, telling all to remain at their posts, with the results both tragic and heroic that we know.

What were the reasons for this persecution? In the first place war leads to irrational violence; in the second the Church, for example Mgr. Yu-pin of Nanking, had compromised itself in the eyes of the Communists by being very openly pro-Chiang Kai-shek. Thirdly some was 'long-distance' revenge for the punishing of the Boxer Rising of 1900. A pagan village here or there would attack a neighbouring Christian village and anni-hilate it; lastly, all the time the implacable hatred of the Com-munists for God and religion was the cause.

Suddenly the sky cleared, persecution was over, the Com-munists were all smiles with the outstretched hand; priests were released and buildings returned. The soldiers were told: 'Hands off the Church.' This next phase lasted from midsummer 1948 till approximately the spring of 1950. Liberty of conscience was the great cry. The Communist armies were coming as liberators from the tyranny of Chiang Kai-shek, for example Mgr. Coté of Suchow in Kiangsi was liberated. Military and political chiefs would pay ceremonious calls on the local clergy.

Why this sudden reversal of policy? The first reason may have been that all over the world public opinion had been thoroughly aroused over the appalling treatment of missionaries. Then this was the period during which the Communists were digesting immense new areas conquered by their armies. It was the time that the whole of China suddenly fell at their feet. They had to limit the hostile element as much as possible until they felt them-selves firmly in the saddle. Besides, the population was not yet sufficiently indoctrinated to support a violent attack on this institution which had given them so much, their schools, their hospitals, their orphanages. . . . Lastly, they wished to keep the economic and social structure of society going, the educational buildings, the hospitals, until such time as they had the personnel to take them all over.

The Christians, having few illusions as to the sincerity of the conquerors or of the lastingness of the peace, did not lose the opportunity afforded by this respite to reorganize themselves. They prepared for a further attack by the distribution of books which would provide the doctrine for the time when priests were once again hunted—as indeed they were soon to be; priests and bishops proletarianized themselves by becoming workers; hundreds of priests and nuns became peasants, farmers, weavers, gardeners, industrial workers, doctors, chemists.

Meanwhile the technique was to choke the Church to death. The children had Communists cadres, were taught Communist songs, were made to spy on their parents and each other. The Communists' technical training colleges gave 'certificates' in three or four months, whereas the other universities' courses last three years. The Catholic University of Tsinku at Tientsin was the last to preserve its independence, Aurora and the Catholic University of Peking (run by the Society of the Divine Word) were already Communist supervised and controlled. But even at Aurora the real power rested with three Soviet professors, three Soviet students and three Soviet servants.[1] Financially the burden was overwhelming, taxes and fines were unrelated either to the supposed offence or to the capacity to pay. However, so long as the foreign supply of money went on, the Communists were quite ready to leave the nominal ownership of these institutions in the hands of the Christians. But a time came when the foreign sources of supply dried up. Then the Government simply confiscated the buildings. All missionaries were already immobilized in their own town, often in their own compound. This could not go on. The end of the story is told in *The Times* of 27th September 1952:

> The reorganization of Chinese universities which has been in progress for the past few months has now been completed, according to an announcement from Peking. One effect of the change is the merging or disappearance of all those universities that were founded and maintained on foreign Christian initiative. The aim has also

[1] This was told me by Fr. Germain, one-time Rector of Aurora.

been to reduce the number of what are now described as comprehensive universities, and to create a number of new technical colleges.

In Peking, the only fully fledged university to remain is the Peking National University, which will absorb Yenching University, the Anglo-American supported missionary institution, which incidentally has produced a whole crop of Communists holding high office in the new régime. Tsinghua University is to become an engineering college and its arts faculty will also be absorbed by the Peking National University. Fujen, the Roman Catholic foundation, is to be absorbed in the National Normal College. There are also to be created in Peking technical colleges specializing in geology, aviation, steel technology, forestry, agricultural mechanization, finance, and law.

The same pattern is evident in other parts of China. In Nanking, Ginling College; in Shanghai, St. John's and the French Roman Catholic Université de l'Aurore; and in Canton, Lingnan University, are all foreign-supported institutions whose identity is to disappear. In each of the cities of Tientsin, Shanghai, Nanking and Canton only one comprehensive university is to remain, while technical colleges similar to those in Peking are to be set up.

Thus ends the phase of missionary higher education in China which has lasted more than half a century; ironically, though perhaps inevitably, it has been ended by a régime in whose ranks many—perhaps even the majority—of its products are to be found.

About March 1950 a more active persecution was brewing. The new scheme was to create a reformed Church to which all the denominations including Catholic would be expected to belong. This movement had been set on foot by Wu Yao-tsung and Chou En-lai. It was this move to separate the Catholics from their allegiance to the Holy See that produced remarkable demonstrations of Christian heroism and numberless martyrs.

Hundreds of heroic episodes might be cited, not only Catholic but Protestant; let us give one of the most stirring. The Communists were trying to drive a wedge between the native Catholics and the foreign central authority, the Pope. For this purpose they chose as special object of attack the Papal representative, Mgr. Riberi. Throughout China meetings were called for the repudiation of Mgr. Riberi and all he stood for. At first some measure of success was claimed. The incident to follow was one of the finest incidents in the stand made by the Christian Catholics in their fight to preserve their loyalty to the Holy See.

The Government began by trying to make Catholics declare that the Internuncio Riberi was a lackey of imperialists, then to repudiate the Pope, then doubtless in the following year to repudiate 'foreign doctrine' or 'Western theology'. The Communists spread rumours that in other parts of the country Catholics were enthusiastically supporting this separatist Church, when in fact the whole Catholic Church in China has shown an unswerving loyalty to the Holy See.

The Government also formed committees of laymen to control the worship in the churches. These joined the reformed Church. If a priest said Mass in one of these churches the faithful refused to go, or if forced to go, refused to join with the priest in the prayers.

On a June Sunday in Chungking,[1] as the faithful were leaving the church after Mass, they were met by a procession which they were forced to join. It was to be a demonstration against the foreign imperialists especially against the Internuncio, Mgr. Riberi.

The Communists were hoping to persuade the Catholics that they could repudiate the Pope's representative, and so save their skins, without repudiating the Pope. Some Catholics had played with the idea, knowing that next they would be asked to repudiate the Pope. This demonstration was the great test case.

'Down with the imperialist Riberi—let the Government expel him' was the cry. The reason for the Communist animus against him was that he had warned the Catholics of the schismatic Church founded by the Communists. The remainder of the incident will follow closely the words of the Hong Kong correspondent of *The Tablet*:

By late afternoon the régime had staged another of its monster Szechwan demonstrations. . . . The day's schedule called for a final summing-up of the aims of the demonstration, to be

[1] cf. *The Times*, February 1951.

delivered to the weary marchers by various 'interested participants'. It was then that Fr. John Tung, aged forty-five, electrified Chungking's 'Progressive Catholics' and the city's officialdom.

Ascending the speaker's rostrum, he traced on himself the sign of the Cross, and began, as all sermons preached in Catholic Churches begin, with the words, 'In the name of the Father and of the Son and of the Holy Ghost.' Then, in the stillness as of a church, he continued, 'The Sacred Heart of Jesus, have mercy on us; the Immaculate Mary Mediatrix of all graces, St. Peter and St. Paul, pray for us.' With a bow to the large portrait of Mao Tze-tung and to his audience, he said, 'The point of what I wish to say is this: "I offer myself as a sacrificial victim to bring about an understanding between the Government and the Church."'

This was unusual enough and unwanted by the Communist organizers. But he went on:

It is those very people, who deny the existence of God and of the immortal soul, who do not recognize the Vicar of Jesus Christ on earth—the Holy Father—and the position of the Hierarchy in relation to the Catholic Church, who would claim that the 'three independencies'[1] programme is merely a patriotic movement. They profess the freedom of religion and admit the spiritual ties between believers and their religious superiors, but by this same 'independence' I am today required to attack the representative of the Holy Father. Tomorrow I shall perhaps be forced to attack the representative of Jesus Christ, the Holy Father. The following day why should I not then be constrained to attack God Himself?

In a ringing tone and in the most solemn manner Fr. Tung went on to declare his Catholic Faith and his disapproval of the Communist campaign to force Catholics to ask for the expulsion of the Pope's representative. Then:

Since the government has time and again insisted that they are not forcing us, but simply directing us, then I ought only to speak from my heart, and not have said yes with my lips, and no in my heart.

[1] These the 'independencies' are 'Three Autonomies' suggested to the Church by the Communists to free them from foreign tutelage.

I ought only to sign those declarations to which I sincerely consent, and not affix my name to those with which I disagree. If I live by deceit and fear death, I become a completely untrustworthy man, of use to no one.

Foreseeing what might happen to him he concluded:

I make these statements now being of a sane mind, and I avow that whatever I may say later in a state of confusion will be entirely invalid. I am a Catholic and desire to love both my country and my religion. I do not wish discord between the two, but if the government cannot work harmoniously with religion, persecution will follow and many victims will be demanded from among Catholics. In such an event it is better that I die right now.

There was complete silence while he spoke, and afterwards the meeting broke up in confusion. The Communists had been defeated in their design. That was the end of the affair. The following Sunday at High Mass in the cathedral the Vicar Capitular read a statement in the name of himself and all the priests who had submitted under pressure, saying: 'We have committed a serious offence to lend our names and presence to the demonstration. We solemnly withdraw our names, conscious of our sin before God and you. We humbly ask pardon for the scandal we have given.'

A few weeks later the blow, that all knew must come, descended upon Fr. John Tung. On the morning of 2nd July he was seized and carried off to prison. He has not been heard of since, but people were saying that he had died in prison after being subjected to appalling torture.

As an example of what happened to many Catholic institutions during the turmoil of the Communist triumph we shall take the history of the Belgian Benedictine foundation at Sichan,[1]

[1] The Benedictine Monastery of SS. Peter and Andrew at Sichan in West China was founded from the Abbey of St. André in Belgium at the request of the Most Rev. Archbishop Celso Constantini, the first Apostolic Delegate in China, with a view to introducing Christian monasticism into the Buddhist province of Szechwan and to aid the newly-erected vicariate of Chungking by the traditional Benedictine apostolate of prayer and work. It was established in the year 1927.

Chungking, in the province of Szechwan, which later, owing to war, removed to Chengtu in 1943.

It was Christmas Day, 1949. The Communists took over the city of Chengtu. Until March of the following year the Benedictines were left more or less free to continue their work in the city. During these three months there were a number of conversions. The Legion of Mary functioned as usual, and non-Catholics could still come to visit and consult the Fathers. In the meantime the Communists were trying to consolidate their control of the city, first by propaganda in order to win the good-will of the people with enticing promises, then by force of arms in suppressing all possible resistance to the régime. Having established themselves in power, they launched their long-expected persecution against all organized religions. The Catholic Church was considered by them to be their most formidable enemy, and therefore the Catholic institutions and organizations in the city were their main target of attack.

The Benedictine monastery, with its well-known affiliations with Chinese professors and students of the city, could not possibly be let go free. The Communists began by petty annoyances: they came to search the monastery at all hours of the day and night; thus they rendered monastic life impossible. They then took away anything they took a fancy to. Finally they had recourse to their most terrible tactic: that is, trying by persuasion and by threat, to excite the Chinese monks to rebel against their European confrères. They wanted to use the former as their instruments to persecute and destroy the latter. Once they had removed the Europeans they would bring the Chinese monks in their turn to subjection. They used the same tactics in their attempt to destroy the hierarchy. They had turned the laity against their priests and the priests against the bishops, thus hoping to destroy the Church from within. They avoided making martyrs at all costs.

The monks were always persecuted on 'political' grounds; they were called imperialists or reactionaries. Here we have the common pattern in the Communist attack throughout China.

In this battle, as through the centuries, the enemy has always under-estimated the power of the Church, thinking it has but an earthly stability, whereas its strength comes from God. They also overlooked the bond of charity which Christ had established between the various members of the Mystical Body, which is the Church.

In spite of threats the Chinese monks, at a public meeting which had been called by the Communists, proclaimed their loyalty to God, to the Holy See and to their monastic family. The European members of the community felt it a privilege to be able to suffer something with their Chinese fellow monks, brethren in Christ. They continued to do what work they could for the Church, replacing the proscribed Legion of Mary by a study circle devoted to those subjects having a direct bearing on Communism. At the same time the Fathers drew up a catechism which contained the questions and answers Catholics should know in times of persecution. They clearly stated the Catholic position on the Communist-sponsored movement of the three autonomies: self-government, self-support and self-propagation.

This state of affairs lasted until the middle of 1951. After that the Communists had recourse to force. They could not tolerate any longer the existence of a monastery, a citadel of resistance in their very midst. They removed the Prior and put him in prison for three months before expelling him. The other European monks were also expelled from China one by one. The Chinese monks were driven from the monastery. At the time of the dispersal sixteen monks lived there, of whom six were Chinese.

This account is not peculiar to the Benedictine monastery, it has been the common lot of the Church: threats, violence, expulsion.

The situation in China as it appeared in 1952 was somewhat as follows. Of the hundred and forty-three dioceses or their equivalents eighty-seven were already without their bishops; forty-three of these had been expelled, seven had died in prison, eighteen were still in prison. The fate of nineteen was unknown. More than two thousand of the foreign priests, out of roughly three thousand, had been expelled, while the number of religious Sisters treated in like manner was much greater. The persecution was not all directed against the foreigner, for more than two hundred Chinese were in prison and over a hundred Chinese had been killed. Of course many foreign priests were still in prison and others had been killed.

On the material side the situation was as bad. All funds had been seized and in an apparently legal way. By the simple method of imposing immense fines for imaginary infringements of the law the Christian institutions, whether Catholic or Protestant, could be, and soon were, reduced to penury. Thus the Rector of Aurora University was fined in Chinese money the equivalent of 1,000,000 American dollars.

Buildings were not spared. Every secondary school, every primary school, every college for further education, most of which were technical, all of them built and manned by Catholics, had by 1953 been confiscated by the Communist Government. The universities were not spared, nor their libraries. The famous Jesuit library at Aurora University was seized. The churches too, except those in the biggest cities—these were left untouched in order to give the appearance of tolerating religion—were taken over and are now used for secular purposes. The numerous great hospitals, the children's homes, the homes for the aged, all in fact, were taken. The same could be said of the Protestant institutions. They have all been purged, confiscated and become centres not of Christian culture but of atheistic propaganda.

The whole of China was put back to school—the Communists call it 'washing the brain'. At 6 a.m. comes a lesson in Communism, no matter what the remainder of the study is, or the work in hand; and again in the evening a lesson to discover whether the morning lesson has been well learned and put into practice. Two hundred to three hundred newspapers in China used to disseminate news; now they all sing the same song. The newspaper is the textbook out of which the 'good' Chinese learn their lesson in the New Way.

Enough people have been liberated from China after periods

in prison for us to get a clear if horrifying picture of conditions undergone by the multitude of confessors for their faith whether Catholic or Protestant. From 4 a.m. till 8 p.m. you are not allowed to close your eyes, you are obliged to remain immobile, warders watching all the time; bright lights dazzle the eyes. At 8 p.m. you are liable to be taken off for an examination. This may last two, four, eight, ten or even twelve hours. Its purpose is to persuade you by exhaustion to sign a document confessing your guilt. This attack on conscience is going on all over China. Two examples will suffice. One priest, Fr. Tiberi, was made to stand for a hundred and eight hours in order to force him to confess his guilt. He would not. They released him; but he was released mad. He lives on in Italy. Another was being conditioned to divulge something he might have heard in Confession. As he felt his resistance collapsing, he cut out his tongue so that he could not speak. He will never speak again.

Besides the secret attack on the conscience in the prison cell, the public attack goes on in savage ferocity. Popular trials take place in all great cities of China. In Peking the stadium can hold 30,000 persons. No one is excused from going. No one is allowed to remain a passive spectator; all must show their approval by vociferations, gesticulations, appeals for punishment on the wretched victims crouching on the platform, usually kneeling with hands tied behind their backs.

The most savage attack of the Communists was against the nuns and particularly against nursing sisters. In Canton in February 1951 five Sisters of Mercy were arraigned before a vast crowd. The 'trial' was broadcast. They were accused of murdering the very children they were in fact trying to save. After cruel imprisonment and humiliating treatment these nuns were expelled the country. No one, not even the judges, believed the accusations. The same mockery of justice was performed before a vast crowd of 80,000 people in Hankow when two American nuns were accused of murdering babies.

The Legion of Mary, another Catholic society, a lay organization, now received the brunt of the Communist attack on the laity. Men and women who before the persecution seemed ordinary folk enough, became, according to the evidence of more than one eyewitness, filled, as the New Testament used to phrase it, with the Holy Spirit. Their heroism amazed even their enemies. Their leaders took special vows: never to miss a meeting, to accept every job for the Legion, never to flee on account of prison or death. Seventy of these legionaries in Shanghai had already died for the Faith by the end of 1953.

The Legion of Mary was begun between the wars in Dublin by Mr. Frank Duff, who is still alive. The Legion is in every corner of the world. Its aim is to bring Christ to all men under the direction of the hierarchy. Its patroness is Mary the Mother of God, its weapons prayer, penance and action.

The setting up of the Legion of Mary today throughout China was the work of the Internuncio Mgr. Riberi. He had known Edel Quinn, Legion Envoy for Africa, and on landing in China he said that the best way of reaching the Chinese nation was the Legion of Mary. In a very short time it was set up in ninety of the dioceses of China. Mgr. Riberi sent Fr. Aidan McGrath to do the work; a great deal of it was also being done by Johanna Hsaio, a heroic young woman, aged only twenty-seven when she was taken by the Communists. She came of an old Catholic family. As men had to have Communist passes, girls were sent instead, to go from place to place. In disguise Johanna went all over North China; and in this way she organized four hundred branches. Her prestige was such that the Communists, believing that the Legion's handbook was really in code, thought that Mary must be a code name for Johanna Hsaio. She was finally seized at the time of the launching of the State Church. They offered her the post of organizer. She refused and prophesied that she would be shot. She was tried and sentenced. It was generally presumed that she was dead. But in fact the court gave her ten years' imprisonment. At the time of writing (1955) she is still in prison.

Mgr. Riberi is reported to have said on one occasion that if one wanted to gauge the stature of the Legion one had to go back to primitive Christianity. If it had not been for the Legion, the Church in China would not have survived.

At the moment of the Communist triumph, in 1949, there was chaos. Then everyone, especially the Legion, expected a persecution. Missionaries, following an old Papal instruction not to throw away lives unnecessarily, had left the country in fair numbers. But orders came from Communist Peking that local government should be set up, that good tolerant rule should be created; no one was to pay off old scores; the missionaries and the Legion were to be left in peace. All that was needed, from the Communist point of view, was that the present generation be subjected to intensive propaganda and they would be converted to the régime.

The unexpected result was that the Legion took over local government in more than one place. Even a bishop set up local defence, a local police, and organized sanitation. There had been no medical services in the Nationalist régime. In one place the Legion organized a complete hospital. This was the period of decent government. The Communists were endeavouring to endear themselves to the people. Even Catholics were saying: these are not real Communists. They got education going; they refused bribes. Prostitutes were sent off the streets, begging became unknown. They preached public virtue. There was a department of Smells!

The missionary field was open. It is true, there was propaganda, but it was not forbidden to have counter-propaganda, for instance, to set up a rival at a Communist meeting. The Communists even encouraged this; it created a crowd. As the Legion was quick to adopt this work, the pleasure of the Communists was soon soured, for the audience usually applauded, not the Communists' arguments, but those of the Catholic Church. The result was a great wave of conversions. One important Church dignitary in China commented that the time was one of mass conversions. He was wrong. Time was on the side of the Communists but they now made their fatal mistake. What with propaganda and education they could have worn out resistance. But they lost their nerve,

they over-emphasized the Catholic success. They looked around
for a way out. It is true that they were, in a sense, in a precarious
position, being only a handful; but they were armed. True also
that meanwhile the Legion had founded a thousand branches
with more than seventeen thousand active members. When the
pressure of persecution started, the numbers even increased. The
Communists seemed to be hesitating. There was at this time
great variation in policy from one area to the other, here persecution, there peace. If the Legion was suppressed under one name,
it rose up under another. What were the Communists to do?
They devised a scheme for a State Church.

Mgr. Riberi had set up on his arrival 'The Catholic Central
Bureau' and placed at its head a Scheut Missionary, Fr. le Grand.
This extremely efficient priest received from all the bishops of
China their decision on the Autonomous Church—they were all
adverse, not to Chinese clergy and self-support in finance, but to
separation from the Holy See. Immediately he sent out that
unanimous decision to every Catholic centre in China. Thus the
Church was forewarned and forearmed. The immediate result was
that he and Fr. McGrath were arrested on the same day. Fr. Joseph
Sing, one of Mgr. Riberi's secretaries, was taken and has died in
prison, the other, Fr. Ch'eng, is still in prison, resisting to the end.

This was the moment when the Legion proved itself. These
lay Catholics of both sexes, brought up in the spirit of absolute
self-sacrifice and loyalty to the Holy See, came forward everywhere in support of the hierarchy's stand. The State Church had
failed. A decree was passed by the Communist Government that
to belong to the Legion was treason and the penalty death. The
formula was: if you forswear the Legion you go free. Now
the dam of hatred burst. More than fifteen million people were
killed, among them many Christians, for a variety of reasons.
Burying alive and similar horrors took place. This alienated the
whole people, which remained sullen, angry and cowed. In
every town of China was set up an anti-Legionary bureau. Yet
where the Legion is, the anti-Christian drive has failed. It strives
against the white flame of utter devotion.

Here is one example of heroism: the priest chaplain of the Legion at Tientsin said he could not sign the Communist document to forswear the Legion. They told him: 'You'll have to be killed.' He replied: 'In all my life I never thought of the possibility of martyrdom, but now it has been offered to me I certainly shall not refuse it.'

The president of the same branch was also brought before the tribunal. When asked to sign he said: 'What good could that shattered life be to me.' It was winter—he was middle-aged. However, he was stripped, and every half-hour water was poured over him. It froze to him and in three hours he was dead. But the effect was to increase the courage of the others.

As a summing up of this phase in the crucifixion of the Church in China here is the letter written in November 1952 by a 'Group of Chinese Catholics' to the Indian delegation to China.

Apart from a certain number of large centres, freedom of worship, although guaranteed by the Constitution, is a mockery pure and simple. The truth is that the dioceses have been devastated spiritually, that their leaders have been expelled, that their Chinese and foreign priests have been driven away, that their churches are occupied, and that most abominable pressure is being brought to bear on individual consciences. In Communist China one cannot hope to live without adopting the materialistic and atheistic principles of the Party.

Our prisoners. . . . They are imprisoned by the hundreds on the pretext of crimes against the fatherland, but in reality on account of their religious convictions. They are arrested one fine day or one fine night, in the street or in their homes, often without a written charge. Taken from their peaceful occupations as Christian ministers, they disappear in the darkness of the night. There are dark holes and over-populated cells where the unhappy prisoners cannot all lie down at the same time and where they must take turns in sleeping. There are cells which are refrigerators in winter and furnaces in summer. Prisoners are obliged from daybreak till dusk to squat, without the least motion, on wooden or cement floors. No movement is permitted. It is a crime to close their eyes. There is complete inactivity for long days, weeks, months. Interrogations are the only break in this monotonous régime. The prisoner appears alone before his judges. He must rely entirely upon his own memory with regard to declarations that he made before; he is not allowed a pencil or paper which would make it possible for him to note some details or some replies that he has given. When he is obliged to make a written declaration, he is not permitted to retain a copy.

If his answers are judged unsatisfactory or insolent, or if he refuses to answer, because any answer would imply apostasy or his own dishonour, he is kept standing for hours, sometimes for days and for entire nights between guards holding tommy-guns. Chains and shackles are put on the prisoners' hands and feet, which make them swell immediately. Like savage beasts they are chained to the walls of their dark holes. They are suspended by their hands until they ask for mercy and agree to talk. . . .[1]

The state of affairs is always fluctuating, but by the end of 1954, only a handful of foreign priests still remained in China, compared with the three thousand before the persecution. It is said that four hundred Chinese priests were in prison. The total number of priests, religious and nuns, Chinese and foreign who had been killed up to the end of 1954 was 166. This figure leaves aside the thousands of both Protestant and Catholic ministers and priests who were tortured to breaking point, the thousands of nameless lay folk who died or were tortured for Christ. This is the hour of darkness; but, as in the days of Diocletian, so today, the sufferings of the martyrs are not unrewarded. The hour of Christ will come. 'Love is strong as death.'[2]

The latest news from China is contained in a letter from Bishop Kiong of Shanghai, printed in *Shanghai Missionaire*, July 1955, 'Tell all men everywhere that the Church of China is not dead, but rather is she more beautiful than ever. True, another attack is about to be launched, but up to now the Church has come out victorious from so many a combat, that on this occasion too, we do not lose courage.'

In the same publication it was recorded that on 6th May 1955, of the six thousand missionary priests who worked in pre-Communist China, only thirty-three still remain, twenty of whom

[1] *The Tablet*, 5th November 1952.   [2] Canticle of Canticles, viii, 6.

were in prison. There were also sixteen foreign nuns and one Brother. They ask incessantly for our prayers.

The love of Christ for China expressed through the ages by the Church, persistent, courageous, unswerving, is like the love of a true lover. It will admit no impediment, nor will it alter when it alteration finds. China may desert or be forced to flee the embrace of Christ, but the love of Christ is an ever fixed mark. No tempests, not the bitterest persecution nor the basest accusations can make Him in His Church turn away. Christ's love bears it out even to the edge of doom.

When will the marriage of these two minds be consummated? At times they have been friends. Then misunderstandings have arisen, the mutual approach has halted, and now the two remain at arm's length.

But one day the mind of Christ and the mind of China will be made one. It is the purpose of this book to help bring that happy consummation about and speed its arrival even if only by one hour.

Appendix I

TRANSLATION OF THE NESTORIAN MONUMENT

(taken from Fr. Semedo's *History of China*)

A RELATION IN THE PRAISE AND ETERNAL MEMORY OF THE LAW OF THE LIGHT
OF TRUTH BROUGHT FROM JUDEA AND PREACHED IN CHINA

A PROLOGUE made by the priest of the kingdom of Judea named Chingching.

Oh how true and profound is the eternal and the incomprehensible most spiritual speaking of time past; He is without beginning, and of time to come He is without end, and always in the same perfection. He took nothing, and with it He made all. He is principal, consisting of Trinity and Unity, yet without any real principle. The Lord Olooyu. He made the four parts of the world in figure of a Cross. He moved the Chaos and made the two principles. There was an alteration made in the abyss, and heaven and earth appeared. Nature at the beginning was pure and exempt from inordinate passions, and the heart was clean without the unruliness of the appetites.

Man came afterwards to fall into the deceits of Satan, who, covering with words the mischief he had plotted, perverted the innocence of the first man. From this principle sprang 365 Sects, which by reason they were so many did none drive away the other, and of all of them was made a net wherein the world was caught. Some chose the creatures and appropriated divinity to them: others were plunged in that error of thinking that all is nothing, and ends in nothing. Others made sacrifices to invite good fortune with: others counterfeit virtue to deceive the world. The understanding corrupted with errors, and the will with passions are altogether obscured. Men walked forward without ever arriving at the end they aimed at. The world was all in a miserable confusion. Man still multiplied the darkness, and losing his way, wandered long time in it, without finding the truth.

Then the Messias, one of the Three Persons, covered his true majesty and making himself a man, appeared unto the world. An angel came to minister the mystery, and a Virgin brought forth the Holy One. A star appeared which gave notice of his birth to those of the kingdom of Persia. They came to offer him Tribute, and all was done according to what had been foretold by the four-and-twenty saints. He published to the world the most true law. He purified their customs and rectified the faith. He cleansed the world. He perfected virtue and therein founded the three virtues. He opened the way to life and shut up that of death. He manifested the bright day and banished the obscure darkness. He conquered the obscure seat, at what time the devil remained wholly subdued, and succoured with his mercy the sinking world, that men might ascend to the habitations of light. After He had perfected his work, He ascended into the heavens at midday. There remained 27 books of holy scripture. There was opened the gate to conversion by means of that water which cleanseth and purifieth. His ministers made use of the holy Cross, they made their abode no more in one place than another, that they might illuminate the whole world. The world being thus reduced to union, men did walk after their example, and thus did they open the way of life and glory.

They suffered their beard to grow, and did show by this means that they were like other men in their external parts. They cut their hair even to the roots upon the top of their head, and by this they showed that they had no internal worldly affections. They kept no servants, the noble and the common men were with them the same thing. They took no riches from men. They gave to the poor that which they had. They fasted and watched to bring the flesh into subjection to the spirit. Seven times a day they offered sacrifices of praise, by which they helped the living and the dead. Every seventh day they did offer. They purified their hearts to receive the holy innocence. The true law hath no name which doth well suit with it and that is able to explain the excellency thereof; therefore because it wanteth another name, we will call it the law of Brightness. The law, if it be not holy, cannot be called great: and if holiness be not answerable to that which the law teacheth, it may not have the same name. But in this law the holiness correspondeth to the law, and the law to the holiness.

If there be not kingly persons to favour it, the law cannot well be propagated; if they receive not the law, they cannot grow truly great. When they and the law do agree, presently the world is enlightened. By this means, at the time, when a king named T'ai Tsung did govern with famous prudence and sanctity, there came from Judea a man of high virtue, by name Alopen, who being guided by the clouds brought the true doctrine. And in the year A.D. 635 he arrived at court. The king commanded the Colao, Fang Hsuan-ling, that he should go and meet him as far as the West, and that he should treat him as his guest with all manner of kindness. He caused this doctrine to be translated in his palace, and seeing the law to be true, he powerfully commanded it should be divulged through the Kingdom, and presently after, he sent forth a royal patent, which contained that which followeth.

The true law hath no determinate name. The ministers therefore go about in every part to teach it unto the world, having no other aim, but to be profitable to those that live in it. In the kingdom of Ta'chin this Alopen, being a man of great virtue, hath brought from so remote a country doctrine and images, and is come to place them in our kingdom. Having well examined that which he proposeth, we find it to be very excellent and without any outward noise, and that it hath its principal foundation even from the creation of the world. His doctrine is brief, neither doth he found his truth in superficial appearances; it bringeth with it the salvation and benefit of men. Wherefore I have thought it convenient that it should be published through our Empire.

He commanded the mandarins of this court of I-ning, that they should build there a great church with 21 ministers, weakening by that means the monarchies of Lao Tzu, head of the sect of Taoists, which was carried in a black chariot towards the West. So the great T'ang being enlightened together with Tao, the holy Gospel came into China, and a little while after, the king commanded that Alopen his picture should be painted on the walls of the temple, where it shineth, and his memory will always shine in the world.

According to the records of the empires of Han and Wei the kingdom of Ta'chin bordereth southward upon the Red Sea, and northward on the Mountains of Pearls, westward on the (forest of the immortals and the Flowery Forests), eastward on the (long winds and the weak waters) and the dead water . . . the country produceth a lake Asphaltitis of fire, balsam, pearls and carbuncles. It hath no robbers, but all live in joyful peace. The Gospel only is allowed in that kingdom, and honours are only conferred on those who are virtuous. Their houses are great, and all is illustrious by their order and good customs.

The great emperor Kao-Tsung, the son of T'ai Tsung, continued with good decorum the intention of his grandfather, enlarging and adorning the works of his father. For he commanded that in all his provinces churches should be built and honours conferred on Alopen, bestowing upon him the title of bishop of the great law, by which law he governed the kingdom of China in great peace, and the church filled the whole country with the prosperity of preaching.

In the year 698 (699) the bonzes of the sect of the pagodas, using their wonted violence, did blaspheme this new and holy law, in this place of Eastern Chou; and in the year 712 some particular persons in the Western Hao with laughter and disparagement did mock at it.

Then one of the chief of the priests, called John, and another of good virtue, named Kie Lie, with some others of their country, priests of great fame, being disengaged from the things of the world, began to take up again that excellent net, and to continue the thread, which was now broken. King Hsüan-Tsung commanded five little kings to come in person to the happy house and to set up altars. Then in the year 742 the pillar of the law, which had been cast down for a while, began to grow great.

King Hsüan-Tsung (c. 742) gave command to Kao Li-Shih that the pictures of the five kings his ancestors should be placed in the churches, with a hundred presents to honour the solemnity. Although the great beards of the Dragon were afar off, yet could they lay hands on their bows and their swords. The brightness which floweth from these pictures maketh them seem as if the kings themselves were present. In the third year of the Tien pao the priest Chi-ho was in Ta'chin who guided by the stars came to China, and beholding the sun came to the emperor who commanded that John and Paul and other priests should be joined unto him to exercise holy works in Hsing-Ching, a place within the palace. Then were hung up the Table(t)s in the churches, the king's letters richly adorned by public order with red and blue colours, and the king's pen filled the emptiness. It mounted on high and transcended the sun. His favours and donatives may be compared to the tops of the mountains of the South, and the abundance of his benefits is equal to the bottom of the eastern sea. Reason is not to be rejected. There is nothing which the saints cannot do; and their deeds are worthy of memory. For this cause king Su-Tsung (756–762) commanded that churches should be built in this Ling-wu and in five cities. He was of an excellent nature and opened the gate to the common prosperity of the kingdom by which means the affairs of the empire began to flourish again.

King T'ai Tsung caused happy times to return again, doing things without labour and trouble. Always at the feast of the Nativity of Christ he sent heavenly perfumes to the royal churches, to honour the ministers of this holy law. Truly, heaven giveth beauty and profit to the world and liberally produceth all things. This king imitated heaven and therefore he knew how to sustain and nourish his subjects.

King Teh Tsung used eight ways of government for to reward the good and chastise the wicked, and nine ways to renew the estate of the gospel. Let us pray to God for him without being ashamed of it. He was a man of much virtue, humble and desirous of peace, and ready to forgive his neighbour and to assist all men with charity. These are the steps of our holy law: to cause the winds and the rains to retire at their seasons, that the world should live in peace, men be well governed and affairs well established, that the living should prosper and the dead be in happiness. All this proceeds from our faith.

The king gave many honourable titles in his court to the priest I-ssŭ, a great preacher of the Law, and also a garment of red colour, because he was peaceable and took delight in doing good to all. He came from afar off into China from the country of Balkh. His virtue surpassed our three famous families; he enlarged the other sciences perfectly. He served the king in the palace and afterwards had his name in the royal book. The little king of Fen-yang Province who had the title of Secretary of State and called himself Kuo-Tzŭ-i served at first in the wars of these parts of the Northern Regions. King Su-Tsung commanded I-ssŭ that he should assist Kuo-Tzŭ-i very much above all the rest. Neither did he for this change his ordinary custom, being the nails and teeth of the Commonwealth, the eyes and ears of the army. He knew well how to distribute his revenue. He was not sparing in anything: he offered a precious gift called poli (crystal) to the church of this place of Lintiguen(?). He gave golden carpets to that of Cie Ki. He repaired the old churches and established the house of the Law, adorning the chambers and galleries thereof, making them shine like flying lights. He laid out his whole strength upon the works of charity; every year he assembled the priests of the four churches, serving them with a good heart and making them honourable entertainment for the space of fifty days. He fed the hungry, clothed the naked, cured the sick and buried the dead.

In the time of Ta So with all his parsimony there was not such goodness as this to be seen. But in the time of this Law we see such men who do such good works as these. For this reason I have graved this stone, that thereby they might be published.

I say then that the true God hath no beginning, but being pure and quiet was always after the same manner. He was the first Artificer of the creation, he uncovered the earth and elevated the heaven. One of the three Persons made himself man for our eternal salvation; he ascended like the sun on high and defeated darkness. In everything he did discover the profound truth.

The illustrious king, being really the first of the first, making use of a fit time, put a stop to men's invention: the heaven was dilated and the earth extended. Most bright is our Law, the which, when the Tang came to the kingdom and propagated the doctrine and builded churches, was as a barque both for the living and the dead, and gave rest to the whole world.

Kao-Tsung, following the example of his great-grandfather, built new churches. The beautiful temples of peace filled the whole earth. The true Law was illustrated; he gave a title of honour to the bishop, and men enjoyed repose.

The wise king Hsüan-Tsung followed the right way; the royal tables were illustrious; the king's letters shone therein. The pictures of the king gave light on high, and all the people did reverence them, and all men had joy and gladness.

When Su-Tsung reigned, he came in person to the church. The holy Sun did shine and the bright clouds swept away the darkness of the night. Prosperity was united to the royal family; misfortunes ceased, the heat of dissentions was abated; he quieted the rumours and he renewed our Empire.

King Tai-Tsung was obedient, in virtue equal to heaven and earth; he gave life unto the people and advancement to their affairs; he exercised works of charity, he offered perfumes to the church. The sun and the moon were united in his person.

When king Chien-chung reigned, he did illustrate famous virtue, and with his arms restored peace to the four seas, and with his learning he pacified 10,000 confines. As a torch he did enlighten the secrets of men; he saw all things as in a glass. He received the Barbarians, who all took rules from him.

The Law is great and perfect and extendeth itself to all things desiring to frame a name for it; I cannot but call it the Divine Law. Kings know best to dispose their affairs. I, who am a subject, can only cause them to be recited on this rich stone, for to magnify our great felicity.

In the Empire of the great T'ang, the second year (A.D. 781) of the Chien-chung, the seventh day of the month of autumn, was this stone erected, Ning-shu being bishop and governing the Church of China. The Mandarin called Lu Hsiu-yes graved this stone with his own hand.

[Fr. Semedo does not give the list of names written on the stone in Syriac and Chinese.]

The History of the Great and Renowned Monarchy of China by Fr. Alvarez Semedo. London, 1655, pp. 158–63.

Appendix II

DATES of some of the more famous Jesuit Missionaries. (Taken from Louis Pfister, S.J.'s *Notices biographiques et bibliographiques*, Shanghai, 1932.)

Missionaries	Birth	Arrival in China	Death
St. Francis Xavier	1506	1552	1552
Fr. Alexander Valignano	1538	?	1606
Fr. Michael Ruggieri	1543	1580	1607
Fr. Matteo Ricci	1552	1583	1610
Fr. Nicholas Longobardi	1556	1597	1654
Fr. Nicholas Trigault	1577	1610	1628
Fr. Alvarez de Semedo	1585	1613	1658
Fr. Jean Terrenz	1576	1621	1630
Fr. Adam Schall	1591	1622	1666
Fr. Alexander de Rhodes	1591	1623	1660
Fr. James Rho	1590	1624	1638
Fr. Martin Martini	1614	1643	1661
Fr. Philippe Couplet	1624?	1659	1692
Fr. Ferdinand Verbiest	1623	1659	1688
Fr. François. Noël	1651	1687	1729
Fr. Jean de Fontanoy	1643	1687	1710
Fr. Joachim Bouvet	1656	1687	1730
Fr. Louis le Comte	1655	1687	1728
Fr. J. Gerbillon	1654	1687	1707
Mgr. Cl. de Visdelou	1656	1687	1737
Fr. Dominique Parrenin	1665	1698	1741
Fr. Jean Baptiste Régis	1663	1698	1738
Fr. S.-M.-A. de Mailla	1669	1703	1748
Br. Joseph Castiglione	?	1715	1776
Fr. Antoine Gaubil	1689	1721	1759
Fr. Joseph-Marie Amiot	1718	1750	1793
Fr. Jean-Jacques de Grammont	1736	1768	1811
Fr. Louis de Poirot	1735	1770	1814

Appendix III

STATISTICS for the Catholic Church in China as given by the last *Les Missions de Chine*, the equivalent of the English *Catholic Directory*, published by the Lazarist Fathers, Shanghai, 1941.

	1939	1941
POPULATION		
Approximate number of inhabitants	483,000,000	486,000,000
Catholics	3,172,504	3,313,398
Catechumens	640,397	512,263
ECCLESIASTICAL DIVISION		
Vicariates and Apostolic Prefectures	138	138
Principal stations with residence	2,538	2,632
Secondary and Christian groups	30,555	30,722
LOCA SACRA		
Churches (holding at least 400 persons)	2,187	2,485
Chapels and oratories	13,106	13,429
PERSONNEL		
Foreign missionaries	2,939	3,112
Chinese priests	1,968	2,186
Foreign lay religious (*religieux laics*)	582	608
Chinese lay religious (*religieux laics*)	731	750
Foreign nuns	2,271	2,372
SEMINARIANS		
At major seminaries	853	1,066
At *petit* seminaries	3,608	3,688
SCHOOLS		
Secondary and superior: Boys	11,838	14,094
Girls	6,663	9,000
Primary superior: Boys	19,032	28,509
Girls	11,546	17,674
Primary lower: Boys	123,996	122,553
Girls	60,996	68,451
For doctrine and rudiments: Boys and girls	204,225	201,577

CHARITABLE INSTITUTIONS	1939	1941
Orphans: Boys	3,910	3,171
Girls	32,839	27,514
Sick admitted to hospitals	100,805	97,129
Cared for in hospices and asylums	10,603	8,898
Consultations in dispensaries	10,514,932	10,510,798

SPIRITUAL FRUITS		
Baptisms of adult catechumens	105,004	82,338
Baptisms of adult catechumens *in articulo mortis*	78,994	81,019
Baptisms of children of Christians	100,116	90,157
Baptisms of child pagans *in articulo mortis*	303,283	273,969
Confirmations	85,784	104,920
Confessions (*annual de precepto*)	1,472,448	1,516,680
Confessions of devotion	10,630,564	11,031,662
Easter Communions	1,385,867	1,482,257
Communions from devotion	29,632,117	31,246,857
Extreme Unctions	37,375	42,057
Marriages (5,559 and 6,160, *in cultu disparitate*)	24,403	25,440

Appendix IV

THE numerical strength of the various Protestant Bodies in China c. 1932–5.[1]

Group	Mission-aries	Chinese evangelical workers	Resident mission stations	Organized churches	Communicants
Adventist	218	669	23	243	15,469
Anglicans	569	970	109	739	34,612
Baptists (CCC)	(98)	(372)	(9)	(390)	(9,782)
Others	395	1,763	57	398	59,204
Brethren	109	44	34	4	2,065
Congregational (CCC)	(191)	(487)	(23)	(413)	(15,057)
Others	85	189	9	218	14,258
Disciples	38	238	5	16	2,127
Evangelical	18	70	6	46	2,924
Friends	28	6	9	11	1,412 (members)
Holiness and Pentecostal	193	189	71	35	9,416
Lutheran (CCC)	256	714	92	378	21,853
Others	185	425	42	106	6,813
Mennonites	37	5	10	—	1,999
Methodists	465	1,712	69	956	78,491
Presbyterian and Reformed (CCC)	(525)	(2,382)	(52)	(443)	(58,113)
Others	238	759	40	256	32,757
United Brethren (CCC)	(10)	(22)	(2)	(8)	(906)
United Church of Canada (CCC)	(231)	(263)	(21)	(196)	(7,557)
China Inland Mission	1,359	3,810	359	1,281	85,345
Church of Christ in China	1,055	3,526	107	1,450	91,415

[1] cf. *The China Year Book*, 1939.

Group	Mission-aries	Chinese evangelical workers	Resident mission stations	Organized churches	Communi-cants
Other Churches	464	570	150	145	14,471
Chinese Home Missionary Society	—	21	—	28	1,596
Independent Churches	—	—	—	—	5,000
TOTALS	5,712	15,680	1,192	6,310	481,227

Note: The numbers given for those bodies which joined the Church of Christ in China are given in brackets because they are given again under that last-named communion. For its creation cf. pp. 254–5.

BIBLIOGRAPHY

THIS is of course not a complete bibliography. It does not for instance contain books on the religions of China, which would themselves be a vast bibliography. Nor does it list the archives throughout the world which contain more material than any single person could ever comb in a lifetime. Here I have given the books that I think of interest, and almost all of which I have used. A few, such as de Mailla's, I have included because I know they are source books, though I myself have not had the use of them. German books I have not read, but I have included one or two which I know from references would be useful to a student.

C.C.S. in this bibliography stands for Collectanea Commissionis Synodalis, Peking.

ADUARTE, FR. DIEGO. *Historia de la Provincia del Santo Rosario de la Orden de Predicadores en Philipinas, Japón y China*, libro II. Manila, 1640.

ANDRÉ-MARIE. *Missions dominicaines dans l'Extrême Orient*. 2 vols. Paris, 1865.

Annals of the Association for the Propagation of the Faith. Dublin, New York, London, 1838–1954.

ANSON, LORD. *A voyage round the world*. London, 1942.

ARIAS, EVARISTO FERNÁNDEZ. *El Beato Sang y Compañeros Mártires del Orden de Predicadores*. Manila, 1893.

BALLOU, ROBERT O. ed. *The Bible of the World*. New York, 1947.

BALTASAR DE SANTA CRUZ, FR. *Tomo segundo de la Historia de la Provincia del Santo Rosario de Philipinas, Japón y China del Sagrado Orden de Predicadores*. Zaragoza, 1693.

BAR, HEBRAEUS. *Political History of the World from the Creation to A.D. 1286*. Tr. E. A. W. Budge. London, 1932.

BARKER, SIR E. 'The Crusades', *Encyclopædia Britannica*, 11th ed.

BARTOLI, DANIELLO. *Dell' Istoria della Compagnia di Gesù, La Cina, I–IV*. Florence, 1832.

BAUDIMENT, LOUIS. *François Pallu, Principal Fondateur de la Société des Missions Étrangères (1626–1684)*. Paris, 1934.

BAUER, THOMAS. *The systematic Destruction of the Catholic Church in China*. New York, 1954.

BAYLE, CONSTANTINO, S.J. *La Expansión misional de España*. Barcelona, 1946.

BEAZLEY, C. R. *The Texts and Versions of John de Piano Carpini and William de Rubruquis* (Hakluyt Society, London, 1903).

Berkeley, Sister Xavier (1861–1944), by M. L. H. Foreword by John C. H. Wu. London, 1949.

BERNARD, HENRI, S.J. *La Découverte de Nestoriens Mongols aux ordos et l'Histoire ancienne du Christianisme en Extrême Orient*. Tientsin, 1935.

Sagesse Chinoise et Philosophie chrétienne, essai sur leurs relations historiques. Tientsin, 1935.

Aux portes de la Chine, Les Missionnaires du seizième siècle (1514–1588). Tientsin, 1933.

Le Père Matthieu Ricci et la Société Chinoise de son temps (1552–1610). 2 vols. Tientsin, 1937. See also Bornet, Paul.

Bibliografia Missionaria, 1935, and yearly, compiled by Fathers G. Rommerskirchen, G. Dindinger and N. Kowalsky, O.M.I.

Bibliography for the Far East. Cf. 'Revue Historique,' vol. 103, pp. 70 ff.

BIERMANN, BENNO, O.P. *Die Anfange der neueren Dominikaner mission in Chine*, 1927. See also *Revue d'histoire des Missions*, 1928, pp. 628 ff.

BINYON, LAURENCE. *Akbar*. London.

BODDE, DERK, see Fung, Yu-lan.

BORNET, PAUL, S.J. *Adam Schall, S.J. Lettres et Mémoires*. Editées par Paul Bornet et Henri Bernard, S.J. Tientsin, 1942.

BOXER, C. R. 'Portuguese and Spanish Rivalry in the Far East during the Seventeenth Century', in *Journal of the Royal Asiatic Society*, 1946, pp. 150–64; 1947, pp. 91–105.

BOXER, C. R., ed. *South China in the XVI century, being the narratives of Galeota Pereira, Fr. Gaspar da Cruz, Fr. Martin de Rada (1550–75)*. Hakluyt Society, 2nd. series, vol. CVI. London, 1953.

BRAGA, J. M. *Igreja de S. Domingos e os dominicanos em Macau*, in *Boletin Ecles: da Diocese da Macau*, XXXVI. Macau, 1938, 1939.

BRANDT, C., SCHWARTZ, B. and FAIRBANK, J. K. *A Documentary History of Chinese Communism*. London, 1952.

BRANDT, J. VAN DEN. *Les Lazaristes en Chine*. Peking, 1936.

BRODRICK, JAMES, S.J. *Saint Francis Xavier (1507–1552)*. London, 1952.

BROOMHALL, M., ed. *Martyred missionaries of the China Inland Mission*. 1901.

BROU, A., S.J. 'L'Église en Chine au XIX–XXᵉ siècle, 1950'. (Unpublished MS. in possession of the Jesuits in Paris, 'Etudes', rue Monsieur.)

'Notes pour servir a l'histoire des origines du clergé indigène en Chine' in *Revue d'histoire des Missions*, 1926, pp. 519–40; 1927, pp. 391–406.

BRUCKER, JOSEPH. Article, 'Rites chinoises' in *Dictionnaire de théologie catholique*.

La Compagnie de Jésus, Esquisse de son institut et de son histoire (1521–1773). 2nd. ed. Paris, 1919.

BUDGE, SIR E. A. WALLIS. *The Monks of Kublai Khan*. London, 1928.

The History of Bar Hebraeus. London, 1932.

CABLE, MILDRED, and FRENCH, FRANCESCA. *Through Jade Gate and Central Asia*. London, 1943.

Cambridge Medieval History, 1911–29.

CAROLL, THOMAS, S.J. *The Educational work of the Catholic China Mission, 1929–39*. In C.C.S., XIV. Peking, 1941.

CARON, FRANÇOIS. *A True Description of the Mighty Kingdoms of Japan and Siam*. London, 1935.

Catholic Encyclopedia. 16 vols. *passim*. New York, 1907–13.

CEREZAL, P., FR. ANGEL, O.S.A. 'Los agustinos españoles en el imperio chino durante los siglos XVII y XVIII', *Illuminare*, mayo-junio, 1934.

CHAN, WING-TSIT. *Religious trends in modern China*. New York, 1953.

CH'ANG-CH'UN. *The Travels of an Alchemist*. Trans. by Arthur Waley. London, 1931.

CHAPPOULIE, HENRI. *Aux origines d'une église: Rome et les missions d'Indochine au XVIIᵉ siècle*. Tome I, II, Paris, 1943, 1948.

CHARLES, PIERRE. *Les Dossiers de l'Action missionnaire*. Vol. I. Louvain, 1939.

CHARVET, R. P., S.J. *Le clergé chinois, 1900–1951*. See also *L'Union missionnaire du clergé français*, April, 1952

CHATELET, ARISTIDE, C.M. *Jean-Gabriel Perboyre de la Congrégation de la Mission, (Lazariste) Martyr*. Paris, 1943.

China Christian Year Book, 1932–33. Shanghai.

China Year Book, The, 1939. Shanghai. Ed. H. G. W. Woodhead.

China Year Book, 1939. London.

Chinese Recorder, The. Foochow 1867–72 called *The Missionary Recorder*. Shanghai 1874–1911 called *The Chinese Recorder and Missionary Journal*. Shanghai 1911 onwards called *The Chinese Recorder*.

COLLINS, MAURICE. *The Great Within*. London, 1941.

Marco Polo. London, 1950.

COMBALUZIER, FERNAND. *Théodoric Pedrini*. See also *Neue Zeitschrift für Missionswissenschaft*. 1952, fasc. 4.

COMTE, L. LE. *Memoires and observations . . . made in a late journey through the empire of China . . . and other manufacturers*. Paris, 1697.

CONFUCIUS. *The Analects* Trans. by W. E. Soothill. Oxford, 1941.

COOK, CAPTAIN. *Voyages*.

CORDIER, HENRI. *Histoire Générale de la Chine*. Paris, 1920.

CORTESAŌ, ARMANDO. *The Suma oriental of Tomé Pires, an Account of the East, from the Red Sea to Japan, written in Malacca and India in 1512–1515. The Book of Francisco Rodrigues . . . in the Red Sea*. Trans. from Portuguese. 2 vols. Hakluyt Society. London, 1944.

COSTE, PIERRE. *La Congrégation de la Mission, dite de Saint-Lazare*. Paris, 1927.

COULING, SAMUEL. *The Encyclopedia Sinica*. London, 1917.

COX, WILLIAM. *Account of the Russian Discoveries between Asia and America to which are added the Conquest of Siberia and the History of the transactions and commerce between Russia and China*. Vol. I. London, 1803.

CREEL, H. G. *Confucius, the Man and the Myth*. London, 1951.

CRONIN, VINCENT. *The Wise Man from the West.* London, 1955.

CROS, P. L., S.J. *S. Franç · Xavier: sa vie et ses lettres.* 2 vols. Paris and Toulouse, 1900.

DAWSON, CHRISTOPHER, ed. *The Mongol Mission.* London, 1955.

DESCOMBRES, P. *Le Collège Général de la Société des Missions Étrangères de Paris (1665–1932).* Hong Kong, 1934.

DEVINE, W. *The Four Churches of Peking.* Tientsin. N.D.

DINDINGER, GIOVANNI, O.M.I. See ROMMERSKIRCHEN, GIOVANNI.

DUCHESNE, L. *The Churches separated from Rome.* London, 1907.

The Early History of the Christian Church. 3 vols. London, 1909–24.

DUFAY, FRANÇOIS. *En Chine, l'Etoile contre la Croix.* 9th edition. Paris, 1954.

DUFAY, F. and HYDE, DOUGLAS. *Red Star versus the Cross.* London, 1954. (This includes some original work by Douglas Hyde.)

DUHR, JOSEPH. See VÄTH, ALFONS, S.J.

EBERHARD, WOLFRAM. *A History of China from the earliest times to the present day.* Trans. E. W. Dickes. London, 1950.

ELIA, PASQUALE M., D', ed. *Fonti Ricciane.* Vols. I–III. Rome, 1949.

ELIA, PASQUALE M. D'. *Catholic Native Episcopacy in China, being an outline of the formation and growth of the Chinese Catholic clergy (1800–1926).* Shanghai, 1927.

Encyclopédie de liturgie et d'archéologie chrétienne. Articles on 'Rites chinoises', 'Nestoriens'. (Brucker, Joseph.)

EYRE, EDWARD (General Editor). *European Civilization, its origin and development.* Maps. Vol. VIII. *The Relations of Europe with Non-European Peoples.* (i) *European Geographical Discovery and Expansion,* pp. 145 ff. A. HILLIARD ATTERIDGE. (ii) *Europe and the Far East,* pp. 595 ff. PÈRE CHARLES. (O.U.P., 1939.)

FARIA Y SOUSA, MANUEL DE. *The Portugûes Asia, or the History of the Discovery and Conquest of India. Containing All their Discoveries from the Coast of Africk to the farthest Parts of China and Japan, etc., etc. . . . .* 3 vols. Trans. Captain John Stevens. London, 1695.

Imperio de la China y cultura evangelisca en él, por los religiosos de la companía. de Jesús, sacado de las noticias del Padre Devaro Semmedo. Lisbon, 1731.

FITZGERALD, C. P. *Revolution in China.* London, 1952.

China, A Short Cultural History. London, 1935.

The Empress Wu. London, 1956.

FITZGERALD, C. P., and YEH, GEORGE. *China, A Short History.* London, 1950.

FLICHE, AUGUSTINE, and VICTOR, MARTIN. *Histoire de l'Église.* Vols. I–XXVI, in progress of publication. Paris, 1941.

FORTESCUE, ADRIAN. *The Lesser Eastern Churches.* London, 1931.

FUNG, YU-LAN. *A History of Chinese Philosophy*. Vol. I. Period of the philosophers (from the beginning to *c*. 100 B.C.). Trans Derk Bodde. Peking and London, 1937. Vol. II. The Period of Classical Learning (from the 2nd century B.C. to the 20th century A.D.). Tr. ditto. London, 1953.

GALLAGHER, L. J., S.J. *China in the sixteenth century: the Journals of Matthew Ricci, 1583-1610*. Tr. from the Latin. Foreword by R. J. Cushing. New York, 1953. (Note: this is a translation of Trigault's editing of Ricci's journal and letters.)

    Commentari S. Francisco Zaverio Sacri 1552-1952 De Antiquis societatis Jesu Missionibus. Coll. Archivum Historicum Societatis Jesu, Anno XXII, Fasc. 43. Rome, 1953.

    The China that was. From the Latin of N. Trigault, S.J. Milwaukee, 1942.

GAUBIL, A., S.J. *Histoire de Gentchiscan et de toute la dynastie des Mongous ses successeurs, conquérants de la Chine*. Paris, 1739.

GENTILI. *Memorie di un Missionario Domenicano nella Cina*. 3 vols. Rome, 1887-8.

GIBB, SIR HAMILTON. *Islam*. London, 1951.

GIENOT, JOSEPH. *Kwangsi, Land of Black Banners*. Herder, 1942.

GILES, H. A. *Confucianism and its Rivals*. New York, 1915.

GILLET, O.P. *Une grande figure de missionaire en Chine. Le Père Vitorio Ricci, Dominicain des Philippines et Apôtre du Fokien*. See also R.H.M. XVI. Paris, 1939.

GINOT, LEONIDE. *La Mission du Su-tschuen au XVIIe siècle: Vie et Apostolat du Mgr. Pottier*. Paris, 1892.

GOFFART, P. *Life of Father Lebbe*. Louvain, 1950.

GONZALEZ, P. JOSÉ MARIA, O.P. *Misiones Dominicanas en China (1700-1750)*. Madrid, 1952.

GOYAE, GEORGES. *Les prêtres des Missions Étrangères*. Mayence, 1932.

GRANET, MARCEL. *La Pensée chinoise*. Paris, 1934.

GREENBERG, MICHAEL. *British Trade and the Opening of China, 1800-1842*. Cambridge, 1951.

GREENE, ROBERT. *Calvary in China*. London, 1954.

GROUSSET, RENÉ. *Histoire de l'Extrême Orient*. 2 vols. Paris, 1929.

    Rise and splendour of the Chinese empire. London, 1952. (Translation of the above.)

    Le conquérant du monde (Vie de Gengis-Khan). Paris, 1944.

    Histoire de la Chine. Paris, 1940.

GUBBELS, NOËL, O.F.M. *Trois siècles d'Apostolat: Histoire du Catholicisme au Hu-Kwang, depuis les origines, 1587 jusqu'à 1870*. Wu-chang, 1934.

GUERREIRO, FERNAO, S.J. *Jahangir and the Jesuits, with an account of the travels of Benedict Goes*. Trans. C. H. Payne. London, 1930.

HAKLUYT, RICHARD. *The Principal Navigations, etc.* Everyman series.

HALDE, P. DU. *The General History of China containing a geographical, historical, chronological, political and physical description of the Empire of China, etc.* London, 1736, 1741.

HAOUISSE, A., BISHOP, S.J. *Foreword to Fifty-six years a missionary in China, the Life of Mother Dominic, Helper of the Holy Souls.* London, 1935.

HAVRET, HENRI. *La stèle chrétienne de Si-ngan-fou.* Variétiés sinologiques. Nos. 7, 12 and 20, parts I, II and III, Shanghai, 1895, 1897, 1902.

HEBRAEUS, BAR. *History.* See BUDGE.

HERMANN, ALBERT. *Historical and Commercial Atlas of China.* Cambridge, Mass., 1935.

HOLM, F. *My Nestorian adventure in China.* 1924.

The Nestorian Monument. Chicago, 1909.

HOWORTH, M. H. *History of the Mongols.* 3 vols. 1876–88.

HSIEH, PING-YING. *Autobiography of a Chinese girl.* Trans. by Tsui-Chi. London, 1943.

HSIUNG, S. I. *The Life of Chiang Kai-shek.* London, 1948.

HUBRECHT, A. C. M. *La Mission de Pékin et les Lazaristes.* Peking, 1939.

Les Origines du clergé indigène en Chine. Peking, 1935.

HUBY, P., S.J., ed. *Christus.* Paris, 1927.

HUC, L'ABBÉ. *Christianity in China, Tartary and Thibet.* 3 vols. London, 1857, 1858.

A Journey through the Chinese Empire.

Dans la Tartarie, nouvelle éd. publiée par H. D'Ardenne de Tizac. Vols. I–III. Paris, 1925.

HUGHES, E. R. *Chinese Philosophy in classical times.* London, 1942.

Invasion of China by the Western World. London, 1937.

HUMMEL, A. W. *Eminent Chinese of the Ch'ing Dynasty.* 2 vols. Washington, D.C., 1943, 1944.

HUNTER, EDWARD. *Brain washing in Red China. The Calculated Destruction of Men's Minds.* New York, 1951.

HU SHIH, DR. *A History of Chinese Philosophy.* 1939.

Islam, the Legacy of. Oxford. Various authors.

JAEGHER, RAYMOND J. DE, and KUHER, IRENE CORBALLY. *The Enemy Within.* New York, 1953.

JANIN, R. P. *The Separated Eastern Churches.* Trans. V. Rev. Canon P. Boylan, M.A., D.Litt., D.D. London, 1933.

JARRIC, FATHER P. DU. *Jahangir and the Jesuits.* Ed. C. H. Payne. London, 1926.

KAMMERER, A. *La découverte de la Chine par les Portugais au XVIème siècle et la cartographie des Portugais, avec des notes toponymie chinoise par P. Pelliot.* Leiden, 1944.

KERN, H., ed. *The Lotus of the True Law.* Oxford, 1884.

KIANG, WEN-HAN. *Chinese Student Movement.* 1948.

KOMROFF, MANUEL. *Contemporaries of Marco Polo, consisting of the travel records to the eastern parts of the world of William of Rubruck (1253–1255); the journey of John of Pian de Carpini (1245–1247); and the Journal of Friar Oderic (1318–1330).* London, 1929.

LAMALLE, EDMOND, S.J. *La Propagande du P. Nicolas Trigault en faveur des Missions de Chine (1616).* In 'Archivum hist. S.J.', IX, Rome, 1940, pp. 49–120.

LAMB, H. *Genghis Khan, the Emperor of all men.* 1928.

LANE, RAYMOND A., BISHOP. *Ambassador in Chains, The Life of Bishop Patrick Byrne.* London, 1956.

Stone in the King's Highway. The Life and Writings of Bishop Francis Xavier Ford.

LATOURETTE, KENNETH SCOTT. *A History of Christian Missions in China.* S.P.C.K., London, 1929.

A History of Modern China. Harmondsworth, 1954.

LAUNAY, ADRIEN. *Mémorial de la Société des Missions Étrangères.* Paris, 1912.

Histoire générale de la Société des Missions Étrangères. 3 vols. Paris, 1894.

Histoire des Missions de la Chine, Mission du Kouang-si. Paris, 1903. See also LY, ANDRÉ.

LECLERQ, CHAN. J. *Vie du Père Lebbe, Le tonnerre qui chante au loin.* Paris, 1955.

LE COMTE. *Nouveaux Mémoires sur l'état présent de la Chine.* 2 vols. Paris, 1697.

LEFEUVRE, JEAN, S.J. *Shanghaï: Les Enfants dans la ville, chronique de la vie chrétiénne; Shanghaï, 1949–1955.* Paris, 1955.

LEGGE, J. *Chinese Classics,* with a translation, critical and exegetical notes, prolegomena and copious indexes. 5 vols. First ed. Hong Kong, 1861–72, revised ed. of Vols. 1 and 2, Oxford, 1893–5.

Lettres édifiantes et curieuses écrites des Missions Étrangères, nouvelle édition. Paris chez J. G. Mérigot le jeune. 1781. Tomes XVI–XXVI. Nouvelle édition, Vols. 1–26. Toulouse, 1810–11. (Vols. 16–20 chiefly on China.)

LEVAUX, LEOPOLD. *Le Père Lebbe, Apôtre de la Chine moderne (1877–1940).* Bruxelles, 1948.

LEY, C. D. *Portuguese Voyages, 1498–1593.* London, 1947.

LIN-LE. *Ti-ping Tien-Kwoh, The History of the Ti-ping Revolution* (including a Narrative of the Author's *Personal Adventures*). 2 vols. London, 1866.

LOPETEGUI, LEON, S.J. 'Contactos entre España y China en el siglo XVI'. In *Misionalia Hispánica.* Vol. 1, pp. 341–52. Madrid, 1944.

LOU, DOM PIERRE CELESTINE (LOU TSENG-TSIANG). *Ways of Confucius and of Christ.* London, 1948.

La rencontre des humanités et la découverte de l'Evangile. Bruges, 1949.

LY, ANDRÉ. *Journal d'André Ly, Prêtre chinois, Missionaire et Notaire Apostolique, 1746–1763.* Latin Text, Intro: A. Launay. Hong Kong, 1924.

MAAS, OTTO, O.F.M. *Father Anthony Caballero, Founder of the Modern Franciscan Missions in China.* In C.C.S., XIII, pp. 709–28. Peking, 1940.
Die Wiederöffnung de Franziskanermission in China in der Neuzeit. Münster, 1926.
Cartas de China. Documentos ineditos sobre misiones franciscanas del siglo XVII. Seville, 1917.
Franciscans in the Middle Kingdom. A Survey of Franciscans in China from the Middle Ages to the Present Time. C.C.S., XI. Peking, 1938.

MAILLE, DE. *Histoire générale de la Chine ou annales de cet empire.* 12 vols.

MANN, H. K. *The Lives of the Popes in the Middle Ages.* Various vols. London, dates various.

MARTINIUS, MARTIN, S.J. *Bellum Tartaricum, or the Conquest of the Gt. and most Renowned Empire of China by the Invasion of the Tartars.* From the Latin. London, 1654.

MASPERO, HENRI. *La Chine Antique.* Paris, 1927.

MCGRAIN. *The Russian Orthodox Mission in China as retold from Russian sources.* In C.C.S. XIII. Peking, 1940.

MCINERNEY, A., O.F.M. *The Spanish Franciscans in the Province of Kiangsi, China, during the years 1685–1813.* New York, 1946.

MCNAIR, H. F. See MORSE, H. B.

MENZ, FR. *Necrologium fratrum minorum in Sinis.* Peking, 1948.

MENDOZA, JUAN GONZÁLEZ DE. *Historia de las cosas más notables, ritos y costumbres, del gran reyno de la China.* Rome, 1585.

MENSAERT, FR. GEORGE. *Sinica Franciscana.* Vol. V. 'Relationes et Epistolace Illumi D. Fr. Bernardini della Chiésa, O.F.M.' Rome, 1954.

MILON, A. *Mémoires de la Congrégation de la Mission, La Chine.* 3 vols. Paris, 1911, 1912.

Missions de Chine, Les. Lazarists Fathers, ed. Shanghai, 1941.

MOGES, LE Mis DE. *Souvenir d'une Ambassade en Chine et au Japon en 1857 et 1858.* Paris, 1860.

MOIDREY, JOSEPH DE. *La Hiérarchie catholique en Chine, en Corée et au Japon (1307–1914).* Zi-ka-wei, 1914.

MONSTERLEET, J. *L'empire de Mao Tsetung, 1949–1954.* Lille, 1954.

Monumenta Serica. Vol. 1. Cura univ. Catholicae Pekini edita sumpt. H. Vetch. Peking, 1935.

Morrison, Robert. Memoirs and Life and Labours of, by his wife. 2 vols. 1839.

MORSE, H. B. *International Relations of the Chinese Empire.* 3 vols. Shanghai, 1910–18.

MORSE, HOSEA BALLOU, and MCNAIR, HARLEY FARNWORTH. *Far Eastern International Relations.* U.S.A., 1931.

MOULE, A. C. *Christians in China before the Year 1550.* S.P.C.K., London, 1930.

NAVARETTE, F. *Account of the Empire of China. . . . Decrees of Popes and Propositions defined at Rome for the Mission to China. . . .* 2 vols. 1703.

Nouvelles lettres édifiantes des missions de la Chine et des Indes Orientales. 8 vols. Paris, 1818–23.

O'CALLAGHAN, JEROME, O.F.M. 'Franciscan Martyrs of the Boxer Rising.' In *Franciscans in China,* 1935–7.

OLIPHANT, LAURENCE. *Narrative of the Earl of Elgin's Mission to China and Japan in the years 1857, '58, '59.* 2 vols. Edinburgh, 1860.

OMAECHEVARRÍA, IGNACIO, O.F.M. 'Fray Martin Ignacio de Loyola, O.F.M.' in *Misionalia Hispánica.* No. 22, 1951.

PALAFOX, M. DE. *Histoire de la conqueste de la Chine . . . trad. par le sieur Colle.* Amsterdam, 1723.

PARRY, ALBERT. 'Russian (Greek Orthodox) Missionaries in China 1687–1917'. In *Pacific Historical Review,* IX (1940), pp. 401–24.

PASTOR, DR. L. *History of the Popes.* Especially Vols. XXXIII and XXXV. Dates various.

PELLIOT, PAUL. 'Les Franciscains en Chine au XVIIᵉ et au XVIIIᵉ siècle.' In *Toung Pao,* XXXIV. Leiden, 1938.

'Chrétiens d'Asie Centrale et d'Extrême Orient' in *Toung Pao,* p. 628. Leiden, 1914.

PELLIOT, PAUL, and MOULE, A. C. *Marco Polo, The Description of the World.* 4 vols. London, 1938.

PFISTER, LOUIS, S.J. *Notices biographiques et bibliographiques sur les Jésuites de l'ancienne mission de Chine, 1552–1773.* 2 vols. Shanghai, 1933.

PINKERTON, JOHN. *A general collection of the best and most interesting voyages and travels in all parts of the world.* 18 vols. London, 1808–14.

PIRES, TOMÉ. See CORTESÃO.

PLATTNER, FELIX ALFRED. *Jesuits Go East, a record of missionary activity in the East, 1541–1786.* Dublin, 1950.

POLO, MARCO. *Travels.* See YULE.

PUECH, H. CH. *Le Manichéisme, son fondateur, sa doctrine.* 1950.

REMY. *Pourpre des Martyrs.* 1953.

RICCI, MATTEO. See TACCHI VENTURI and PASQUALE M. D'ELIA.

RIPA, MATTEO. *Memoirs, during 13 years residence at the court of Peking, in the service of the emperor of China.* Trans. F. Prandi. London, 1846.

Storia della Fondazione della Congregazione e del Collegio de' Cinesi sotto il titolo della S. Famiglia di G.C. 3 vols. Naples, 1832.

ROMMERSKIRCHEN, GIOVANNI, O.M.I. *Bibliografia Missionaria*, 1935, and yearly. Rome.

ROWBOTHAM, ARNOLD R. *Missionary and Mandarin.* California, 1942.

RUNCIMAN, STEVEN. *A History of the Crusades.* 3 vols. Cambridge, 1951–4.

RYAN, J. P. 'American contribution to the Catholic Missionary effort in China in the XX century'. In *Catholic Historical Review.* Washington, 1945.

SÁ, A. BASILIO DE. *Documentação para a história das missoês do padroado portugûes do Oriente Insolíndia.* Vol. 1 (*1506–1549*). Lisbon, 1954.

SADDHARMA-PUNDARÎKA. *The Lotus of the True Law.* In 'Sacred Books of the East', series edited by F. Max Müller. Trans. H. Kern. Oxford, Clarendon Press, 1884.

SAEKI, P. Y. *The Nestorian Monument in China.* London, 1916.

SANCHEZ, J. G., O.P. 'Las Misiones dominicanas de China en la primera década del Siglo XIX'. In *Misiones Dominicanas*, XXII, Avila, 1939. Cf. also XXIII, XXIV.

SCHALL, ADAM, S.J. *Lettres et mémoires de, I—Relation historique.* Tientsin, 1942.

SCHUTTE, JOSEF, S.J. *Valignanos missionsgrundsätze für Japan.* Rome, 1951.

SCHYNS, JOSEPH. *Aveux Spontanés.* Brussels, 1953.

SEMEDO, F. ALVAREZ A PORTUGHESS. *The History of the Great and Renowned Monarchy of China, wherein all the particular provinces are accurately described . . . lately written in Italian by . . . after he had resided 20 years at the Court and other famous cities of that Kingdom.* Now put into English by a person of Quality and illustrated . . . to satisfie the curious and advance the Trade of Great Britain. Map. London, 1655.

SERVIÈRE, J. DE LA. *Les Anciennes missions de la Compagnie de Jésus en Chine* (*1552–1814*). Shanghai, 1924.

La nouvelle mission du Kiangnan (*1840–1922*). Shanghai, 1925.

SHIRLEY-PRICE, L. *Confucius and Christ, a Christian estimate of Confucius.* Westminster, 1951.

SILVA REGIO. *Documentação para a história das missôes padroado portugues do Oriente coligida e anotada por.* 6 vols. Lisbon, *c.* 1951.

Sinica Franciscana. Vols. I–V. Cf. A. van den Wyngaert and G. Mensaert. Florence and Rome, 1929–54.

SOOTHILL, W. E. *The Analects of Confucius.* Oxford, 1941.

STEIN, SIR AUREL. *On Ancient Central-Asian Tracks.* London, 1933.

SUIGO, FATHER CARLO. *In the Land of Mao Tse-tung.* London, 1953.

SUN YAT-SEN. *San Min Chu I. The Three Principles of the People.* Shanghai, 1927.

San Min Chu I. The Three Principles. Trans. F. W. Price. Shanghai, 1927.

SYKES, SIR PERCY. *The Quest for Cathay*. London, 1936. (Containing some good maps.)
A History of Exploration. London.

TACCHI VENTURI, PIETRO. *Opere Storiche del P. Matteo Ricci S.J.* 2 vols. Macerata, 1911–13 (also new ed. by D'Elia, Pasquale M., S.J.).

TACHARD, G. *Voyage de Siam, des pères Jésuites envoyez par le Roy aux Indes et à la Chine.* . . . Paris, 1686.
English translation of above. *A Relation of a voyage to Siam.* . . . London, 1688.

TARN, W. W. *The Greeks in Bactria and India*. Cambridge, 1938.

TAYLOR, DR., and MRS. HOWARD. *Hudson Taylor and the China Inland Mission. The Growth of a Work of God*. London, 1919.
Hudson Taylor in the Early Years. London.

TEIXEIRA, P. MANUEL. *Macau e a Su Diocese*. Vols. I, II, III. Macau, 1940.

TELLIER, MICHEL LE, S.J. *Défense des nouveaux chrestiens et des missionnaires de la Chine, du Japon et des Indes*. Paris, 1687.

THEINER, A. *Il Seminario Ecclesiastico*. Roma, 1834.

THOMAS, A. *Histoire de la Mission de Pékin depuis les Origines jusqu'à l'Arrivée des Lazaristes*. Paris, 1923.
Histoire de la Mission de Pékin depuis l'arrivée des Lazaristes jusqu'à la Révolte des Boxers. 2 vols. Paris, 1923, 1926.

TISSERANT, E. CARDINAL. Article in *Dictionnaire de Théologie Catholique*. Tome XI, col. 157–323.

TOYNBEE, A. J. *A Study of History*. Vols. I–X. Oxford, 1934–54.
Journey to China, or things which are seen. 1931.

TRIGAULT, NICHOLAS, S.J. *The China that Was: China as discovered by the Jesuits at the close of the 16 cent*. Trans. by L. J. Gallagher, S.J. Milwaukee, 1942.
Histoire de l'expédition Chrestienne au Royaume de la Chine . . . tirée des mémoires du R. P. Matthieu Ricci. Lille, 1617.

TSUI CHI. *A short history of Chinese Civilisation*. London, 1942.

VÄTH, ALFONS, S.J. *Johann Adam Schall von Bell, S.J. Missionar en China Kaiserlicher Astronom und Ratgeber am Hof von Peking*. Koln, 1933. (Joseph Duhr adapted above into French. Bruxelles, 1936.)

VAULX, BERNARD DE. *Histoire des Missions Catholiques françaises*. Paris, 1951.
Les plus beaux textes sur les missions. Paris, 1954.

VIANI, P. *Historia delle cose operati nella China Da Monsignor Gio Ambrogio Mezzabarbe*. Cologne, 1740.

WADDING, LUKE. *Annales Ordinins Minorum*. 8 vols. 1625–54.

WALEY, ARTHUR. *170 Chinese Poems*. London, 1939.
The Temple and other Poems. London, 1925.
Three Ways of Thought in Ancient China. London, 1939.
The Analects of Confucius Translated and Annotated. London, 1938.

WILHELM, R. *A Short History of Chinese Civilisation.* Trans. by J. Joshua. New York, 1929.

WILLAERT, L. *Correspondance de Fernand Verbiest de la Compagnie de Jésus (1623–1688).* Bruxelles, 1938.

WOLFERSTAN, BERTRAM. *The Catholic Church in China from 1860 to 1907.* London, 1909.

WOODHEAD, H. G. W. *The China Year Book, 1939.* Shanghai.

WU, JOHN C. H. *Beyond East and West.* New York, 1951.

WYNGAERT, ANASTASIUS VAN DEN, O.F.M. *Sinica Franciscana.* Vols. I–V. Florence and Rome, 1929–54.

Jean de Monte Corvin, O.F.M., premier Evêque de Khanbalig (1247–1328). Lille, 1924.

XAVIER, ST. FRANCIS, cf. Callagher, L. J., *Commentari S. Francisco.*

YU-LAN, F. *The Spirit of Chinese philosophy.* Trans. and ed. by E. R. Hughes. 1950.

YULE, SIR HENRY. *Cathay and the Way Thither.* New ed. by Henri Cordier. 4 vols. London, 1913–16.

The Book of Sir Marco Polo with Henri Cordier's Notes and Addenda. 3 vols. London, 1920–9.

YUTANG, LIN. *Wisdom of Confucius.* U.S.A., 1943.

The Importance of Living. New York, n.d.

INDEX OF TOPICS

INDEX OF PEOPLE AND PLACES